Scribes of Gastronomy

Scribes of Gastronomy

Representations of Food and Drink

in Imperial Chinese Literature

Edited by Isaac Yue and Siufu Tang

香港大學出版社

HONG KONG UNIVERSITY PRESS

Hong Kong University Press
The University of Hong Kong
Pokfulam Road
Hong Kong
www.hkupress.org

ISBN 978-988-8139-97-2 *(Hardback)*
ISBN 978-988-8139-98-9 *(Paperback)*

British Library Cataloguing-in-Publication Data
A catalogue record for this book is available from the British Library.

10   9   8   7   6   5   4   3   2   1

Printed and bound by Goodrich Int'l Printing Co., Ltd. in Hong Kong, China

Contents

Contributors

Duncan Campbell, a New Zealander, teaches Chinese history and culture and classical Chinese language and literature at the Australian National University in Canberra, Australia. His research focuses on aspects of the material and literary culture of the late imperial period in China, with specific reference to private gardens and libraries.

Tak Kam Chan is a scholar in modern Chinese and Hong Kong literature, as well as a prize-winning poet, essayist and novelist. His publications include eight academic books, nine collections of creative work and a novel. He has taught at Lingnan University, and currently teaches at Hong Kong Baptist University.

Louise Edwards is professor of modern China studies at the University of Hong Kong. She is a fellow of the Australian Academy of the Humanities, the Academy of the Social Sciences of Australia and the Hong Kong Academy of the Humanities. Her most recent sole authored book is *Gender, Politics and Democracy: Women's Suffrage in China* (Stanford UP, 2008) and her major work relating to *Honglou meng* is *Men and Women in Qing China: Gender in the Red Chamber Dream* (E. J. Brill, 1994). Her current research focuses on gendered cultures of war in China and kinaesthetic modernity.

Ronald Egan is professor of Sinology at Stanford University's Department of East Asian Languages and Cultures. He works on Tang and Song literature, aesthetics, and literary culture. He is the author of books on Ouyang Xiu and Su Shi. His most recent work is a reappraisal of Li Qingzhao and contested views of her through time, entitled *The Burden of Female Talent: The Poet Li Qingzhao and Her History in China* (Harvard University, forthcoming).

Charles Kwong was educated at the University of Hong Kong, Oxford and Yale. He had taught in the US, and is currently professor of Chinese and translation as well as adjunct professor of philosophy at Lingnan University. His academic work includes four books, and his translations include rendering the Chinese texts for a book of paintings into English. He has also published twenty collections of classical Chinese poems and two collections of modern Chinese prose essays.

Siufu Tang is assistant professor in the School of Chinese, the University of Hong Kong. His research focuses mainly on early Confucianism and its relevance to the modern world. He has published papers on various aspects of the thought of the early Confucian thinker Xunzi, and also on Confucianism and liberalism. He is currently working on a project about the understanding of self and authenticity in the *Xunzi*.

Nicholas Morrow Williams is research assistant professor at the Mr. Simon Suen and Mrs. Mary Suen Sino-Humanitas Institute of Hong Kong Baptist University. His research focuses on Six Dynasties and Tang poetry.

Isaac Yue is assistant professor of Chinese in the University of Hong Kong. His research interest falls into two broad areas: nineteenth-century China-West studies and imperial Chinese literature since the Song dynasty. He has published in these fields in such journals as *Victorian Literature and Culture*, *Journal of Oriental Studies*, and *Études Chinoises*.

1
Food and the Literati

The Gastronomic Discourse of Imperial Chinese Literature

Siufu Tang and Isaac Yue

It has been observed that while all other life feeds, the human species eats.[1] The act of 'eating', which distinguishes humans from other forms of life, has brought about the phenomenon of different cultures pursuing dissimilar diets and having distinctive ways of preparing food. Since for each culture, food is symbolic in a unique way, the study of one's cultural gastronomical practices enables an introspective examination of one's own cultural traditions as well as facilitates the understanding of other cultures around the world.

The Chinese take pride in their food culture and the fact that their ethnical culinary excellence is recognized internationally. To quote the late Chang Kwang-chih, 'That Chinese cuisine is the greatest in the world is highly debatable and is essentially irrelevant. But few can take exception to the statement that few other cultures are as food oriented as the Chinese.'[2] In fact, not only does gastronomy occupy a central role in the development of Chinese civilization, it also represents a theme of some importance in literary productions, with the language of food manifesting itself in multifarious ways throughout different eras, serving a variety of purposes, and encompassing genres. Examples can be as far-ranging as the stanzas on food and wine in the *Classic of Poetry* (*Shi jing* 詩經) or in Su Shi's 蘇軾 (1037–1101) enunciation of the attainment of culinary perfection, and the articulation of the refinement of dining in *The Dream of the Red Chamber* (*Honglou meng* 紅樓夢). From these literatures, it is possible to extract different layers of interpretation in respect to the references to food, ranging from the historic to the aesthetic. As Roel Sterckx observes, 'food is omnipresent in reality, in simile and in metaphor [of China]'.[3] The unique appeal of food and its special cultural significance within Chinese society cannot be underestimated.

The purpose of this present volume is to engage the fledging genre of food literature in global academia from a Chinese perspective. By considering the textual representations of food in relation to the agendas of the writers, the type of text in which they appear, and the context under which nourishment is evoked as a literary motif, the contributors to this project hope to add to the understanding of the cultural and social significance of food in the Chinese literary tradition.

Food, Moral Education, and the Way of the *Taotie*

Whereas the English lexicon contains words such as gourmet, aristologist, gourmand, epicure, and gastrologer to describe a person who is acquainted with the fine art of dining, in Chinese this person would be referred to as a *laotao* 老饕, a derivative of the mythical *taotie* 饕餮. As a beast of legend, the nature and the origin of the *taotie* continue to be a subject of scholarly debate.[4] Traditionally, the *taotie* has been associated with a beast-like motif on ritual vessels on the one hand, and with voracious appetite on the other. Such an association was made as early as in the *Spring and Autumn Annals of Lü* (*Lüshi chunqiu* 呂氏春秋):[5]

> The *taotie* that is inscribed on the tripods of the Zhou dynasty has a head but not a body. It devours people but does not swallow them, and damages its own body as a result. This demonstrates retribution. It is the same for those who do immoral acts. 周鼎著饕餮，有首無身，食人未咽，害及其身，以言報更也。為不善亦然。[6]

Three elements of the passage are worthy of our attention. First, the passage mentions the tripod of the Zhou dynasty, which is an important ritual vessel. In early China, rites (*li* 禮) were originally performed as sacrifices to gods and ancestors and later became governing norms for social and political life as well. Ever since the elaboration of the concept by early Confucianism, especially in the hands of Confucius, Mencius and Xunzi, 'rites' has become an encompassing term for spiritual and moral norms, covering nearly every aspect of Chinese life. Second, the passage talks about eating. The mythical beast *taotie* eats human beings but does not swallow them, presumably choking itself out of hastiness. Eating in itself, in particular as a necessary means of life maintenance, is innocuous. However there are good and bad ways of eating. The *taotie's* way of eating can be seen as wrong for two reasons. Not only does it eat human beings, but it eats them improperly by not swallowing. Such a bad way of eating thus brings about harm, not merely to others but especially to the *taotie* itself. The results of such an improper way of eating bring out the third important element of the passage, which is that of moral evaluation and moral education. The passage concludes that immoral acts lead to retribution and bring harms to the actor, just as the *taotie* harms itself by eating in the wrong way. This early passage about the *taotie* tactfully conjoins three elements: rites as moral norms, the act of eating, and moral education, and sets an example of using food for moral and cultural representation.

This linkage between food and moral education is also explored in another account of the *taotie* in *The Chronicle of Zuo* (*Zuo zhuan* 左傳). Here, the *taotie*, a depraved descendent of a certain Jinyun clan 縉雲氏, is compared to the three evils of the world and appears as greedy as it is voracious.[7] Although the two accounts differ in the sense that the human origin of the *taotie*, as found in the latter, is completely replaced by elements of bestiality in the former, its connotation as an eater and a devourer conveys one consistent moral message: what is wrong with the *taotie* is not its love for food and drink, but its indulgence without limitations and at the expense of other concerns (which brings harms not only to others but also to itself).[8]

This association of the *taotie* with the negative qualities of gluttony, ravenousness, and an insatiable appetite—a theme that remains relevant in such later work as Du Fu's 杜甫 (712–770) 'Muntjac' (*ji* 麂), in which the image of the beast as an eater is evoked to critique the self-indulging greed of the upper class during the Tang dynasty[9]—is indicative of the conventional Chinese perception of an innate relationship between eating and moral education. The *taotie*, both as a motif on ritual vessels and as a symbol for gluttony, seems a perfect example of the cultural representation of food in China. Food, on the one hand, can be an essential element of the highest and the most solemn rites of China. Yet, on the other hand, it might also be the source of temptation, and be accompanied by moral corruption and deprivation. We believe, it is as a medium of myriad possible representations that food occupies a central role in Chinese culture and society.

The usage of food for moral education is, in fact, a tradition that is traceable to as early a time as was recorded in the *Classic of Poetry*. In the poem 'Mian Man' 綿蠻, for example, we find the following lines:

綿蠻黃鳥　There is that little oriole,
止於丘阿　Resting on a bend of the mound.
道之云遠　The way is distant,
我勞如何　And I am very much wearied.
飲之食之　Give me drink, give me food;
教之誨之　Inform me, teach me;
命彼後車　Order one of the attending carriages,
謂之載之　And tell them to carry me.[10]

The two lines that concern us, 'Give me drink, give me food; Inform me, teach me', not only illustrate the way the two concepts are bound together in a matter-of-fact manner, but the fact that they are quoted with approval by Xunzi 荀子, who uses them to illustrate the two essential aspects of a kingly government—that of satisfying material needs and that of providing moral guidance—[11] further demonstrates the degree to which these concepts have been adopted and endorsed by Chinese thinkers. In *Mencius* (*Mengzi* 孟子), the importance of food for the cultivation of morality and virtue is also emphasized in the repetition of the belief that normal people must first be well fed and clothed before they can be taught virtue.[12] Although Mencius also suggests that when someone is filled with virtue, it is possible for that person to have no regard for fine food, he returns to the point with another poem from the *Classic of Poetry*,[13] which reads: 'Having filled us with drink; Having filled us with virtue' 既醉以酒，既飽以德.[14] While the exact meaning of these lines is open to interpretation, the perceptible analogy between spirits and virtue serves to validate an inherent connection between food and morality (with the former being regarded as prerequisite to the achievement of the later); that just as we might be drunk with spirits, we can also be full with virtue.

It is along this same vein that in the *Book of Rites* (*Li ji* 禮記), rites—the Confucian generic name for norms—are stated to have had their beginnings in food and drink. As James Legge surmises, it was first through various forms of food and drink that ancient people expressed their reverence to spirits and gods.[15] The idea that food and drink could be invested with meanings and feelings so rich as to become the medium for cultural activities represents a parallel development to such classics as *Mencius* and the *Classic of Poetry*, in which the moral qualities of food are established and expounded. However, food and drink are more than simply the medium for rites and other cultural activities, and it is not as though they could be discarded and replaced by better means of expression. On the one hand, the fact that food and drink are the means of subsistence for all human beings, and could hardly be discarded is recognized and accepted. On the other hand, rites actually represent the proper way of living a good human life, including eating and drinking well. Xunzi, when explaining the origin of rites, also points out that the primary function of rites is to nourish people. By nourishment, Xunzi means the proper satisfaction of human desires, among which those for food and drink are prominent.[16] Similarly, it is recorded in the *Doctrine of the Mean* (*Zhongyong* 中庸) that Confucius once commented that while everybody eats and drinks, rarely do they know the flavours.[17] It thus seems deducible that it is precisely through rites that someone can truly appreciate the flavours of food and drink. That is, food and drink gain their proper taste and proper meaning within a good human life only when structured by rites. Only in such a way can a person truly enjoy food and drink to their fullest. Xunzi suggests that only when nature (including desires of food and drink) is joined with artifice (*wei* 偽, predominantly rites) can the true order of humanity be established.[18] What Xunzi means is that a life that is truly human requires both the natural desires and their embellishment in cultural forms like rites. Xunzi's suggestion can also be seen as an elaboration of Confucius' famous statement that the nobleman (*junzi* 君子) must be well-matched in raw substance (*zhi* 質) and cultural embellishment (*wen* 文).[19] Given such an understanding, food and drink can be seen as essential medium for the embellishment of our natural desires. It is through the cultural and social representations invested in food and drink that we eat like humans and not merely feed like animals. Such a Confucian understanding might also help to explain the central roles played by food and drink in Chinese culture.

One example of Chinese cultural representations of food and drink can be found in sacrificial rites. As offerings in sacrificial rites, food and drink are not only compatible with rites, but in fact are mutually constitutive to a large extent. Throughout Chinese history, they occupy a central role not only in the mundane but also in the religious and spiritual dimension. Offerings of food and drink to ancestors have been the exemplary component of Chinese ancestor-oriented rites, which are identified by scholars as keys to Chinese culture.[20] One early description of the use of food and drink in various sacrificial rites appears in the *Xunzi*:

> At the Grand *Xiang* sacrifice, the *zun* goblet holding the dark liquid is offered up, raw fish is placed on the *zu* offering table, and the grand broth is served first. This is to honour the root of food and drink. At the *Xiang* sacrifice, the *zun* goblet holding the dark liquid is offered first, and then distilled and sweet spirits are served as well; panicum and setaria millet are served first, and then rice and sorghum are offered as well. At the regular sacrifice, the grand broth is offered up, and then ample viands are served. This is to pay honour to the root but also make familiar employment.
>
> 大饗，尚玄尊，俎生魚，先大羹，貴食飲之本也。饗，尚玄尊而用酒醴，先黍稷而飯稻粱。祭，齊大羹而飽庶羞，貴本而親用也。[21]

The above passage is aimed at explicating the guiding principle of rites, which is to pay honour to the root but also make familiar employment. The ubiquitous presence of food and drink in these sacrificial rites clearly illustrates their essential role in early China's spiritual activities. Such a central role of food and drink is confirmed by a similar yet less detailed account in the *Book of Rites*, where it is said that blood is used for the border sacrifice (*jiao* 郊), raw flesh for the great offering (*da xiang* 大饗), sodden flesh for sacrifices of three presentations (*san xian* 三獻), and roast meat for sacrifices of one presentation (*yi xian* 一獻).[22] If anything was considered sacred in early China, it was the sacrificial rite. The border sacrifice which made an offering to Heaven (*tian* 天) and the great offering to the imperial ancestors surely ranked among the most solemn of ceremonies.

The fact that food and drink are an integral and essential component of sacred rites testifies to their potency of spiritual representation.

In summary, in Chinese culture food and drink are more than mundane items for bodily nourishment. As E. N. Anderson suggests, 'As a marker of social status, ritual status, special occasions, and other social facts, food became less a source of nutrients than a means of communication.'[23] Regardless of whether there is a sharp contrast between the sacred and the mundane in Chinese culture, it remains true that food and drink constitute a versatile medium for bridging aspects of life and for bearing various cultural images. It is such a rich potentiality, we would like to suggest, that has been captured and extended by literary works in imperial China with nearly endless representations.

The Politics of Food and Drink as a Literary Motif

In the *Romance of the Three Kingdoms* (*Sanguo yanyi* 三國演義), having finally defeated the barbarian leader Meng Huo 孟獲 and brought lasting peace to the Southern regions, one final challenge stands before Zhuge Liang 諸葛亮 (181–234) and his endeavour to refocus his attention on the war effort against Sima Yi 司馬懿 (179–251):

> It was autumn, the ninth month of the year, when the vanguard reached the River Lu. Suddenly, thick clouds darkened the sky and fierce winds blew. Told that the troops could not cross, [Zhuge] Kongming turned to Meng Huo for advice. Meng Huo said, 'An evil spirit has cursed this water; those who would pass must appease him by sacrifice.' 'What would appease the spirit?' Kongming asked. 'In olden times,' Meng Huo explained, 'when the god worked his wrath, they sacrificed forty-nine human heads—seven times seven—a black ox and a white sheep; then the winds would ease, the waters would subside, and years of plenty would follow.'
>
> 時值九月秋天，忽然陰雲布合，狂風驟起；兵不能渡，回報孔明。孔明遂問孟獲，獲曰：「此水原有猖神作禍，往來者必須祭之。」孔明曰：「用何物祭享？」獲曰：「舊時國中因猖神作禍，用七七四十九顆人頭並黑牛白羊祭之，自然風恬浪靜，更兼連年豐稔。」[24]

Zhuge, the protagonist of the novel and the embodiment of traditional Chinese virtues such as wisdom and compassion, is understandably reluctant to pacify the volatile spirit with live human sacrifices. He comes up with an alternative solution:

> [Kongming] ordered his army cooks to slaughter oxen and horses and to compound a doughy preparation in the shape of a human head with a stuffing of beef and lamb; it was called 'dough-head'. That night on the bank of the Lu, Kongming set up an incense stand, laid out the offerings, and lined up forty-nine lamps. He then

raised streamers high to summon lost souls and placed the dough-heads on the ground. At the third watch Kongming, wearing a gilded headdress and a cloak of crane feathers, personally officiated at the sacrifice as Dong Jue read out the text.

〔孔明〕喚行廚宰殺牛馬；和麵為劑，塑成人頭，內以牛羊等肉代之，名曰「饅頭」。當夜於瀘水岸上，設香案，鋪祭物，列燈四十九盞，揚幡招魂；將饅頭等物，陳設於地。三更時分，孔明金冠鶴氅，親自臨祭，令董厥讀祭文。[25]

Although historically, the novel is probably incorrect in attributing the invention of the dough-head (*mantou* 饅頭) to Zhuge—the idea is first recorded in the Song dynasty text *Compound Source of Matters and Facts* (*Shiwu jiyuan* 事物紀原)[26]—the portrayal of his replacement of a human sacrifice with the sacrifice of the dough-heads demonstrates the significance of food as a literary motif— one which is consciously evoked by the story to enhance the characterization of Zhuge as a humanitarian captain of war. In addition, it highlights several important cultural facts, the most important being its reflection of society's cultural value in the emphasis of the moral superiority (and legitimacy) of the Han state, which is demarcated from the southern barbarians through the concepts of compassion and benevolence (*ren* 仁). Thus, although *Romance* is not a work that is commonly associated with food and drink, especially when compared to other classical novels such as *Red Chamber*, *Gold, Vase, and Plum Blossom* (*Jinpingmei* 金瓶梅) or the *Scholars* (*Rulin waishi* 儒林外史), the political importance of gastronomy to Chinese society is effectively demonstrated not only on the literary level as a powerful entity that contributes to the progress of the plot, but culturally as an important tool to distinguish the symbolic superiority of the Han culture.

Such gastronomic and culinary discourse reaffirms our reading of the role of food within the Chinese literary convention—as a concept that connotes more than straightforward carnal pleasures. We have seen that in ancient China, a perceived connection between gastronomy and morality was central to writings on food and other food-related concepts (such as the *taotie*). We have also suggested that such an illustration is actually dependent on the understanding that food and drink constitute the medium for cultural representation. It seems natural then, that following the legitimization of Confucianism during the Han dynasty and its subsequent politicization, the representation of food in literature also became more and more complex over time, especially since the distinctions between morality, politics, and culture became blurred to the point that 'neither politics nor morality had its independence, and the boundary between them was not clearly determined'.[27] In the rich repository of food metaphors in China's poetic tradition since the Tang dynasty, we not only find evidence of the continuation of the ancient tradition of associating morality with the gustatory, but also traces of the apparent expansion of this tradition—in the sense that the usage of food imagery as a means to express a wider range of personal and cultural politics became increasingly common. Examples include Li Shangyin's 李商隱 (c. 812–858) three interlinked and inter-implicated poems—'The Teasing of the Cherry by a Hundred Fruits' (*Baiguo chao yingtao* 百果嘲櫻桃), 'The Response of the Cherry' (*Yingtao da* 櫻桃答) and 'Teasing the Cherry' (*Chao yingtao* 嘲櫻桃)—in which the conventional application of food as an allegory to beauty (aesthetics) is powerfully combined with the poet's observation of contemporary corruption and moral degradation, which interjects a political dimension to the overall message of the poems,[28] and the image of the rotten fruit in many of Du Fu's poems, which serves as a parallel reflection of the physical and psychological decline of the elderly poet, who lived in poverty and drifted from place to place.[29] Besides reaffirming China's rich tradition of interleaving morality, along with its expanding implications, in the literary presentation of food, such evocations also implicate the Imperial Chinese writers' expanding awareness of the significance of the subject of food as a medium for the conveyance of issues of more wider ranging and profound social phenomena.

It should, however, be noted that the transcendence of food from physical nourishment to literary device, on which various moral, cultural, and political associations are formulated, is observable beyond the contextual characteristics of a text. For instance, in the *Notes from Chouchi* (*Chouchi biji* 仇池筆記), we find the following poem concerning a steamed pork dish that is allegedly composed by a monk dressed in purple (*Ziyi shi* 紫衣師):

嘴長毛短淺含臕	Its snout is long and its coat is short,
久同山中食藥苗	With a bit of fat it is raised on mountainous herbs;
蒸處已將蕉葉裹	It is wrapped in a layer of banana leaf and steamed,
熟時兼用杏漿澆	When cooked it is eaten with an apricot sauce;
紅鮮雅稱金盤飣	Its colour is red and it is served on a golden plate,
熟軟真堪玉箸挑	Its texture is soft enough to be picked apart by jade chopsticks;
若把膻根來比並	To compare it to a dish of lamb,
膻根自合吃藤條	The lamb is as fitting as the rattan.[30]

Regardless of the authenticity of the story, the fact that the topic of food is approached in such a playful manner illustrates the extent to which writers began to look to food, as both a type of sustenance and an art form, for various literary articulations. Moreover, such a poetic approach to both the process of eating and the preparation for the meal shows a new appreciation of food as delightful and worthy of celebration—an important psychological development that paves way not only for the expressiveness of such poems on food by Su Shi and Lu You 陸游 (1125–1210), but also for the legitimization of recipe writing as an art form, in anticipation of the emergence and popularity of such texts as Yuan Mei's 袁枚 (1716–1797) *The Recipes from the Sui Garden* (*Suiyuan shidan* 隨園食單). To borrow Ye Jiaying's 葉嘉瑩 comment on the 'wine poems' of Tao Qian 陶潛 (365–427)—that beyond the poet's personal experience and philosophies on life they also embody 'the historical belief and cultural values of ancient China'[31]—there may indeed be no better way to appreciate the politics of Chinese writings than through the subject of gastronomy.

Having observed a number of ways that Chinese literature deals with the theme of food, there is one rational question that needs to be answered: Why food? According to Michel Jeanneret:

> We live in a divided world, a world in which physical and mental pleasures are compartmentalized and ordered into a hierarchy: they either conflict with each other or are mutually exclusive. All sorts of ideological barriers exist between sense and the senses, between intellectual activity and the consumption of natural produce … the banquet is the one thing that overcomes this division and allows for the reconciliation of opposites … The combination of words and food in a convivial scene gives rise to a special moment when thought and the senses enhance rather than just tolerate each other.[32]

Although the scope of Jeanneret's research focuses on the European Renaissance, his statement nevertheless reflects a universal truth that fittingly summarizes the attraction of food to the Chinese writers, as well as the development of their fascination with the interrelationship between thought and the senses. This is especially the case given that food and drink in Chinese culture traverse the mundane and the solemn and bridge natural desire and cultural embellishment. Besides the tradition that is invested in the moral implications of food, through writing about the acts of eating and drinking, it becomes possible for the writer's personal experiences to transcend the microscopic level to reflect a greater cultural ideology shared by society. By charting the way the motif of food reveals and reflects such cultural, social, and political ideologies, as well as the strategy behind the individual authors' engagement and interaction with gastronomy and its literary implications, the potential of Chinese food literature not only holds the key to the long tradition of development of nutrition and culinary practice in ancient China, but more importantly, is reflective of the way Chinese society saw and interpreted the world throughout the imperial dynasties and up through modern times.

Chinese Food Literature through the Imperial Dynasties

The aim of this volume is to consider the cultural, social, and personal significance of the subject of food in imperial Chinese literature. We hope to do this
by exploring the ways these themes are presented in the writings of different
periods and by authors of dissimilar backgrounds, in order to illuminate some
of the many important implications of literary representations of the trope of
gastronomy.

If the evocation of food and drink in ancient Chinese literature holds special
significance in the embodiment of moralistic ideals, then wine, as an intoxicating
agent and a somewhat extravagant commodity, brings a unique perspective to
this intrinsic relationship between gastronomy, literature, and Chinese morality.
In 'From Conservatism to Romanticism: Wine and Prose-Writing from Pre-Qin to
Jin', Tak Kam Chan draws our attention to the unique place of wine within the
trope of food literature by charting the changing prosaic conceptualization of this
substance from the pre-Qin era to Wei-Jin period. By observing the way wine in
Pre-Qin prose is mostly alluded to in a restrictive manner and in association with
the aristocracy's sacrificial rites and social feasts, Chan notes the existence of a
clear moral censure of over-drinking, which changed in Han times when wine
drinking became a common activity among the literati class. Although moral
censure retained its influence throughout this transition, wine increasingly took
up the role in poetry as an intensifier of sensation or a reliever of sorrow and
worry. The positive perception of wine culminated in its synonymity with spiritual independence in the Wei-Jin era.

In 'The Morality of Drunkenness in Chinese Literature of the Third Century
CE', Nicholas Morrow Williams follows up Chan's scholarship and examines
the textual representation of wine during the Wei-Jin era. Unlike Chan's mac-
roscopic registration of the transformative evocation of wine through several
centuries of Chinese prose, Williams microscopically considers the polarizing
approaches to alcohol by the Han dynasty Daoist and Confucian traditions
and focuses upon the contention between the former's celebration of drunkenness and the latter's prohibitive stance. He draws our attention to the fact that
writers of the third century CE not only recognized but endeavoured to resolve
this dilemma in their writings. For example, in spite of their different political
agendas and affiliations, representative figures from the period, ranging from
Cao Cao 曹操 (155–220) to Ruan Ji 阮籍 (210–263) to Liu Ling 劉伶 (221–300), all,
to different extents, endeavoured to make sense of these two extreme interpretations of wine in their writings and displayed the predilection to debate the issue

with moralizing overtones. By paying close attention to their writings, Williams examines the political, social, and philosophical ramifications that are achieved by these writers in their literary representation of drunkenness and considers their significance in terms of establishing a literary convention for the integration of the 'authenticity and spontaneity of drunkenness into their everyday lives and convictions'.

In 'Making Poetry with Alcohol: Wine-Consumption in Tao Qian, Li Bai, and Su Shi', Charles Kwong demonstrates the significance of the wine eulogy in the poetic works of Tao Qian, Li Bai 李白 (701–762) and Su Shi. Noting the importance of wine as an ancient poetic motif in China's literary tradition, Kwong begins his argument by examining the way the various associative dimensions of wine came to their first apex of expression in the poetry of Tao Qian. As the masters of Tang poetry continued to develop existing themes of wine in relation to various facets of literati life, the extraordinary quality and flavour of Li Bai's poems, with celestial ingredients and seasonings, exemplified another height of the literary representation of wine. Song poetry and beyond took on a 'popular turn', featuring more wine drinking among the common folk. The usage of wine as a means of social criticism by these poets also received broader attention. The symbolic use of wine became more restricted in *ci* 詞 poetry and was largely limited to associations with negative feelings such as sadness or frustration. Yet there was a minority of song lyrics marked with tones of 'alcoholic vitality', especially in the works of Su Shi. Kwong's study demonstrates how certain aspects of wine, such as its use as a social catalyst, as an intensifier of emotions, and as an anaesthetic, have largely remained constant and how other aspects have been transformed through the enlightening experiences of philosophy and art.

In 'The Interplay of Social and Literary History: Tea in the Poetry of the Middle Historical Period', the historical and social importance of drink in Chinese literature is once again at the centre of investigation; but instead of wine, Ronald Egan considers the importance of tea in China's poetic tradition and proposes the possibility of using it as a means to gain a better understanding of the economic, cultural, and political changes that took place within the Tang-Song transition. By juxtaposing such changes with the dissimilar treatments of tea in the poetries of these two periods, Ronald Egan notes a similar change in the poetic expressiveness of tea and contemplates its potential as a means to gauge society's changing attitude toward leisure and connoisseurship. Because like alcohol, tea is a beverage that is not only popular in China[33] but also appeals to generations of writers as a subject of poetic expression, through paying close attention to the differences of tone in the poetic elucidation of tea in the Tang-Song period and by charting its parallel migration from the confinement of the monasteries to the urban setting, Egan's study importantly highlights the interest in food as a poetic motif during the Tang and the Song dynasties and reminds us once more of the implicit connection between this subject and society at large.

As food became more and more of an item associated with luxury and extravagance after the Song dynasty, its literary evocation also gained a different connotation in its reflection of this social change. In 'The Obsessive Gourmet: Zhang Dai on Food and Drink', Duncan M. Campbell contributes to our understanding of this growing culture of connoisseurship with a fascinating discussion of the Ming dynasty essayist Zhang Dai 張岱 (1597–1684?) and his philosophies of diet and food. Although Zhang's most representative work in this area, *Laotao ji* 老饕集, is no longer extant, by referencing his other food-related writings such as an epistolary on Zhang Donggu 張東谷 and the preface to *Laotao ji* (which has fortunately survived), Campbell is not only able to determine Zhang's stance on gastronomy and trace a correlation between his taste in food and his upbringing and outlook on life, but more importantly to consider the significance of food writing in relation to historicity. As Campbell surmises, 'Zhang Dai's engagement in this discourse of food and eating, and his compilation of his book of recipes, should best be understood in terms of a specific moment in time, the late Ming dynasty.' It is through such a perspective that Campbell acutely demonstrates an existing interrelationship between food and society in which, as shown by Zhang's presentation of food, gastronomy effectively becomes a reflective paradigm of the literati's social concerns. Campbell's conclusive statement concerning the importance of food as 'a highly moralized [discourse] that had implications of the most serious kind about political legitimacy and historical continuity' further emphasizes the importance of food literature during this period, as evidenced on both the micro level of the individual and the macro level of how the extant societal and cultural discourse on food is interpreted through the act of writing.

Along similar veins, Isaac Yue, in 'Tasting the Lotus: Food, Drink and the Objectification of the Female Body in *Gold, Vase, and Plum Blossom*', looks at the interconnection between literary conception and the implications of gastronomy as manifested in late Ming society. Instead of approaching the subject from a historical and social perspective and contemplating the textual representation of food as reflective of such cultural paradigms, Yue concentrates on the materialization of this discourse in the novel tradition and examines the significance of the motif of food in *Gold, Vase, and Plum Blossom*—an important novel that is considered by C. T. Hsia to be full of 'contradictory moral and religious assumptions'[34] that are typical of the late Ming period. In examining this text that is

primarily conceived of in terms of its sexual politics and eroticism, and appreciated by critics such as Martin W. Huang for its 'ramifications of private desires
and how people are simultaneously driven and consumed by these desires',[35]
Yue argues for the importance of food in the work as not only illustrative of
the dining habits of late Ming society, but as a strategic literary theme that is
consciously intended by the author to complement the overt sexual politics of
the novel. His study of the linguistic and contextual evocation of food in the
novel, beside shedding light on the self-positioning of the work within the tradition of food literature in China, also highlights the way this tradition is evoked/
manipulated by the author as a means to establish the social position of women
as well as the overall gender dynamics of the text.

Next we move from one canonical novel to another, in 'Eating and Drinking
in a Red Chambered Dream', Louise Edwards examines the significance of gastronomy in the most celebrated novel in imperial China, *The Dream of the Red
Chamber* by Cao Xueqin 曹雪芹. The premise of Edwards's argument concerns
the way food and drink are entwined with the key messages of the novel—the
tragedy of impermanence and the impossibility of maintaining purity in an
impure world—and the evocation of these tropes delineate the boundaries
between purity and profanity. For example, while alcohol consumption within
the Prospect Garden (*Daguan yuan* 大觀園) by pure, young women brings no ill
effect and is in fact likened to a magical fairy party, excessive drinking outside
of the garden results in disaster. Similarly, although a separate kitchen is set up
to specially serve the residents of the Prospect Garden so as to protect the purity
inside, there is no stopping the entry of outside food which signals the polluting effect of the profane world outside. By considering the ways in which such
examples from the novel bear testimony to the close relationship between food
and ethical values, Edwards reveals the extent to which the concept of eating
and drinking is used by Cao to set up the gradual and inevitable pollution of the
purity of the Prospect Garden by the profane world outside.

In David Knechtges' opinion, the subject of food in Chinese literature is 'as
inexhaustible as the vast variety of Chinese cuisine'.[36] By investigating textual
representations of food in relation to the agendas of the writers, the types of text
in which they appear, and the context under which nourishment is evoked as a
literary motif, it is hoped that this project will not only contribute to the understanding of the cultural and social significance of food in the Chinese literary tradition, but also lead to other studies of this kind and encourage more discussion
on China's rich and unique gastronomic tradition from a literary perspective.

2
From Conservatism to Romanticism

Wine and Prose-Writing from Pre-Qin to Jin

Tak Kam Chan

Wine has emerged as a recurring theme in classical Chinese prose in its three thousand years of historical development. At least three points of general significance may be kept in mind in studying early prose writings related to wine. First, wine was a luxury in ancient China; making wine required a lot of labour and grain. Second, the consumption of wine can produce diametrically opposite effects: duly enjoyed on ceremonial occasions, wine may foster a harmonious feeling between a ruler and his ministers and subjects, yet excessive drinking may cause chaos and even ruin human relationships or corrupt government in serious cases. Such diverse effects are well reflected in prose writings prior to the Tang dynasty, attesting to a cultural phenomenon fraught with potential tensions. Third, drinking is seen as an activity that facilitates artistic creation. Literati whose spirits wander in surreal drunken states feel more connected to the pulse of the universe, which enables them to capture the kaleidoscopic changes of the natural environment. One may say that studying the wine motif in early Chinese literati prose-writing can help us understand the ancient elite's way of feeling and thinking. Wine traverses between culture and daily life, between abstraction and concreteness; it is a catalyst as well as an object of art, playing a meaningful role in the historical development of classical Chinese prose.

Wine and Prohibition of Drinking in Ancient (Pre-Qin) Prose

True to the Chinese cultural tradition, references to drinking in early Chinese literature do not start with the merry enjoyment of wine but with the prohibition of drinking. It is believed that Yu 禹, the founder of the Xia dynasty, was the first ruler to propose the prohibition of wine:

> Yi Di, daughter of Emperor [Yao or Shun], made delicious wine and offered it to Yu as a tribute. After tasting its sweetness, Yu kept Yi Di at a distance and never touched the fine wine again, saying that wine would destroy someone's kingdom some day.

帝〔堯或舜〕女儀狄作酒而美，進之禹，禹飲而甘之，遂疏儀狄而絕旨酒。曰，後世必有以酒亡其國者。[1]

Yu is a wise ruler who knows the potential danger of fine wine. Yet his descendant Jie 桀 is notorious for drinking excessively, 'wasting labour and using up people's money to build a wine pond with a bank of dregs, indulging in effeminate pleasure and gathering three thousand people to drink at the strike of a drum' 罷民力，殫民財，為酒池糟隄，縱靡靡之樂，一鼓而牛飲者三千人.[2] The evil effects of a ruler's drinking addiction are fully revealed: waste of labour, abandonment to lust, neglect of official affairs and the fact that every drinker belongs to the ruling class—all are signs leading to political doom. The Shang dynasty that overthrew the Xia ended in a similar way. From the large number of drinking vessels unearthed at the ruins of the Shang capital (*Yinxu* 殷墟), like *jue* 爵, *jia* 斝, *he* 盉, *gong* 觥, *you* 卣, *zun* 尊, *yi* 彝, *lei* 罍, etc., one might infer that the Shang was probably a wine-indulging dynasty (at least among the ruling classes), with a drunkard King Zhou 紂 as its last ruler. After overthrowing the Shang, Ji Dan 姬旦, Duke of Zhou 周公 (?–? BCE), wrote the famous 'Announcement against Drinking' (*Jiu gao* 酒誥) for his people, the first piece of wine-prohibiting writing in recorded Chinese history. He criticizes King Zhou of Shang as follows:

> He was simply obsessed with drinking and refused to refrain from pleasure. He had a perverse and cruel heart with no fear of death. He behaved badly at Yin [Shang's capital] without worrying about its fall. No fragrant sacrifices ascended to Heaven; only people's grievances and drunken officials' rank alcoholic odour did. Thus Heaven showed no love for Yin and sent down destruction.
>
> 惟荒腆於酒，不惟自息、乃逸。厥心疾很，不克畏死；辜在商邑，越殷國滅無罹。弗惟德馨香、祀登聞於天，誕惟民怨。庶群自酒，腥聞在上；故天降喪於殷，罔愛於殷。[3]

The warning relates the immorality of excessive drinking to irreverence toward the Lord-on-High, so that to avoid His repeated punishment, people might be more willing to follow the Duke of Zhou's advice. In any case, making wine required a large amount of grain, and thus needed to be regulated in a simple agricultural society without overtaxing the food supply. Any drinking behaviour not restrained by proper etiquette was regarded as a moral hazard.

It is possible that the Duke of Zhou's serious approach muted early Chinese interest in wine, with the result that discussions of drinking are rare in ancient philosophical prose. The wine recorded in the 'Wine Rites of the District Symposium' 鄉飲酒禮 in the *Book of Etiquette* (*Yili* 儀禮) merely serves as a component of ritualistic formalities. It may be noted that Confucius 孔子 (551–479 BCE), a reverent admirer of the Duke of Zhou, holds a comparatively relaxed attitude to wine: 'only in wine does [the *junzi* 君子] set no limits, but he never drinks himself to confusion'.[4] As long as one does not lose one's senses, drinking is acceptable to the morally noble man. Confucius also once states, 'Serving high ministers when abroad and family elders when home; conscious of no neglect in funeral matters; not be overwhelmed by wine—how could such things be difficult for me?'[5] The inner-worldly sage is quite confident about maintaining self-control amid the activity of drinking, but such an attitude is relatively rare among pre-Qin thinkers.

Interestingly enough, neither Zhuang Zhou 莊周 (c. 369–286 BCE), known as a champion of carefree spontaneity in his philosophical prose, nor his followers who edited the book of *Zhuangzi* 莊子, wrote much about drinking. It is stated in the 'Mastering Life' 達生 chapter that 'If a drunkard falls from a carriage, he would not die even though the carriage is moving at full speed. His bones and joints are the same as other people, but he would not get hurt like them because his spirit remains wholesome' 夫醉者之墜車，雖疾不死。骨節與人同而犯害與人異，其神全也。[6] This example of a partially conscious drunkard that remains unhurt in a vehicular accident illustrates the point that anyone in tune with the Way of Nature and undistracted by human fear has the best chance of avoiding injury by external agents. Of course this does not mean Zhuangzi endorses drinking: a well-known saying from the 'The Mountain Tree' 山木 chapter states, 'Friendship between gentlemen is mild like water; that between petty people is sweet like *li*' 君子之交淡若水，小人之交甘若醴。[7] *Li* is refined wine, and is used here as a metaphor for the association between petty people whose material interests intoxicate them. A third wine-related statement in the *Zhuangzi* is found in the 'Imputed Words' 寓言 chapter, where three types of language (imputed words, repeated words, and goblet words)[8] are mentioned. Among these, 'goblet' in 'goblet words' 卮言 is a kind of wine cup, and annotators offer varying interpretations of it. If *zhi* is taken as an empty wine vessel, goblet words could refer to 'empty', unbiased language that reflects reality as it is;[9] thus it would be misguided to interpret the term as 'blabber when drunk' or 'fragmented language'. Zhuangzi's own philosophy is clear and penetrating, without ever descending into blabber. It is important to remember that in keeping with Zhuangzi's philosophy, wine is used in this chapter as an analogy rather than an actual substance; to pick up a wine cup and claim to incarnate Zhuangzi's Way, as some literati did in later generations, is simply reflective of wishful understanding. Zhuangzi is a free and easy but sober man in his philosophical work.

Only a story in the *Liezi* 列子, commonly regarded as a Daoist work, briefly shows a positive defence of wine in ancient China. Zichan 子產 (Gongsun

Qiao 公孫僑, ?–522 BCE), a statesman of the state of Zheng 鄭, has an elder brother Gongsun Chao 公孫朝 who is extremely fond of wine. The latter's story is recorded in the 'Yang Zhu' 楊朱 chapter, and his unbridled behaviour is described as follows:

> Chao's house stores a thousand pots of wine and piles of yeast, so one can already smell the grain mesh from a hundred paces away. When he indulges in drinking, he forgets all about the world's disputes, human fortune, personal possessions, gradations of familial closeness as well as the joys and sorrows of life and death. He remains oblivious even if natural and man-made disasters come together before him.
> 朝之室也，聚酒千鐘，積麴成封，望門百步，糟漿之氣逆於人鼻。方其荒於酒也，不知世道之爭危，人理之悔吝，室內之有亡，九族之親疏，存亡之哀樂也。雖水火兵刃交于前，弗知也。[10]

Zichan tries in vain to exhort his brother to give up drinking. Gongsun Chao's reasoning is that life is short, and already he feels 'too full to be able to drink without restraint' 患腹溢而不得恣口之飲. Chao despises concepts like humanity, righteousness and morality. Compared to Zhuangzi, he seems much closer to being a model of the Wei-Jin 魏晉 Pure Conversationists, as well as a role model for those who enter 'Drunkenland' 醉鄉, voluntarily or involuntarily. Zichan's position is closer to the practical Confucianist Xunzi 荀子 (c. 313–238 BCE), who spares no effort lashing at Confucian scholars unworthy of the name, calling them 'base *ru*'.[11] In 'Contra Twelve Philosophers' 非十二子, Xunzi dismisses such scholars as creatures of excessive eating and drinking instead of upright and well-mannered gentlemen, criticizing them for their 'muddle and blindness amid wine, food, music and women' 酒食聲色之中，則瞞瞞然，瞑瞑然.[12] In this he is in agreement with Mencius 孟子 (c. 372–289 BCE), who stresses moral conduct over vain pursuits. His famous story 'The Qi Man with a Wife and Concubine' 齊人有一妻一妾 in the 'Li lou' 離婁 chapter of *Mencius* 孟子 digs at the vulgar person who eats and drinks sacrificial leftovers at graveyards and deceives his wife and concubine by pretending to have social connections with wealthy people. Drinking is vanity here.

As the two main schools of thought in the late Zhou, both Confucianism and Daoism (the latter if only by implication) were set against excessive drinking for different reasons. Confucianism saw wild drinking as leading to social disorder, personal corruption and dereliction of public duties, and so advocated regulating drinking within the domain of rites. Daoism rarely touched on the positive effects of drinking, probably because it teaches that only a clear-headed person can attain the highest reaches of spiritual cultivation. The consequences of getting drunk are mostly negative in pre-Qin 先秦 works and records. Only one person seemed to have benefited greatly from his circumstantial drunkenness, namely Duke Wen of Jin 晉文公 (697–628 BCE), known as Chonger 重耳 prior to coming to power. Having escaped to the state of Qi 齊, whose king found him a wife and bestowed many presents upon him, Chonger nursed little motivation to return to his own state and reclaim his position. His wife, who exhorted him in vain to return to Jin, plotted with one of his attendants to get him drunk and carried out of Qi in 637 BCE.

Wine and the Emerging Temperament: Drinking Scenes in Han-Wei-Jin Prose

Most pre-Qin prose, then, voiced a negative view on wine, which was clearly an extension of the theme of prohibiting excessive drinking. By the Han dynasty, the heavily moral tone against drinking seemed to have receded a little, or at least came to be blended with a more positive appreciation of drinking as a reflection of heroic spirit or genuine friendship. This more comprehensive appraisal of the activity of drinking may be related to the expansive spirit of the unified Han empire or even a more confident view of history. Take the historical prose of Sima Qian 司馬遷 (c. 145–87 BCE) for example: his *Records of the Grand Historian* 史記 describes many important drinkers and drinking scenes, including the famous assassin Jing Ke 荊軻 (d. 227 BCE) in 'Biographies of Assassins' 刺客列傳:

> Jing Ke loved wine. He drank with his dog butcher friend and Gao Jianli in the market in Yan every day. When they became heavily drunk, Gao would play the string instrument *zhu*, accompanied by Jing singing in the market. They were happy together, yet within a moment they would wail to each other as if nobody was around. While Jing spent much time with drinkers, he was a thoughtful person and liked to read.
>
> 荊軻嗜酒，日與狗屠及高漸離飲於燕市，酒酣以往，高漸離擊筑，荊軻和而歌於市中，相樂也，已而相泣，旁若無人者。荊軻雖游於酒人乎，然其為人沉深好書。[13]

As a matter of fact, these two assassins who failed in their attempt to assassinate the First Emperor of Qin 秦始皇 were ordinary people who could not afford to drink wine all the time, let alone run wild and fail in their official duties after getting drunk. They had no constant assets and roved from place to place, waiting for a chance to serve the aristocrats. What they counted on was their prowess—capable of changing history given favourable special conditions. Such is the historical viewpoint of Sima Qian: however humble his birth, man is the creator of history. To properly reflect this viewpoint, Sima Qian must show the complete face of the portrayed characters. Drinking scenes, along with the characters' words and actions, highlight their role on the stage of history. Jing Ke and

Gao Jianli were not mere passers-by in the turbulent Warring States era, but men of deep emotional substance whose sense of commitment thrust them forward to serve the state of Yan against the dominant Qin. Wine drinking is an integral part of Sima Qian's portrayal of his lively heroic characters.

Slips and errors arising from drunkenness often repeat in history. In *Records of the Grand Historian*, it is recorded in 'Biographies of the Marquis of Weiqi and Marquis of Wu'an' 魏其武安侯列傳 that Guan Fu 灌夫, a general with military achievement, upset the prime minister Tian Fen 田蚡 (Marquis of Wu'an) at a banquet and was sentenced to death along with his entire family. Criticizing the statesman who framed a good man because of a minor quibble after getting drunk, Sima Qian is quite sympathetic about Guan Fu's embroilment in the political conflict of imperial concubines. Sima Qian describes him as 'upright, wine-loving and not obsequious' 為人剛直使酒，不好面諛,[14] putting him more or less in the same category as Jing Ke—people who act in a frank, forthright manner. Though drunkenness cost him his life, wine seems to be symbolic of Guan Fu's bold, fearless spirit, and only those who value genuine friendship can drink freely together.

Most readers of *Records of the Grand Historian* enjoy the 'Hongmen Banquet' 鴻門宴 episode concerning Xiang Yu 項羽 (232–202 BCE). The most touching detail in this episode is probably the scene when Fan Kuai 樊噲, a general in the camp of Xiang's rival Liu Bang 劉邦 (256–195 BCE), bursts into Xiang's tent to plead Liu Bang's case. Xiang unexpectedly offers Fan a large cup of wine and calls him a hero, without doing him any harm (see 'Annals of Xiang Yu' 項羽本紀). Here, offering wine represents a gesture of respect for the heroic spirit. Interestingly, when Sima Qian was found guilty on account of defending Li Ling 李陵, he observed that he had 'never shared wine' 未嘗置杯酒[15] with Li, by way of pointing out that they were not close friends. Here wine is seen as yet another positive symbol—of friendship.

In the prose writings of the Wei and Jin dynasties, wine drinking seems to be marked less by heroic spirit and pure affection, than by the political considerations of rulers and the plaintiveness of the oppressed. Cao Cao 曹操 (155–220), de facto ruler of the last two decades of the Han, once imposed a prohibition on wine in order to prevent social turbulences. Kong Rong 孔融 (153–208) wrote to express his discontent, especially since he thought Cao Cao was a wine-loving poet himself. As Lu Xun 魯迅 (1881–1936) shrewdly observes, 'as a man of business, Cao Cao had no choice but to do it' 因曹操是個辦事人，所以不得不這樣做,[16] even against his own habits. As for Kong Rong, he aroused Cao Cao's anger and hastened his own execution. In practical terms, it would have been better for him either to stay silent, or to get drunk and feign madness.

Unlike Kong Rong, many literati of the Wei-Jin era learned not to voice their discontent in public. Mindful that unexpected adversities might arrive at any time, they drank in order to preserve their lives and enhance a precarious sense of existence. They seemed to be carefree and indulgent on the surface, but were in fact laden with inner worries and misery. *A New Account of Tales of the World* 世說新語, known for its truthful reflection of the Wei-Jin literati's lives, records many stories of famous literati of the time drinking all day, remaining drunk and acting wildly (especially in the 'Ren dan' 任誕 chapter): 'rather than leaving a name after death, why not enjoy a cup of wine right now?' 使我有身後名，不如即時一杯酒[17] While most traditional literati loved fame, Zhang Han 張翰 (fl. late third century) would rather have given up his official position than the pleasure of wine. Drinking had become a symbol of individual freedom.

It can be seen from the above sketch that if the role of wine was seen in the context of morality, politics and human relationships in pre-Han literature, drinking gradually earned a more independent status since the Han. While a close examination of *fu* 賦, a mixed genre of prose and poetry prevalent in the Han, lies beyond the scope of the present essay, it may be noted in passing that the Chinese literati's detailed writing on wine was first seen in Han *fu*. In keeping with the basic principle of detailed objective description in writing Han *fu*, there are various works that contain concrete accounts of wine drinking and its functions and effects, including several pieces with wine as their title, e.g. 'Wine *fu*' 酒賦 by Zou Yang 鄒陽 (?–120 BCE), Yang Xiong 揚雄 (53–18 BCE), Wang Can 王粲 (177–217) and Cao Zhi 曹植 (192–232). In addition, drinking scenes also appear in other pieces such as Mei Sheng's 枚乘 (d. 140 BCE) 'Seven Stimuli' 七發, Ban Gu's 班固 (32–92) '*Fu* on Two Capitals' 兩都賦 and Zhang Heng's 張衡 (78–139) '*Fu* on the South Capital' 南都賦. In order to help the emperor display the prosperity of the regime as well as the grandeur and solemnity of court ceremonies, *fu* writers of the Han often tried to write something in a grand 'exhibitionist' spirit. As an integral component of ceremonies and rituals, wine drinking was one of the emperor's means of gaining the support of officials and common people; for their part, government officials and literati needed to maintain self-control on these drinking occasions.[18] Han *fu* writers often remind people not to drink excessively, but most descriptions of drinking scenes or the history of wine actually convey a sense of excitement. Despite giving weak and perfunctory warnings against drinking at the end of the pieces, *fu* often ends up affirming drinking rather than denigrating it, encouraging people to drink in order to reach beyond secular restraints. For example, Cao Zhi's 'Wine *fu*' carries an implication of breaking social barriers, and seems to go against his father Cao Cao's prohibition on wine.[19] That said, this mode of enjoyment was still deemed improper if carried to excess.[20]

Since drinking was not heavily censured in the Jin dynasty, there continued to be *fu* works that discuss the merits and demerits of wine. For example, an 'Admonition to Stop Drinking' 斷酒戒 by Yu Chan 庾闡 (fl. early fourth century) adopts a negative attitude towards drinking, on the ground that 'intemperance sacrifices true essence' 任欲喪真, yet the prohibitionist's stance is somewhat weakened in the face of the drunkard's defence that 'open-minded people drink to their contentment without restraint, letting go of trifles and getting through to the great Way' 達人暢而不壅，抑其小節而濟大通.[21] In fact, making use of the conversational feature of this genre, the *fu* writer skilfully puts together two different functions—'to satirize' and 'to encourage'—in the same piece of writing, his attitude to any given issue being manifested in the relative weight of satire and encouragement in a particular piece. Among all the *fu* writings on wine, Liu Ling's 劉伶 (c. 221–300) 'Encomium to the Power of Wine' 酒德頌 is probably the most famous one, describing the drunken state of the main character in a lively manner:

> There is a great man who regards all time since creation as a day, ten thousand years as a moment ... Holding his pot and wine instrument, the great man enjoys the mellow wine in his cup ... He nurses neither thought nor worry, but remains happy and carefree ... He does not feel the effects of coldness or heat, or any desire for personal gain. He surveys all things disturbing one another like duckweed ever floating on the rivers.
>
> 有大人先生者，以天地為一朝，萬朝為須臾，……先生於是方捧罌承槽，銜杯漱醪。……無思無慮，其樂陶陶。……不覺寒暑之切肌，利欲之感情。俯觀萬物，擾擾焉如江漢三載浮萍。[22]

The writings of Cao Zhi, Liu Ling and Yu Chan on wine (and similar pieces by others like Zou Yang, Yang Xiong, Wang Can, etc.) should be seen as a continuing tradition. They help to show that wine has a positive meaning not only in personal but also in social terms. For the common people, wine is an agent of merriment available to the poor and inferior. While drinking freely and becoming intoxicated, they can discard social conventions and move away from political constraints. They need not envy the rich and kneel before the powerful, but can attain a carefree state of no desire. Figures like prefects of mores, young aristocrats and gentry hermits become targets of satire, while drinking wise men and 'great men' are the truly lofty spirits. Far from being repulsive, their drunken state is an elevation of their life.

Unity with the Way and Nature

From Liu Ling's biography in the *History of the Jin Dynasty* 晉書, we know that he is an intellectual follower of Zhuang Zhou's otherworldly spirit, with 'no restraints on his affection, always belittling the mundane world and seeing the equality of all things in his heart. Tranquil and taciturn, he did not make friends recklessly' 放情肆志，常以細宇宙齊萬物為心，澹默少言，不妄交.[23] He formed the 'Seven Worthies of the Bamboo Grove' 竹林七賢 with several kindred spirits, including Ruan Ji 阮籍 (210–263) and Ji Kang 嵇康 (224–263), whose temperaments were similar to his. Ruan and Ji's prose writing often contain characters similar to the 'great man' in Liu Ling's 'Encomium to the Power of Wine'. Ruan has a piece entitled 'Biography of the Great Man' 大人先生傳, in which the main character revolts against the secular world and yearns for Nature: 'He regards ten thousand *li* as a step and a thousand years as a day. He does not travel for a purpose or live in one place, but is in quest of the Way with no other commitment' 以萬里為一步，以千歲為一朝。行不赴而居不處，求乎大道而無所寓.[24] Ji states directly that he always drinks excessively, and that his character makes him unfit to be a government official; thus he scolds those friends who recommend him for a post. Ruan's 'great man' does not drink, and his philosophy reflects the rational side of those retiring from the world. Ji's writing, on the other hand, reveals the emotional conflict of a person refusing to serve as an official: he cared about the common people, yet refused to be associated with corrupt political power and would rather stay out of officialdom, so that he could remain 'self-contented and carefree' 自得而無悶.[25]

Throughout the Wei-Jin era, the anxiety and instability of existence remained a concern for many literati who found themselves out of tune with the turbulent times and violent political environment. A sense of existential transience persisted in the relatively stable years of the Eastern Jin, and drinking enabled the literati to comprehend the transience of life in a deeper way. Writers laden with a sense of life's vicissitudes or attempting to escape from politics often used drinking parties as occasions to get closer to Nature, in the hope of seeking happiness and release. In the 'Preface to the Orchid Pavilion Collection [of Poems]' 蘭亭集序, Wang Xizhi 王羲之 (303–361) sums up not a few literati's state of mind:

> Human beings come to know each other, yet life passes swiftly by … Although people make different choices and differ in nature in terms of quietude and restlessness, when they meet something gratifying to the self, they will become happy and contented, forgetting the onset of old age; yet once they feel weary of it, their mood changes with the circumstances, and regret follows.

夫人之相與，俯仰一世……雖取舍萬殊，靜躁不同，當其欣於所遇，暫得於己，快
然自足，不知老之將至；及其所之既倦，情隨事遷，感慨係之矣。[26]

Amid the beautiful scenery of Nature, drinking enhances the writer's pleasure
and deepens his sense of life. Scholars of later ages certainly need not imitate
the Orchid Pavilion literati's refined enjoyment of the *qushui liushang* 曲水流觴
game (channelling water into a winding stream on which wine cups are floated),
but the spirit of drinking in Nature is a timelessly inspiring experience. From
those living in semi-exile because of demotion to those stumbling along a bumpy
path in life, scholars gain extra creative inspiration or a special visa of the landscape and the Way as compensation. As an important subgenre of Chinese prose,
travel writing also began to appear in this era with a broad artistic awakening to
the grandeur of Nature, and literary writing continued to deepen with a sense
of the interplay of the subjective and the objective spirit in Nature. Man is part
of objective Nature, yet the human subject is able to perceive and experience it.
What is more, the paradox of this double identity of subject-object can be transformed through a certain degree of intoxication into inspiration for the creative
imagination.

The most famous Jin writer known for drinking and living in Nature is
undoubtedly Tao Yuanming 陶淵明 (365–427). He often mentions drinking in his
works, and put together a sequence of twenty poems entitled 'Drinking Wine' 飲
酒, one of which states the spiritual meaning of drinking clearly: 'Unable to feel
my own self, / Would I know the importance of other things? / Deeply lost in
where I linger, / There are deep flavours in wine!' 不覺知有我，安知物為貴。悠
悠迷所留，酒中有深味。[27]

Allowing one to forget about constraints in reality, drinking is thus conducive
to writing. Tao's love for wine is not just escapism but part of his nature. At the
age of forty, he worked as a local government official for another brief period,
admitting frankly that he did it because income from public fields enabled him
to make good wine. But he left officialdom only after three months, and his
affinity for wine seemed to become even stronger. Wine has become his close
friend, the social bond between him and his fellow farmers, and a catalyst for
his art—his poetry and prose are full of the wine subject. Tao's portraits of his
maternal grandfather Meng Jia 孟嘉, of the autobiographical 'Gentleman of the
Five Willows' 五柳先生, of himself in 'Return Home *fu*' 歸去來兮辭 and 'Self-
Elegy' 自祭文, are all about people who enjoy drinking without becoming dis-
orderly. Without wine, there might have been less inspiration, fewer poems and
compositions; he might have lost part of his intimate relationship with pure,
simple Nature and part of his creative source. Without wine, Tao would have

found it harder to rise to a higher spiritual level that enables him to forget his frustrations and hardships in life.

Tao Yuanming's drinking is a kind of aesthetic praxis, different from Liu Ling and Ruan Ji's drinking as a passive revolt against the secular world. Tao deeply inspired later writers who admired his personality and his works, as well as those who followed his reclusive path. Wine offers inspiration, expands the personality, and enables one to resist suppression of the individual in reality. Its positive effect is to allow one to return to his true nature, and live a life where he can better direct his own destiny. One notes that in his famous prose work 'Peach Blossom Spring' 桃花源記, the residents welcome the fisherman with food and wine, showing that prohibition of drinking is not needed in a society where human nature is not suppressed.

Conclusion

From collective memory to cultural inheritance, from prohibition to drinking, wine has been an important topic in classical Chinese literature, permeating different levels of creative composition. As a literary topic, its significance lies not only in terms of quantity, but also in its genre-shaping influence. In pre-Qin times, statements about wine are mainly found in historical and philosophical texts, which serve as background, memory and teachings underlying literary composition. More detailed descriptions of the phenomenon of drinking are found in the Han period's historical prose and 'rhyme-prose', with a less dogmatic and deeper humanistic tone. After the Wei-Jin period, wine came to be linked to Daoist philosophy, helping writers to rediscover their sense of self, to explore an often submerged spirit beneath their social role, and so expand their artistic experience. In the process, wine became an element that facilitated and accompanied the development of travel prose literature in later times; but that is a long story beyond the present discussion.

While drinking always kept its social function in traditional Chinese culture, and at times even continued to serve as an escape from political affairs,[28] wine became more and more a matter of individual spiritual and aesthetic experience in traditional literati culture. Since Tang times, literati rarely displayed the kind of wild behaviour seen in the Wei-Jin era while they were drinking; and that, perhaps more than the Wei-Jin 'Pure Conversationists', helped to maintain a living relationship between wine and a kind of 'romanticism' 風流 in Chinese culture and literature.

3
The Morality of Drunkenness in Chinese Literature of the Third Century CE

Nicholas Morrow Williams

Sobriety diminishes, discriminates, and says no; drunkenness expands, unites, and says yes. It is in fact the great exciter of the YES function in man. It brings its votary from the chill periphery of things to the radiant core. It makes him for the moment one with truth.[1]

—William James

It is not wine that intoxicates, but men who intoxicate themselves.
酒不醉人人自醉

—Proverb

Introduction: The Moral Ambiguity of Alcohol

The symbolic significance of alcohol and drunkenness is ambivalent, encompassing both its intense pleasures and unruly consequences.[2] We find this ambivalence stated neatly in the definition of 'alcohol' given by Xu Shen 許慎 (c. 58–147 CE):

> 'Alcohol' (*jiu*) means 'to achieve' (*jiu*). It is what is used to achieve the good and evil in human nature. It is composed of 水 and 酉, and 酉 is also the phonetic. It also means 'to produce', since it is what produces good and bad fortune. In ancient times Yi Di invented unfiltered ale. Yu tasted it and found it excellent, but then exiled Yi Di. Du Kang invented rice wine.
> 酒就也。所以就人性之善惡。從水酉，酉亦聲。一曰造也，吉凶所造起也。古者儀狄作酒醪，禹嘗之而美，遂疏儀狄。杜康作秫酒。[3]

Xu Shen begins with a paronomastic gloss that introduces the duality of alcohol. It is something like a catalyst that can help to realize both the positive and negative potential of human beings. The origin stories recounted in the second half of the entry make clear that this ambivalence was present even at the invention of alcohol in China. The exile of Yi Di is the primeval example of the suspicion directed at alcohol, even by those like Yu who appreciated its taste. Alcohol can encourage both good and evil tendencies, so its role in society at large is ambiguous, but it stands in particular tension to the interests of the state, and its successful invention was followed immediately by the banishment of its inventor. As we shall see below, both the good and evil consequences of alcohol would continue to reverberate in Chinese culture, reaching a climax after the fall of the Eastern Han.

The rewards of drinking are recognized as early as the *Classic of Poetry* 詩經, which praises its health benefits: 'Make this spring wine, / To aid your bushy-browed longevity' 為此春酒，以介眉壽.[4] There are some curious anecdotes that attribute similar functions to alcohol, as in the *Shenyi jing* 神異經 (Classic of the divine and marvellous):

> In the wastes to the northwest there is a Wine Spring. When people drink this wine, it is delicious as meat, clear as a mirror. Above the spring there is a jade goblet. When you take one goblet, another goblet appears. It is as permanent as Heaven and Earth and will never dry up. Those who drink this wine live forever.
> 西北荒中有酒泉。人飲此酒，酒美如肉，清如鏡。其上有玉樽，取一樽，復一樽出。與天地同休，無乾時。飲此酒人，不死長生。[5]

These associations of alcohol and longevity are not unlike the contemporary scientific claim that red wine, drunk in moderation, can promote longevity. However, this positive association of alcohol is an individual and even selfish one. The immortality granted by the alcoholic spring belongs to a realm outside of civilization, isolated from human society. The pleasure of drunkenness was something private and even taboo; as Li Bai wrote: 'If you should reach wine's true delight, / Don't tell the sober people a word!' 但得酒中趣，毋為醒者傳.[6] Though Li Bai's statements of this point of view are most famous, there are numerous earlier precedents, of which Yu Xin's couplet is perhaps most succinct: 'When you have a glass of wine before your eyes, / Who would speak of fame that outlasts death?' 眼前一杯酒，誰論身後名.[7] In poetry, alcohol was typically presented as an aid for enjoyment of the present moment, and also a way to evade the concerns of the sober and serious.

The *Zhuangzi* uses drunkenness as a metaphor for the ideal form of escape from societal pressures. It presents drunkenness (with admiration) as a kind of escape from worldly dangers, a lesser form of the sage's indifference:

> When a drunken man is thrown from a cart, swiftly though he falls it does not kill him. His bones and joints are the same as another man's, yet he is not harmed as another man would be, because of the integrity of his spirit. He rides without knowing it, falls without knowing it; life and death, astonishment and fear, find no entry into his breast, and so he does not shrink from hitting things. If this is true even of a man who gets his integrity from wine, how much more is it true of those who get it from Heaven! The sage hides himself in Heaven, and therefore nothing can harm him.

夫醉者之墜車，雖疾不死。骨節與人同而犯害與人異，其神全也，乘亦不知也，墜
亦不知也，死生驚懼不入乎其胷中，是故遌物而不慴。彼得全於酒而猶若是，而況
得全於天乎？聖人藏於天，故莫之能傷也。[8]

This kind of praise for drunkenness uses exactly the same terms with which a Confucian might anathematize drinking as vice. For both, alcohol would be a tool that allows people to forget their obligations, to become numb to customary pressures, and to achieve a kind of liberation that is effectively antisocial.

Thus praise for alcohol prepared the way for a moralistic denunciation of exactly the same properties. Alcohol consumed in excess leads inevitably to destructive and antisocial behaviour, as recognized in the *Li ji* 禮記 (Book of rites):

> Feeding pigs and making wine [to prepare for a feast] do not in themselves lead to disaster. But lawsuits grow increasingly frequent, and it is the pouring of wine that incurs the disaster. Thus the former kings made the drinking rituals on this account. The ritual of offering wine, making the hundred obeisances of guest and host, allow people to drink all day long but never become drunk. This was the measure taken by the former kings to ward off disasters incurred by wine. Wine and feasting are used to create shared happiness; music is used to demonstrate virtue; and the rites are used to stave off excess.
>
> 夫豢豕為酒，非以為禍也，而獄訟益繁，則酒之流生禍也。是故先王因為酒禮，壹
> 獻之禮，賓主百拜，終日飲酒而不得醉焉；此先王之所以備酒禍也。故酒食者所以
> 合歡也；樂者所以象德也；禮者所以綴淫也。[9]

Here we see an especially stark tension between the disordering power of alcohol and social harmony. With proper ritual protocols established, certainly, people may drink 'all day' without even becoming intoxicated, so alcohol is not actually prohibited. But its singular potency must be sharply curtailed, or it is constantly in danger of creating 'excess' (*yin* 淫).

One way to describe these contrasting depictions of alcohol's role in early China would be to say that Confucianism prohibited excessive drinking, while Daoism celebrated it. However, abstractions of 'Confucian' or 'Daoist' doctrine are misleading; in fact, the dual perspectives on alcohol are ultimately inextricable from one another, aspects of the same deep ambiguity with respect to alcohol's social function. They share a view of alcohol as fundamentally dangerous to social cohesion and political control. Paradoxically, alcohol also forms one element of ritual activities, but only when properly moderated. It was during the decline and fall of the Eastern Han, though, that the contradictions surrounding alcohol reached a heightened intensity. In this essay I aim to explore how literary depictions of it evolved in China during the third century CE, with a focus on the problem of accommodating its tempting pleasures with the higher demands of politics. In fact, the apparently minor question of alcohol and its prohibition turns out to be symptomatic of the larger political questions of the era.[10]

The cultural role of alcohol in Western literature has been ambiguous also. One of the most powerful demonstrations of this ambiguity is the Euripides play *Bacchae*.[11] The Bacchae are the female worshippers of the god Dionysus, who are driven into a violent frenzy by their worship. The King Pentheus seeks to ban the Dionysus cult from his kingdom, and ends up being slaughtered and eaten by a band of Bacchae, including his own mother. The message is that the violent, chaotic powers of alcohol cannot be prohibited completely, but have to be accommodated by society, by means of devices like the rites of Dionysus. The play's depiction of the Dionysian cult, combining ecstatic joy and inhuman brutality, suggests the variety of responses induced by alcohol. I cite this violent example to remind the reader that, although we may be accustomed to approach a poem about drinking (by Li Bai 李白 [701–762], especially) with a knowing smile, or perhaps a puritanical scowl, the emotions wine unleashes may also be passionate, disturbing, or revelatory. As Xu Shen showed in his definition of the term, the problem of alcohol is inseparable from that of good and evil.

The Third-Century Reconceptualization of Alcohol

The tension between alcohol and proper government reached a height during the rule of Cao Cao 曹操 (155–220) in the Jian'an era. Cao Cao and his courtiers famously enjoyed symposia of wine and poetry that established a precedent for Chinese literati culture, yet Cao Cao also made an edict prohibiting alcohol (in 207 CE). Unlike American Prohibitionists, Cao Cao was pleased to permit drinking and even to partake himself, but practical political goals necessarily took precedence over private temptations.[12] The response to his edict was the first sign of a novel trend in Chinese discourse on alcohol. Kong Rong 孔融 (153–208), one of the Seven Masters of the Jian'an Period, was a vociferous critic during his service under late Eastern Han warlords Dong Zhuo 董卓 and Cao Cao. In his inimitable fashion, he wrote two letters critiquing Cao's policy. It is worth quoting the first letter in full for its rhetorical flair and polemical stance:[13]

> When your lordship first came, your countrymen all clapped their hands and leapt with joy, looking upon you as sovereign. 'Once you had arrived',[14] though, you promulgated the ban on alcohol.
>
> 公初當來，邦人咸抃舞踊躍，以望我后。亦既至止，酒禁施行。[15]
>
> Alcohol has exerted its power for a very long time. The sage-kings of antiquity would 'make offerings to the Supreme Lord and sacrifices to the ancestors':[16] there

is nothing like alcohol for appealing to the spirits and pacifying men, to aid the ten thousand states.

酒之為德久矣，古先哲王，類帝禋宗，和神定人，以濟萬國，非酒莫以也。[17]

Heaven bestowed the luminescence of the Wine Stars, Earth set the precinct of the Wine Spring, and men too have the power instilled by sweet wine.[18] Yao, without his thousand cups, would have had no way to establish a general peace; Confucius, without his hundred goblets, would never have achieved his supreme sageliness.[19] When Fan Kuai dispelled disaster at Hongmen, had it not been for the pork shoulder and cup of wine, he would not have brandished his rage.[20] The servant of Zhao, when he went east to rescue the king, would not have been impassioned had he not been led on by goblets of wine.[21] Emperor Gaozu, had he not slain the white serpent while intoxicated, would not have revealed his numinous spirit.[22] Yuan Ang, without the power of strong wine, would not have saved his life.[23] Dingguo, had he not gotten inebriated with a *hu* of wine [20 litres], could not have made such legal decisions.[24] Master Li, because he was a drinker of Gaoyang, showed merit for the Han.[25] Qu Yuan, because he did not feed off the dregs and swallow the light wine, faced disaster in Chu.[26] From this point of view, what does wine have to offend against the ruler?

天垂酒星之曜，地列酒泉之郡，人有旨酒之德。堯非千鐘，無以建太平，孔非百觚，無以堪上聖。樊噲解厄鴻門，非彘肩鐘酒，無以奮其怒。趙之廝養，東迎其王，非引巵酒，無以激其氣。高祖非醉斬白蛇，無以揚其靈。袁盎非醇醪之力，無以脫其命。定國非酣飲一斛，無以決其法。故酈生以高陽酒徒，著功於漢。屈原不餔糟歠醨，身困於楚。猶是觀之，酒何負於治者哉。[27]

Kong Rong's selective history of drinking takes a number of liberties, but this comical aspect should not detract from its seriousness. Kong ended up paying with his life for exactly this kind of opposition to Cao Cao, and he was surely aware of that danger. Kong's historical examples are all pointedly chosen and vividly described, ranging from Confucius himself, and other sages and emperors, to heroic ministers and officials. In some cases they are merely examples of admirable people who chose to drink, but in other cases alcohol plays an important and useful role in the event. Perhaps the most striking example, though, is that of Qu Yuan: in Kong's literal interpretation of the fisherman's tale, Qu Yuan's error was his failure to become drunk like his contemporaries. His excessive determination to remain ethically pure led to his ruin. One modern Chinese commentary suggests that this allusion is inappropriately chosen to convey Kong's message, but this surely reflects the latter-day Qu Yuan cult more than the sensibilities of Kong's era.[28] Two centuries earlier Yang Xiong 揚雄 (53 BCE–18) himself had critiqued Qu Yuan in two separate pieces, so there was a precedent for such critique within the Confucian tradition. Later on Xie Wan 謝萬 (321–361) would also side with the fisherman over Qu Yuan in his 'On Eight Worthies' 八賢論.[29]

The exceptional character of this anecdote within Kong's litany suggests it has a special significance for his message. Besides its acceptability to the sages, and its proven success at heightening people's courage, or usefulness in dulling the perception of enemies, wine represents an entire political and philosophical outlook: the accommodations and compromises proposed by the fisherman, in contrast to the dogmatism and puritanical morality of Qu Yuan. This is a perfect rebuttal to the authoritarian ban on alcohol initiated by Cao Cao, since Kong is critiquing both the policy itself, and also the dictatorial manner in which the policy was formed. Here he is diverging from Yang Xiong, who in a brief piece, the 'Admonition on Wine' 酒箴, had humorously contrasted the rigid absolutism of the water pitcher, which ends up 'smashed on a brick' 為瓵所䨍, with the flexible service of the leather wine bag, which is carried in and out of palaces.[30] Yang's true sympathies seem to lie with the incorruptible water pitcher, while the popularity of the wine bag represents the worldly success of court sycophants. For Kong the moral absolutism of prohibition is evidently the greater evil, so he sides with the fisherman and the drinker over both Qu Yuan and Yang Xiong.

We have another, briefer letter from Kong on the same subject, restating his argument in response to a reply from Cao Cao.[31] But this substitutes for the panache of the first letter a lawyerly feat of argument. To Cao's claim that alcohol has caused states to fall in the past, Kong responds that excessive devotion to women or even to Confucian morality had likewise caused kingdoms to fall, but that Cao does not on that account ban either women or morality. In fact, neither extant letter gives a full sense of Kong's point of view. His willingness to criticize Cao Cao repeatedly and openly seems to display the integrity and honesty of a Qu Yuan, and in the end he suffered a similar fate, being executed by Cao Cao for a manufactured intrigue. What comes through clearly from the first letter though is a resistance to control. Alcohol is a catalyst for all kinds of passions and virtues, and Cao Cao's ban on alcohol was thus a ban on diverse impulses that conflicted with state interests. A state that had no place for alcohol would scarcely have room for an eccentric like Kong Rong either.

What comes across only indistinctly in Kong Rong becomes a prominent theme in later Wei and Jin literature. Two by Cao Zhi 曹植 (192–232) and Wang Can 王粲 (177–217) follow the typical *fu* practice of presenting both sides of the debate, first praising alcohol and then criticizing it. The moralistic and teetotalling conclusions seem to follow the model set by Cao Cao's ban, with Cao Zhi calling alcohol 'the source of decadence and falsity' 淫荒之源. Both these *fu* present both sides in the debate on alcohol, and even present the case in favour more energetically, but they are returning to the familiar dichotomy—alcohol as both aid to enjoyment and destroyer of virtue, with a moralistic conclusion. In a slightly later *fu*, Zhang Zai 張載 celebrates Ling 酃 wine (from Ling prefecture, east of modern Hengyang, Hunan) as an inexhaustible resource for humanity in '*Fu* on Ling Wine' 酃酒賦:[32]

> The sages and worthies first created it,
> We honour them for transmitting the merit that does not fade,
> And praise the early recognition of [Du] Kang and [Yi] Di,
> Who also acted in accordance with Heaven and obliging the people.
> Setting the Wine Banner beside the Dark Constellations,
> They made sweet wine to please their spirits.
> Both wise and foolish shared a fondness for it,
> Like the level bearing of the Great Transformation.
> There is no thing that can move without change,
> Although it stays in the old it still renews the new.
> Passing through rise and decline without loss,
> Through one hundred ages ever regarded as a treasure.
> 惟聖賢之興作，貴垂功而不泯。嘉康狄之先識，亦應天而順民。擬酒旗於玄象，造甘醴以怡神。雖賢愚而同好，似大化之齊均。物無往而不變，獨居舊而彌新。經盛衰而無廢，歷百代而作珍。

But he still feels the need to add a moralizing epilogue that condemns drinking with an allusion to the 'Announcement against Drinking' 酒誥 from the *Shang shu*.

Thus these *fu* on the whole recapitulate conventional and dualistic attitudes towards drinking. We find truly original stances towards alcohol only with the Seven Worthies of the Bamboo Grove 竹林七賢, who are the heirs of Kong Rong and other late Eastern Han eccentrics.[33] These arise as part of a general trend towards nonconformity, which found its expression in all aspects of culture, from nudity to filial piety.[34] The historical evaluation of these eccentrics raises an important question, whether their eccentricity expresses authentic feeling, or merely an elite fad just as conventionalized as any earlier ritual behaviour. Michael Nylan has offered a trenchant critique of the appraisal of Han and Wei-Jin eccentrics as 'individualists', arguing that the modern Western concept of 'individualism' should not be applied to them.[35] But 'individualism' is a problematic term when used to describe modern cultures as well: note that de Tocqueville, to whom Nylan attributes the modern concept, himself disparages it as a disturbed sentiment that leads to isolation: 'Individualism is a mature and calm feeling, which disposes each member of the community to sever himself from the mass of his fellow-creatures, and to draw apart with his family and friends … individualism proceeds more from erroneous judgment than from depraved feelings'.[36] Though it is true that Tocqueville presents the concept as an American invention, that does not mean it could not be applied to other cultures with heuristic value. In fact, the very ambiguity with which Tocqueville defines the term seems remarkably accurate with reference to the Seven Worthies of the Bamboo Grove, who could also be accused of drawing apart from their family and friends. In any case, their eccentricity was not entirely superficial. The non-conformity of someone like Kong Rong was a political stance for which he gave his life, and in that sense takes on an enduring significance beyond the fashions of his contemporaries. It was in this special context that the state of drunkenness itself took on a serious role in Chinese culture and politics.

Liu Ling 劉伶 (c. 221–300) is the representative figure for this phenomenon, since he is renowned above all for his drinking. Even for Liu, drinking is never an innocent act but always rich with symbolism. One famous anecdote suggests a whole universe of thought behind his seemingly spontaneous behaviour:

> Liu Ling was always drinking to excess, so that he became bold and unrestrained. He would sometimes remove his clothes and be naked in his room. People saw and mocked him for it, but Ling said: 'For me, Heaven and Earth are the rafters and roof of my house; this chamber is just the trousers of my garment. What are you gentle-men doing inside my trousers?'
>
> 劉伶恒縱酒放達，或脫衣裸形在屋中，人見譏之。伶曰：「我以天地為棟宇，屋室為褲衣，諸君何為入我褲中？」[37]

This idea that the entire cosmos was as immediately present as a suit of clothing has precedents throughout the *Zhuangzi*, and evinces a transcendence of social, moral, and physical distinctions that seems essentially Daoist. As presented in the anecdote, though, this kind of attitude is also intimately connected to drinking. Part of the humour of the story is the ambiguity about whether Liu's attitude derives from serious philosophical premises or drunken bravado. Yet alcohol is not incidental to the philosophical message either, since alcohol naturally helps one to ignore the same distinctions that Daoist thought seeks to transcend.

Liu Ling presents this argument at greater length in his famous 'Encomium to the Power of Wine' 酒德頌. The phrase *jiude* 酒德 ('the virtue/power of alcohol') itself suggests the ambiguous power of wine. The phrase is used pejoratively in the *Shujing*:

> No one is so far astray and out of order as the King of Yin, consumed by the power of alcohol!
>
> 無若殷王受之迷亂，酗於酒德哉！[38]

Liu Ling adapts the same phrase with solely positive connotations, finding the highest virtue in drunkenness:

> There was a Master Great Man:
> For him all Heaven and Earth were in a day,
> A myriad ages passing in an instant.
> The Sun and Moon were his door and window,
> The Eight Wastes his garden paths.
> He travelled without carriage or footstep,
> Inhabited no room or hut.
> He made of Heaven a curtain and of Earth a mat,
> Following his whims as he pleased.
> Each time stopped, he took up a wine jar and lifted a gourd;
> Each time he moved, he brought his wine jar and raised his pot.
> Wine was his sole pursuit:
> What else should he know?
> There was a splendid young nobleman,
> And a gentleman of tablet and sash.
> They heard of his reputation,
> And discussed the reason for it.
> They shook their sleeves and waved their lapels,
> Glared at each other and gnashed their teeth.
> Setting forth opinions on the rites and laws,
> Truth and falsity rose up in contention.
> And the Master
> Then lifted up a jar and brought a vat,
> Poured a cup and swallowed the dregs.
> He flourished his hair and squatted down,
> Made a pillow of yeast and a mat of lees.
> Without a thought, without a care,
> His happiness was overflowing.
> At times he was drunk,
> And at times he would wake.
> He listens so quietly he could not hear the sound of thunder,
> Looks so closely he could not see the mass of Mount Tai.
> He would not notice the chill or heat cutting his skin,
> Nor feel any emotion of interest or desire.
> He looks down at the profusion of the myriad things,
> Like duckweed floating in the Jiang and Han,

And these two worthies wait beside him,
Like the wasp and the moth larva.[39]

有大人先生，以天地為一朝，萬期為須臾，日月為扃牖，八荒為庭衢。行無轍迹，
居無室廬，幕天席地，縱意所如。止則操卮執瓢，動則挈榼提壺。唯酒是務，焉知
其餘。有貴介公子，縉紳處士。聞吾風聲，議其所以。乃奮袂攘襟，怒目切齒，陳
說禮法，是非鋒起。先生於是，方奉罌承槽，銜杯漱醪，奮髯箕踞，枕麴藉糟，無
思無慮，其樂陶陶。兀爾而醉，慌爾而醒。靜聽不聞雷霆之聲，熟視不見泰山之
形，不覺寒暑之切肌，利欲之感情。俯觀萬物，擾擾焉如江漢之載浮萍。二豪侍
側，焉如蜾蠃之與螟蛉。[40]

The first section of the poem describes the awesome powers and universal perspective of the Great Man. This is somewhat conventional, recalling various characters in *Zhuangzi* but perhaps especially Sima Xiangru's 司馬相如 (179–117 BCE) ('*Fu* on the Great Man' 大人賦, which presents Emperor Wu of Han in the role of the shaman-poet of *Chuci* 楚辭 poetry, who traverses the universe in his mystic quest. Whereas in that tradition the hero's transcendence of worldly limitations derives from his moral and spiritual cultivation, the unique source of this Great Man's powers is alcohol. We may recall again the analogy provided by *Zhuangzi* and *Liezi* between the sage's philosophical indifference and the drunkard's alcoholic indifference. Liu Ling replaces the analogy by a total equation of the two states, with comic effect.

The remainder of the poem introduces two additional characters to act as a foil for the Great Man (who himself has little personality). Their heated argument contrasts with the Great Man's detachment. The poem then concludes with a reference to the popular superstition about the wasp and moth larvae: supposedly the wasp would adopt the larvae as its own children.[41] Yang Xiong uses the story as an example of students learning to imitate their teachers, like the disciples of Confucius, so the allusion contributes to the overall portrait of the drunkard-as-sage. Again it is more than a little amusing to think of drunkenness as a self-perpetuating tradition, in the manner of Confucian doctrine. But the record of the *Shishuo xinyu* 世說新語 and other sources show that Liu Ling, the Seven Worthies of the Bamboo Grove, and other Wei-Jin elites actually did follow the example of this Master Great Man.

Anecdotes about Liu Ling's friend Ruan Ji 阮籍 (210–263), the great poet, are similarly drenched in alcohol. Later writers tend to bowdlerize these anecdotes by means of their interpretation of Ruan Ji as a patriot disturbed by the usurpation of the Sima clan and the founding of the Jin dynasty. One *Shishuo xinyu* anecdote describes Ruan's drunkenness as a way of alleviating his grief:

Wang Xiaobo asked Wang Da: 'How does Ruan Ji compare with Sima Xiangru?'
Wang Da: 'Ruan Ji has a block in his chest, so he must use wine to dissolve it.'
王孝伯問王大：「阮籍何如司馬相如？」王大曰：「阮籍胸中壘塊，故須酒澆之。」[42]

This anecdote is ambiguous, but clearly locates the causes of Ruan Ji's drinking in psychological and personal motives. But other historical anecdotes about Ruan Ji give a more complicated picture. His drunkenness does not come across as a mere consolation, but a fundamental component of his relationship with society, as in the following passages from Ruan Ji's biography in the *Jin shu*:

Ji originally had the ambition of saving the world. During the Wei and Jin disasters befell the realm, and few famous gentlemen survived intact. Ji thus refused to participate in worldly affairs, and regularly drank to excess. Emperor Wen[43] originally wanted to make a proposal of marriage to Ji on behalf of Emperor Wu, but Ji was drunk for sixty days, so Emperor Wen could not speak to him and gave up. Zhong Hui repeatedly tried to ask him about contemporary events, hoping to implicate him based on his responses, but Ji always escaped by means of his drunken stupor. When Emperor Wen started to assist in governance, Ji once casually said to him: 'I have visited Dongping and admired the local customs and scenery.' The emperor was greatly pleased, and appointed him prefect of Dongping. Ji rode a donkey to the post, and when he arrived destroyed all the screens and barriers within the offices, so that those inside and outside could look at each other. His decrees were impartial and restrained, and he returned after ten days … Ji had heard that the kitchen staff for the infantry were expert at brewing, and had stored up over three hundred *hu* of wine.[44] He asked to serve as colonel of infantry. He disregarded all worldly events, and although he went to assist in administration, he always entertained himself inside the office, and joined in all the daily feasts. When the emperor was refusing the Nine Bequests, the nobility all wanted to persuade him to accept, and they asked Ji to write the formal request. Ji was dead-drunk and neglected to do it. When they sent a messenger to his office to pick up the letter, the messenger saw him leaning on his desk in a drunken stupor. When the messenger told him about this, Ji wrote out the request on his desk, and had the messenger copy it, without making any corrections or deletions. His refined and forceful composition was much praised by contemporaries.

籍本有濟世志，屬魏晉之際，天下多故，名士少有全者，籍由是不與世事，遂酣飲為常。文帝初欲為武帝求婚於籍，籍醉六十日，不得言而止。鍾會數以時事問之，欲因其可否而致之罪，皆以酣醉獲免。及文帝輔政，籍嘗從容言於帝曰：「籍平生曾游東平，樂其風土。」帝大悅，即拜東平相。籍乘驢到郡，壞府舍屏鄣，使內外相望，法令清簡，旬日而還。……籍聞步兵廚營人善釀，有貯酒三百斛，乃求為步兵校尉。遺落世事，雖去佐職，恒游府內，朝宴必與焉。會帝讓九錫，公卿將勸進，使籍為其辭。籍沈醉忘作，臨詣府，使取之，見籍方據案醉眠。使者以告，籍便書案，使寫之，無所改竄。辭甚清壯，為時所重。[45]

These entertaining but ultimately puzzling anecdotes may be apocryphal. I take them as important evidence of the cultural trend represented by Ruan Ji, even if some of the details are not necessarily historically accurate. These miscellaneous stories suggest two larger frames within which to perceive Ruan's drinking. First is that of drunkenness as a way to hide oneself, to escape from politics, and to avoid the dangers of partisan commitment. This idea is represented most strongly in the story of Ruan Ji evading the questioning of Zhong Hui. Zhong Hui would actually contribute to the death of Ruan's friend Xi Kang 嵇康 (223–262) by quoting a comment of Xi Kang to Sima Zhao 司馬昭 (211–265), so this was a serious threat. This is certainly an important aspect of Ruan Ji's biography, and the basis for the tradition of his drunkenness as a calculated pose.

An alternate pattern that becomes visible in these anecdotes, though, is that Ruan's drunkenness was actually consistent with skilful work and competent administration. When Ruan Ji arrives in Dongping he eliminates all the barriers in the offices, allowing administrators and common people to look at each other directly. Rather than ignoring the business of government, he is actually governing in an ideal manner. One might call this kind of leadership an example of Daoist quietism, but it is also consistent with a Confucian tradition of government by moral example. We also see examples of Ruan's admirable behaviour even while he is drunk. The letter he drafted spontaneously, without any need for revisions, is one example. But others show him exhibiting virtuous restraint even in the midst of a drunken escapade:

> There was a lady in the house next to Ruan's who was beautiful to look at. She had a shop selling wine. Ruan and Wang Anfeng would often drink wine with her. When Ruan got drunk, he would fall asleep beside her. Her husband at first was highly suspicious, but when he observed them, he saw that Ruan had no further intentions.
>
> 阮公鄰家婦有美色，當壚酤酒。阮與王安豐常從婦飲酒，阮醉，便眠其婦側。夫始殊疑之，伺察，終無他意。[46]

This story was perhaps inspired by the literary tradition of works on 'restraining the passions', describing a man's virtuous restraint in front of the temptations of a beautiful seductress.[47] The curious thing about it, though, is how it combines that theme with Ruan's drunkenness. In all these stories about Ruan Ji there is never a suggestion that Ruan is following the example of the *Li ji*, drinking all day without becoming intoxicated. To the contrary, he is already drunk at the beginning of most of the anecdotes about him, and yet one kind of decadent excess turns out to be consistent with other virtues.

Another set of famous anecdotes relates to Ruan's violation of ritual protocol. After the death of his mother, though overcome with grief, Ruan continued to eat meat and drink alcohol with abandon.[48] In another anecdote, he is criticized for visiting his sister-in-law in violation of protocol, and responds: 'Were the rites established for men like me?' 禮豈為我輩設也.[49] These stories might seem to be nothing more than a demonstration of Ruan's extreme egotism, but it is clear that he was admired by contemporaries and later observers, whether in spite of or actually because of these violations. The compound *wobei* 我輩 in Ruan's reply is of special significance here, suggesting that in some of the anecdotes that Ruan might act as a model for others as well. Like most other anecdotes in the *Shishuo xinyu*, those about him frequently involve friends, associates, and other contemporaries, so his behaviour is not totally selfish, but often acts as a stimulus or model for others. Ruan's freedom and willingness to act spontaneously suggest a value system more capacious than the traditional one, a sense of propriety that allows more variety according to individual needs.

Most of Ruan's lapses are linked to excessive drinking, itself yet another violation of ritual propriety, but one that is fundamentally social. Drunkenness is not merely a pose for Ruan Ji, because it is fundamentally related to some of the other values that he holds dear. It is an encouragement to act spontaneously, to ignore social convention, and to achieve one's own desires. Alcohol is a material and also symbolic counterpart to the more abstract ideas that animate and inspire Ruan and his contemporaries. As Donald Holzman has observed, drinking plays a relatively small part in Ruan's poetry. On the other hand, given the copious testimony of his contemporaries, we may suspect that even Ruan's idealized recluse-sage, described at length in the 'Biography of Master Great Man' 大人先生傳, achieved something of his equanimity and superiority by means of drinking.[50] It seems significant that this most ambitious statement of Ruan's worldview chooses for its protagonist the same name as that of Liu Ling's 'Encomium to the Power of Wine'. Though this epic work does not mention drunkenness itself, the Great Man shares the features of Liu Ling's hero, living on an epic scale in harmony with the entire universe. He is not a recluse who shuns the world but a 'Great Man' who has mastered it.

This point of view has to be seen in context of the major philosophical movement that sprang up in Ruan Ji's lifetime, *xuanxue* 玄學. The major thinkers of the movement were Wang Bi 王弼 and He Yan 何晏, famous for their subtle commentaries. Their key philosophical contribution was ontological investigation of the origin of all things in *wu* 無, 'nonbeing'. But *xuanxue* had ramifications for the culture at large, not merely abstract philosophy, especially through its attempted reconciliation of Confucian and Daoist thought. As Paul Kroll has pointed out, the term *xuan* itself refers to something dark but not entirely impenetrable, to a liminal state that is obscure but not entirely so.[51] This sense accords nicely with the sense of rapprochement between Confucian doctrine and Daoist mysticism. The Seven Worthies of the Bamboo Grove reflected this movement both in their poetry and in their reflective essays.[52] They sought to reconceive Confucian ritual in a way consistent with the spontaneity and naturalness of the Way. In this light we can understand better why alcohol played an important role in their thought. After all, as we have seen, alcohol maintained an ambivalent position, forming part of Confucian ritual but also challenging ritual restraint. Ruan Ji and Liu Ling drew out that pre-existing ambivalence even farther to suit their worldviews, creating a new kind of lifestyle and social relations based not on cautious, limited use of alcohol, but on wild drunkenness. Yet their drunkenness was never as casual or extreme as it appeared, but constrained within a new set of values and conventions.

The view that Ruan Ji's drunkenness was merely a calculated defence against implication in political intrigue has always been implausible, because he drank so much that he ended up drawing even more attention to himself in the end. The view that it was a protest against political corruption is more plausible, but still fails to take seriously the inherent significance of drinking itself. This reflects the opprobrium traditionally directed against drunkards both by dour moralists and longevity-obsessed recluses. One could not, certainly not seriously, advocate that everyone should become a drunkard. But Ruan Ji never did so; instead he asked only, 'Were the rites established for men like me?' His drunkenness was not merely a protest but a serious challenge to the conformity imposed by all sober ideologies, whether Confucian or not.

None of these writers who celebrated drunkenness has a fully developed political theory, but it is still possible to read into their works a perspective within the tradition of political philosophy, as Hsiao Kung-ch'üan has done. He argues that the general trend of the *xuanxue* thinkers and other contemporaries was along the lines of the *wuwei* doctrine of the *Daodejing*,[53] but that Bao Jingyan 鮑敬言 went beyond this to advocate a theory of *wujun* 無君 'without a monarch'.[54] Moreover, he affiliates Ruan Ji and Tao Qian with the same school, based on a relatively small sample from their literary compositions. This was not a theory of anarchy, however. When Ruan Ji writes in the 'Biography of Master Great Man' that 'Then without a lord the common things were all stabilized, / Without vassals the myriad affairs were ordered' 蓋無君而庶物定，無臣而萬事理, he is imagining a natural order with no need for a conventional monarch. But this would not be a state of chaos; instead it would be naturally and spontaneously ordered, with some new hierarchy. Though he never proposes any direct route by which to reach that state, the freedom of drunkenness is at least a symbolic first step in the direction of that spontaneous order.

Conclusion: A Fleeting Intoxication?

I have pointed out in this chapter some features of the representation of alcohol and drunkenness during the third century CE that were, if not unprecedented, at least unprecedented in scope. Whether the drunken ecstasies of Kong Rong, Liu Ling, and Ruan Ji left any long-lasting impact on the future development of Chinese civilization is a question that would require a much larger study to explore seriously. The special relationship of Wei-Jin literati to wine has long been appreciated. Lu Xun's 魯迅 famous article 'Wei Jin fengdu ji wenzhang yu yao ji jiu zhi guanxi' 魏晉風度及文章與藥及酒之關係 distinguishes the attitudes corresponding to the drug-takers and the drinkers of the period:

> By consuming drugs one could become an immortal, and an immortal could look upon the ordinary people with disdain; drinking wine one could not become an immortal, and instead just acted perfunctorily.
> 吃藥可以成仙，仙是可以驕視俗人的；飲酒不會成仙，所以敷衍了事。[55]

In other words, the literati who sought elixirs of immortality and aspired to reclusion could be disdainful of political realities, and ironically met with violent death because of their naiveté. But the devotees of alcohol could not achieve the same serene detachment from everyday demands, and instead made compromises. Like a number of Lu Xun's other comments in this essay, this one seems to reflect his own contemporary concerns as much as historical fact. After all, Kong Rong seems like an obvious counterexample. Moreover, *fuyan liaoshi* 敷衍了事 ('acted perfunctorily') seems like a poor description of Ruan Ji, whatever one's ultimate appraisal of his character. But Lu Xun's comment is still a perceptive one in the way that it links together drinking and a particular attitude towards life.

Although their unique perspective had few imitators later on, some remnant of it did survive in altered form. Drinking became a literati pastime that was almost entirely harmless; a form of relaxation and escape from the frustrations of the political sphere. The most famous drinker of the Wei-Jin period is one I have not mentioned so far in this paper, Tao Qian 陶潛 (365–427). He lived more than a century after the Seven Worthies and his literary presentation of drinking is quite different from theirs. He does not share the same grandiose pretensions for alcohol that we have seen above. Much more typical is the elegiac mood of this poem from his famous series 'Poems on Drinking Wine' 飲酒詩:

秋菊有佳色	Autumn chrysanthemums have a fair hue,
裛露掇其英	Drenched in dew I pluck their blossoms.
汎此忘憂物	Steeping this thing for forgetting sadness,
遠我遺世情	I feel remote my desire to leave this world.[56]
一觴雖獨進	Though one goblet may advance alone,
杯盡壺自傾	When cup is drained the pot leans of itself.
日入群動息	At set of sun all movement comes to rest,
歸鳥趨入林	Returning birds turn back to the woods.
嘯傲東軒下	Whistling in pride beneath the eastern corridor,
聊復得此生	For a while I've got my life back again. [57]

The phrase 'thing for forgetting sadness' later becomes a conventional term for alcohol, though Lu Qinli here refers to the chrysanthemums themselves. In this poem we see the subtle appreciation of the older man for a soothing drink to accompany his declining years, the 'season of mists and mellow fruitfulness', quite unlike the mad intoxications of Liu Ling or Ruan Ji. As so often, Tao mentions the chrysanthemums, which not only form a part of his country landscape, but are also something he ingested in hopes of extending his life. Here we return to the wine spring that bestows immortality, the point of view from which alcohol is more useful for its possible health benefits than for spiritual insights. It is one fixture of a life in reclusion and an escape from political danger, but the focus is not on inebriation itself, as is so often the case for the Seven Worthies. Part of the pleasure of these drinking poems is their modulated stance of detachment, toying with a kind of escapism yet returning constantly to 'this life', the immediate and practical. In that sense they may demonstrate a far more restrained, mature, and aestheticized version of the drunkenness of earlier poets.[58] Similarly Wang Ji 王績 (590–644) borrows many of the reclusive tropes of Tao Qian in his 'Records of a Drunken Village' 醉鄉記, describing a utopia isolated from the violence of history and politics. Ding Xiang Warner has argued that Wang Ji's drunkenness is primarily allegorical, which might differentiate it further from Liu Ling or Ruan Ji's more literal celebration of drinking itself.[59]

Drinking in traditional China always had profound political, social, and philosophical ramifications, but these varied greatly with the times, even among a group of poets as superficially similar as Ruan Ji, Tao Qian, and Wang Ji. What is especially noteworthy about the drinkers of the third century is how they attempted to integrate the authenticity and spontaneity of drunkenness into their everyday lives and convictions. There is a certain ecstatic sense of total awareness occasionally intimated by someone who has drunk to excess, what William James calls being 'for the moment one with truth', a sensation that is hard to recall even after sobering up. What these eccentric drinkers of the third century did was to try to retain that insight of drunken ecstasy the morning after as well. It may have been a paradoxical attempt, but reading their works may still provoke some useful insights for later readers, whether stone sober, extra-sensorily drunk, or only slightly tipsy.

4
Making Poetry with Alcohol

Wine Consumption in Tao Qian, Li Bai and Su Shi

Charles Kwong

Overview: Wine in Pre-Qin to Jin Poetry

Wine has been a motif in Chinese poetry since the *Classic of Poetry* (*Shi jing* 詩經, eleventh–sixth century BCE).[1] In its early days, wine was mostly associated with the aristocracy's sacrificial rituals and social feasts, for it was a luxury product predicated on the surrender of precious grains. In due course it took on various functions and meanings in literati culture: as social catalyst and moral corruptor, emotional anaesthetic and intensifier, later as psychological liberator, artistic inspiration and spiritual transporter. Exciting and numbing the rational mind chemically, wine can be an aid to merriment and an agent of social-emotive bonding if imbibed in moderation, a disruptor of moral consciousness and temporary exorcist of grief if consumed to excess. In later times it also became an intensifier of emotions, a stupefying drug facilitating political and psychological escapism, and a philosophical transporter sending one's spirit to a transcendent plane, including a proven elevation of the creative impulse. This essay explores the uses and cultural meanings of wine in classical Chinese poetry via the works of the famous wine poets Tao Qian 陶潛 (365–427), Li Bai 李白 (701–762) and Su Shi 蘇軾 (1037–1101). It is not naive to ask: why does Li Bai's wine taste more delicious than others can savour?

The status of wine as a luxury item in early days explains why in the *Classic of Poetry*, it features much less frequently in the folk songs of 'Airs of the States' 國風[2] than in the 'Major Odes' 大雅 and 'Hymns' 頌 writing of ruling-class sacrificial rituals,[3] or the 'Minor Odes' 小雅[4] that sing of upper-class feast gatherings. For instance, one finds this sacrificial celebration of an 'Abundant Year' 豐年 (Poem 279) in the 'Zhou hymns' 周頌, generally seen as the oldest stratum in the *Shi jing*:

為酒為醴　We make wine and sweet liquor
烝畀祖妣　As offering to the ancestral gods of earth and grains,
以洽百禮　Together with other sacrificial items,
降福孔皆　To bring down blessings broadly to all.[5]

Since wine was consumed at sacrificial rituals that were also social occasions, it was natural for wine to be a part of social gatherings among the upper class, as seen in the 'Minor Odes':

小雅 · 賓之初筵　**Poem 220, When Guests First Take Their Seats**

賓之初筵　When the guests first take their seats,
溫溫其恭　How mild and decorous they are!
......　. . .
彼醉不臧　Those who are drunk behave badly;
不醉反恥　Those who are not feel ashamed.[6]

Noticeable in the description of merriment in Ode 220 is an embedded warning against excess and indulgence that rises to a sharp, grave pitch in the more politically solemn 'Major Odes':

大雅 · 蕩　**Poem 255, Vast**

天不緬爾以酒　Heaven did not let you [Yin] indulge in wine,
不義從式　　And follow ways against virtue.

It can be seen from such excerpts that to the Zhou (1046–256 BCE) elite, wine is most aptly used with food as offering to the spirits in supplication of blessings. This association of wine with heavenly blessings and secular government underlines the vigilance that drinking must not precipitate social, political or religious disorder. While wine is accepted as an aid to social merriment, there is a clear moral voice against intemperate drinking, intensifying to a grave warning against political downfall in Poem 255 (also Poem 256). Indeed the *Shi jing*'s solemn pieces carry a recurrent charge of drunkenness against the Shang. This moral-political tone is typical of the Zhou dynastic temper, resounded most forcefully by the Duke of Zhou 周公旦, younger brother of the founding King Wu 武王, in the *Book of History* (*Shang shu* 尚書).[7] His serious tone does not surprise one, for in terms of moral sobriety, none of the main ethical and religious traditions sanction indulgence in drinking, e.g. Christianity, Islam and Buddhism.[8]

　　This moral censure of over-drinking reflects mainstream thought in pre-Qin philosophical literature, albeit Confucius 孔子 (551–479 BCE) himself seems to hold a more relaxed view of wine,[9] and it is Mencius 孟子 (371–289 BCE) who shows greater vigilance about 'insatiability in drinking [as] intemperance' 樂酒無厭謂之亡 (*Mencius* 1B.4).[10] Daoism does not talk about wine often, but the *Laozi*'s point on 'the five tastes injur[ing] one's palate' 五味令人口爽 (Ch. 12) warns against sensory indulgence of any kind.[11] The *Zhuangzi* offers no unified view on wine: anecdotes write of it as a medium that frees man from his fear or mask towards unity with Dao and true expression, but also liken association between petty people to 'sweet wine' 小人之交甘若醴.[12] Contrary to later views in the Wei-Jin era, the *Zhuangzi* itself gives no endorsement of wine as an agent of spiritual transcendence. As for *Songs of the South* (*Chu ci* 楚辭), they make few mentions of wine other than its use in spirit-related rituals,[13] but do reiterate the grave Confucian sanction against drunkenness. Qu Yuan 屈原 (340–278 BCE) insists on his lone sobriety in an inebriated world in 'The Fisherman' 漁父, reinforcing the linkage of wine to corruption and muddle-headedness.[14] He does not understand the fisherman recluse's point of view: 'The sage is not fettered by material circumstances … If people are all drunk, why not eat their dregs and gulp their wine?' 聖人不凝滯於物，……眾人皆醉，何不餔其糟而歠其醨？ While the recluse offers no endorsement of wine, the association of drinking with a kind of spiritual freedom can be traced to this work.

By Han times drinking was common among the literati. While moral censure and political constraint of alcoholic indulgence remain, the 'identity' of wine was expanding. It was not just a socializing agent spurring a merry mood, but a fitting carrier and intensifier of feelings at parting moments, a reminder of emotional ties between friends.[15] As the literati's outlook on life darkened amid political purges and uprisings in the latter years of the Han, wine also came to be linked to the *carpe diem* theme, as an intensifier of sensations amid a deep sense of existential transience and uncertainty. This is seen in the *yuefu* 樂府 songs and ballads,[16] the 'Nineteen Ancient Poems' 古詩十九首 as well as poems by literati poets:

相和歌辭 · 西門行   **West Gate Ballad**

今日不作樂	If you don't make merry today,
當待何時	What moment are you waiting for?
……	. . .
釀美酒	Brew good wine,
……	. . .
可用解憂愁	It can unknot worry and grief.
人生不滿百	Human life reaches not a hundred,
常懷千歲憂	Yet ever he harbours worries of a thousand years.

古詩十九首 其十三   **Nineteen Ancient Poems, No. 13**

服食求神仙	Those who take drugs in quest of immortality
多為藥所誤	Mostly fall victim to their potions.
不如飲美酒	Better to drink fine wine,
被服紈與素	And clothe yourself in soft and white silk!

曹操 短歌行   **Song in Short Metre, by Cao Cao**

| 譬如朝露 | Life is like morning dew, |
| 去日苦多 | Days gone so abound |

....

何以解憂　How to unknot worries?

惟有杜康　There is only wine.[17]

Common to the poems is a resigned and pessimistic outlook on life, a feeling of incarceration in 'worry and grief' to be 'unknot', and a lack of existential faith itself. As the literati's sense of life and death grew more poignant, the function of wine as a reliever of sorrow and worries also expanded and deepened. Even Cao Cao (155–220), the iron-fisted general and despotic politician, voices the feeling that life's brief hours should be captured and savoured with wine. Compared with a search for immortality (also pursued by some members of the upper class), wine offers at least a more tangible and accessible form of 'real' enjoyment.

On the other hand, we see a new, affirmative dimension to the psychological effects of wine as fuel to the heroic spirit and even poetic inspiration. Never a poet, the first Han emperor Liu Bang 劉邦 (256–195 BCE) wrote the 'Great Wind Song' 大風歌 after getting thoroughly drunk.[18] The overall perception of wine has become less negative and more multidimensional by Han times, so that Ban Gu 班固 (32–92) calls wine a 'fine blessing from Heaven' 天之美祿.[19] If the Jian'an poets use wine to dispel sorrow, that grief is at least rooted in sentiments of a more heroic vein, so that the wine tastes more spirited as well. Drinking in 'Song in Short Metre', Cao Cao longs to emulate the Duke of Zhou's virtue (周公吐哺，天下歸心); Wang Can 王粲 (177–217), serving Cao Cao on his military campaigns, speaks of celebratory 'wine and meat overflowing river islets' 酒肉踰川坻 following a victorious battle.[20]

It is fair to say that wine often took on the flavour of the times. For the 'Seven Worthies of the Bamboo Grove' 竹林七賢, whose lives spanned the transition years between the Wei and Jin, wine dwindled into a means of survival: staying drunk and feigning madness were the best ways to distance oneself from politics and persecution.[21] The expansive, heroic air of Jian'an has retreated into an inward, self-protective sentiment, and the drinking act reflects this shrunken spirit. See No. 64 of Ruan Ji's 阮籍 (210–263) 'Expressing Sentiments' 詠懷 poems:

臨觴多哀楚　Cup before me, I feel much sorrow;

思我故時人　I think of friends of old times.

對酒不能言　Facing wine, I cannot speak—

淒愴懷酸辛　Melancholy blends with bitterness.

Instead of easing sadness, wine locks the negative feelings within the poet's heart; indulgence in drinking became a tragic way of anaesthetizing the spirit and the senses for sheer survival. In fact, one can trace a continuing emotive dialectic between wine and a strain of melancholy in the entire course of the Wei-Jin era, for while the Eastern Jin (317–420) years were politically less perilous and capricious on the whole than the preceding century, the intense fear of Ruan Ji's age probably diffused into some kind of general existential anxiety about the transience of life and fickleness of destiny, so that Wang Xizhi 王羲之 (303–361), drinking with friends in spring amid Nature, would grievously lament how delight 'turns into a trace bygone in the twinkling of an eye' 俯仰之間，已為陳跡 (Preface to the Lanting Collection [of Poems] 蘭亭集序).

In more positive terms, it was also during the so-called 'Neo-Daoist' Wei-Jin era that wine became linked to Daoism in terms of the spiritual freedom it fosters, although philosophical Daoism transcends dependence on any external agent to achieve inner autonomy. One secular basis for this process is that wine is a psychological equalizer: when people get half drunk, 'the inferior forget their humbleness, and the destitute forget their poverty' 卑者忘賤，寠者忘貧.[22] 'Forgetfulness' 忘 is indeed a Daoist state of mind, and writing an 'Encomium to the Power of Wine' 酒德頌, Liu Ling 劉伶 (c. 221–300) depicts a transcendent 'great man' whose 'only affair is drinking' 唯酒是務.[23] If Liu is a little dramatic in his words, the meaning of wine as an element of culture was truly enriched when the literati linked it to a more quotidian mode of reclusion and spiritual freedom. Thus Zhang Han 張翰 (c. 258–c. 319), who resigned his official post out of a love of liberty and autonomy, says 'rather than leaving a name for posterity, I'd rather enjoy a cup of wine here and now' 使我有身後名，不如即時一杯酒.[24] In the course of the Wei-Jin era, free drinking became almost synonymous with spiritual independence. From a larger perspective, there is little doubt that from the Zhou to the Wei-Jin eras, the meanings of wine shifted in gravity from the moral, social and political planes to spiritual and aesthetic dimensions, and from Confucian to assumed Daoist positions. To the extent that Daoism is supra-rational in spirit and drinking tends towards anti-rational effects, it is not difficult to see how some literati would associate Daoism with wine.

From Comfort to Transcendence: Wine in the Poetry of Tao Qian

All these associative dimensions of wine came to their first high point of expression in the poetry of Tao Qian, in which the element of drinking recurs with visibly high frequency.[25] Tao does not get drunk to drown out the world like the Seven Worthies of the Bamboo Grove: while there are moments when he uses wine to dispel melancholy, he usually drinks with a genuine sense of freedom and enjoyment amid his reclusive life. Instead of getting thoroughly drunk like Ruan Ji and others, Tao only reaches a tipsy state, like his maternal grandfather Meng Jia 孟嘉

who 'never turns unruly' after drinking.[26] As the preface to the 'Drinking Wine' poems 飲酒詩 states, Tao 'would always write a few lines to amuse [him]self after getting drunk' 既醉之後，輒題數句自娛—testimony to an increment of creative inspiration which wine can help release, and to the broad range of states that the term 醉 can indicate.[27] It is notable that the partly autobiographical 'Gentleman of the Five Willows' 五柳先生 'drinks to contentment and writes poems to delight his heart' 酣觴賦詩，以樂其志, and that in his 'Elegiac Self-Address' 自祭文, the poet also depicts himself as 'drinking to contentment and writing poems' 酣飲賦詩; wine and writing are paired to describe the subject's life, as though one leads logically to the other. In addition, while the Bamboo Grove literati drink with friends of their own class, Tao extends the delight of the activity by drinking with fellow neighbour farmers of a different social stratum. Above all, Tao becomes China's first great wine poet because it helps to transport him to a level of spiritual transcendence beyond the experience or expression of his predecessors and contemporaries. One may sum up by saying that materially, wine is linked to Nature, writing and fellowship in Tao's poetry; psychologically, it is linked to personal contentment and solitude, social bonding, artistic creativity and spiritual transcendence.

Among the most indelible impressions left by Tao Qian's poetry, one easily recalls the moments of relish when he first tastes the nectar of freedom after his permanent retreat from politics, or those scenes after farm work where the relaxing wine, sometimes shared with neighbours, forms an integral part of his contented life:

歸去來兮辭 'Return Home' *fu*

携幼入室	Holding the children by the hand, I enter the house,
有酒盈罇	Where there is wine filling a jug.
引壺觴以自酌	Taking the jug and a cup, I pour for myself;
眄庭柯以怡顏	A sideways glance at the courtyard trees warms my face.

歸園田居五首其五 Return to Farmstead Living, No. 5

漉我新熟酒	I strain my newly ripened wine,
隻鷄招近局	And to a single chicken treat my neighbours.
日入室中暗	As the sun sets the house turns dark;
荊薪代明燭	Thorn firewood serves as bright candles.

移居二首之二 Moving House, No. 2

過門更相呼	As we pass the doors, we hail each other,
有酒斟酌之	And if there's wine we pour and share some.
農務各自歸	After farm work each returns to his home;
閑暇輒相思	In our leisure we always think of each other.

癸卯歲始春懷　**In Early Spring of the Year Guimao [403], Singing of the**
古田舍二首其二　　**Past in My Farmhouse, No. 2**
日入相與歸　When the sun sets we return home together,
壺漿勞近鄰　And to a jug of wine I treat my close neighbours.

庚戌歲九月中於　**In the Ninth Month of the Year Gengxu [410], Harvesting**
西田穫早稻　　**the Early Rice in the West Field**
盥濯息簷下　Having washed my hands and feet, I rest beneath the eaves;
斗酒散襟顏　A measure of wine relaxes my bosom and face.

Enjoyed at home amid the compensating delight of family and Nature, at times in the company of fellow farmers, wine is savoured together with sweaty labour, well-earned leisure, domestic joy and neighbourly affection. Sparkling in the primitive light at dusk and an enlightening *ziran* 自然, wine has gone far beyond its material properties; it is blended into a rewarding life of self-discovery and self-reliance, into a spirit of rustic simplicity living in existential peace.

Yet for all his delight in Nature and his sense of warmth among family and friends, Tao's poetry also reveals an indelible loneliness in the recesses of his being. Now and then he would 'stroll out alone with my shadow as company', or try to lose himself in wine:

停雲　**Motionless Clouds**
靜寄東軒　Quietly I settle by the eastern eaves,
春醪獨撫　Holding the spring wine alone.
……　　…
安得促席　Where is he whom I can set my mat near
說彼平生　And talk of everything in life?

時運　**Progression of the Seasons**
清琴橫床　The clear lute lies across its stand;
濁酒半壺　Cloudy wine half fills the jug.
黃唐莫逮　Huang[di] and Tang[-Yao][28] cannot be reached:
慨獨在余　Sadness is singularly with me.

In the above lines it is the recurrent character 獨 (singularly alone) that stands out, deepened by leisure and quietude. While Tao never re-entered officialdom after 405, the eremitic choice is taken by the idealistic *shi* 士 only to await better times. The 'valiant aspirations traversing beyond the four seas' 猛志逸四海, of 'bringing great benefit to humankind' 大濟於蒼生,[29] entail a deep sense of loss and frustration rooted in an undying wish for social fulfilment before his life expires. 'The Former Master's bequeathed teaching— / Would I ever abandon it!' 先師遺訓，余豈云墜 he writes in 'Trees in Bloom' 榮木. If the Gentleman of the Five Willows can be carefree in his drinking, 'living out his life unmindful of gain and loss' 忘懷得失，以此自終, Tao resorts to wine partly as temporary solace for his truncated social purpose, and even for his domestic disappointment as a father. As his visionary ardour sags at moments under the weariness of a battered spirit, what has enhanced his happier moods often turns into an anaesthetic:

九日閑居　**Double Ninth, Living in Retirement**
酒能祛百慮　Wine can drive out a hundred cares;
菊解制頹齡　Chrysanthemum can arrest decaying years.
如何蓬廬士　How can the scholar in the thatched hut
空視時運傾　Helplessly witness the seasons pass?

己酉歲九月九日　**Ninth Day of Ninth Month in the Year Jiyou [409]**
萬化相尋繹　A myriad transformations follow one another;
人生豈不勞　Is human life not toilsome?
……　　　. . .
何以稱我情　How can I satisfy my feelings?
濁酒且自陶　With cloudy wine just let me enjoy myself.

雜詩 十二首其二　**Miscellaneous Poems, No. 2**
欲言無予和　I wish to talk, but there is none to answer;
揮杯勸孤影　I raise my cup and urge my lonely shadow.
日月擲人去　The sun and moon cast off man and depart;
有志不獲騁　My aspirations are not given free rein.

責子　**Admonishing My Sons**
雖有五男兒　Although I have five sons,
總不好紙筆　None is fond of paper and brush.
……　　　. . .
天運苟如此　If my Heaven-assigned lot be such,
且進杯中物　Just let me take the thing in the cup!

飲酒詩 二十首其七　**Drinking Wine Poems, No. 7**
泛此忘憂物　I float [the chrysanthemums on] this care-forgetting thing,
遠我遺世情　Roaming afar my feelings that leave the world behind.
……　　　. . .
嘯傲東軒下　I whistle freely below the eastern eaves,
聊復得此生　Having somehow regained my life again.

In poems of this nature, wine is savoured amid a sense of decaying health, passing seasons, heavy solitude, toilsome life, frustrated aspirations and self-mocking resignation to fate. While Tao knows that drinking will only 'shorten his life' 促齡—as the Spirit explains to the Body in 'Body, Shadow, Spirit' 形影神—the poet continues to rely on the 'care-forgetting thing' to 'drive out a hundred cares' and consign his 'lonely shadow' to oblivion. At such moments, sobering up always means a return to his social concerns, including the bleak world, which he has formally left but cannot forget altogether.

As a matter of fact, Tao Qian once describes a vain attempt to give up drinking:

止酒　Stopping Wine

平生不止酒	All my life I've never stopped drinking;
止酒情無喜	When I stopped my feelings knew no joy.
暮止不安寢	If I stopped in the evening I could not sleep;
晨止不能起	If I stopped in the morning I could not get up.
日日欲止之	Every day I wanted to stop,
營衛止不理	But if I stopped my pulse and circulation turned erratic.

Using the word 'stop' 止 in every line, at once self-exhorting and self-affirming, this playful poem reflects a serious tension between mind and heart, dialectically irresolvable in that wine has become part of the poet's bloodstream. As he openly admits without abashment, Tao loves wine too much to be able to give it up, for the pleasure is not just physical but spiritual as well:

連雨獨飲　Drinking Alone in the Rainy Season

故老贈余酒	An old fellow sent me a gift of wine,
乃言飲得仙	And said drinking it makes one immortal.
試酌百情遠	I try a cup, a hundred cares are gone,
重觴忽忘天	A few more, and all at once I forget Heaven.
天豈去此哉	Is Heaven removed from here?
任真無所先	Following truthfulness dissolves all priorities.

飲酒詩 其十四　Drinking Wine Poems, No. 14

父老雜亂言	The old men break into random babbling,
觴酌失行次	Pouring from the jar out of turn.
不覺知有我	Aware no more of my own self,
安知物為貴	How would I know what things to prize?
悠悠迷所留	Leisurely rapt in where I linger—
酒中有深味	There are deep flavours in the wine!

The poet describes how wine makes him 'forget Heaven' and become 'unaware of the self', fostering his instinct to 'follow truthfulness' that 'dissolves all priorities' and 'things to prize'. One recalls how the English nature poet William Cowper (1731–1800) speaks of the need for the proud intellect's 'mercurial powers' to yield to a 'quiescent' meditativeness before cosmic understanding is possible, believing ' 'Tis thus the understanding takes repose / In indolent vacuity of thought, / And sleeps and is refresh'd'.[30] Now Cowper's frame of mind is of course non-Daoist, but the state of an unassertive 'quiescence' and 'indolent vacuity' is not without affinity to Zhuangzi's notion of the 'mind fasting' (Ch. 4 'The Human World' 人間世), until emptied of preconceptions, desires and 'selfhood', it becomes impartially receptive and freely responsive. William Wordsworth (1770–1850) has related how, 'with an eye made quiet by the power / Of harmony … We see into the life of things'.[31] In Tao's poems this intuitive vision of quiet harmony is facilitated by wine, which dissolves even the reality of Heaven and blurs the distinctions imposed by the fragmenting mind, leaving his transcendent spirit 'leisurely rapt in the deep flavours' of cosmic unity beyond the elders' social hilarity. One can make the point that inner spiritual transcendence is ultimately not dependent on any external agent, but that does not negate the expedient value of wine as a means that can help to liberate the spirit.

With Tao Qian, then, the significance of wine as poetic subject reached an unprecedented level. Other poets continued to write about drinking in its various uses in daily life,[32] but no one up to the end of the Six Dynasties era exceeds the range of Tao's expression on the subject. Perhaps only one extra point needs to be made briefly at this juncture. We have noted from the context of Liu Bang's poem how wine serves as an enhancer of heroic spirit. Later poets have continued to write in a similar vein, such as Zuo Si 左思 (c. 250–c. 305) and Tao Qian writing of Jing Ke's 荊軻 drinking as part of his patriotic image.[33] Yet in the 'Ballad of Mulan' 木蘭詩, there is no mention of wine as an aid or 'objective correlative' to the female protagonist's heroic spirit (the point about the ballad's composition or revision in the Tang is immaterial here). While some later female poets like Li Qingzhao 李清照 (1084–1151) and Zhu Shuzhen 朱淑真 (c. 1078–c. 1138) do mention wine—the former seems to get drunk often both to suppress and to preserve memory[34]—the ballad helps to show that drinking was a largely male activity.

'Wine Immortal'[35] and the Force of Personality: Wine in the Poetry of Li Bai

From early Zhou to Wei-Jin times and the Southern-Northern Dynasties, the development of the cultural significance of wine and its poetic expression is largely complete. The Tang poets did not add too much in substance, but the masters of *shi* continued to develop existing themes and write about wine in relation to various facets of literati life (e.g. social merriment, alleviation of grief, parting), often with more artistic force and refinement than their predecessors. Wang Han's 王翰 (c. 687–after 735) 'Liangzhou Poem' 涼州詞, for instance, represents a subgenre of 'frontier poetry' 邊塞詩 that sings of a heightened heroic spirit, crystallizing in the images of the grape wine and phosphorescent cup the heroism (and helplessness) of soldiers engaged in defending and expanding the borders of the empire:[36]

葡萄美酒夜光杯	Delicious grape wine, cup that glows at night;
欲飲琵琶馬上催	About to drink, *pipa* music on horseback urges us on.
醉臥沙場君莫笑	Don't you laugh if we lie drunken on the battlefield—
古來征戰幾人回	Since ancient times, how many have returned from war?

Meng Haoran 孟浩然 (689–740) and Wang Wei 王維 (c. 692–761), on the other hand, write of drinking in the context of country life and close fellowship with a semi-reclusive touch in the manner of Tao Qian, though neither Meng nor Wang has first-hand farming experience:

孟浩然 過故人莊　Visiting a Friend's Farm, by Meng Haoran

開軒面場圃	Opening the window, we face the fields and garden;
把酒話桑麻	Wine in hand, we talk of mulberry and hemp.
待到重陽日	Wait until Double Ninth [Festival] comes around,
還來就菊花	And I'll come again for the chrysanthemums.

While Meng cannot speak of 'mulberry and hemp' with the same persuasion as Tao Qian (cf. 'Return to Farmstead Living', No. 2 〈歸園田居〉其二), the poem blends wine and friendship, quietude and freedom together in a relaxing Daoist ambience of peace and harmony.[37]

Yet however refined or heroic the artistic touch of the above poets may be, it is really the work of Li Bai that sends the Chinese poet's drinking experience to the threshold (or reality) of a supramundane realm. This is fundamentally due to the poet's unique personality, imaginative genius and celestial chemistry with wine, rather than anything in abstract concept or design. Let us first take a look at Du Fu's 杜甫 (712–770) poetic testimony:

飲中八仙歌　Song of the Eight Drinking Immortals

李白一斗詩百篇	Li Bai dashes off a hundred poems after a measure of wine,
長安市上酒家眠	And falls asleep in the market tavern in Chang'an.
天子呼來不上船	Summoned by the Son of Heaven, he does not board the boat,
自稱臣是酒中仙	Claiming 'your subject is an immortal of wine!'

As the most celebrated wine poet in Chinese literature, Li Bai's image comes across vividly: even when inebriated, a poet bold enough to turn down the Son of Heaven's summons can only be a 'banished immortal' who stands logically above and beyond the rules of the earth. That Du Fu's portrayal may be more truth than exaggeration—that wine releases and elevates the creative inspiration—can be seen in the self-portrait of another writer Zhang Yue 張說 (667–730), and in Li Bai's description of the famous calligrapher Huaisu 懷素 (725–785):

張說 醉中作   Written While Drunk, by Zhang Yue

醉後樂無極   Once drunk, my delight knows no limits—

彌勝未醉時   Even better than before I'm drunk.

動容皆是舞   My movements all turn into dance,

出語總成詩   And every expression comes out a poem!

李白 草書歌行   Song of Grass Script, by Li Bai

吾師醉後倚繩床   My master, now drunk, leans by the corded bed,

須臾掃盡數千張   And in an instant dashes through thousands of sheets.

飄風驟雨驚颯颯   Swift wind and sudden rain startle with their speed,

落花飛雪何茫茫   Falling petals and flying snow—how blurry and vast!

Such spirited description of the link between wine and the creative impulse— especially the creativity of a spontaneous temperament—cannot be found in pre-Tang poetry.

One of the unique aspects of Li Bai's art is that he simply envisions and writes on a much larger scale than other poets in quantity and in dynamism, with a touch so sure and natural that the term 'hyperbole' cannot be legitimately applied to him. The lines below give some sense of how the 'banished immortal' drinks wine:

襄陽歌   Song of Xiangyang

百年三萬六千日   Thirty-six thousand days in a hundred years;

一日須傾三百杯   Let's swallow three hundred cups a day!

將進酒   Bring the Wine!

烹羊宰牛且為樂   Boil the mutton, roast the beef—just let's be merry,

會須一飲三百杯   And at one bout make it three hundred cups!

Three hundred cups a day for thirty-six thousand days—such is the natural scale of Li Bai's vision and existence. The Brobdingnagian dimensions are in keeping with the 'white hair three thousand fathoms' 白髮三千丈 of a giant heroic drinker, who travels freely scaling mountains 'forty-eight thousand fathoms' high 天台四萬八千丈[38] as an aboriginal inhabitant of the universe:

友人會宿　**A Night with a Friend**
醉來臥空山　Drunk, we lie down in the empty hills,
天地及衾枕　Heaven and earth are our quilt and pillow.

Indeed, even when the poet drinks and feels alone, his spirit remains robust and expansive:

月下獨酌 四首之一　**Drinking Alone beneath the Moon, No. 1**
花間一壺酒　Amid the blossoms, with a pot of wine,
獨酌無相親　I drink alone, without a friend.
舉杯邀明月　I raise my cup to invite the bright moon;
對影成三人　Facing my shadow, we make three.

The main point in this poem is not that 'the moon knows not how to drink' 月既不解飲, or whether they will 'ever join in passionless revels' 永結無情遊, as the ensuing lines in the poem suggest. What stands out most clearly is how easy and natural the poet feels in beckoning to the moon as a drinking companion, so that the wine almost seems to take on a celestial luminescence.

It may be noted in passing that the 'wine immortal' does not always need to drink. When he stays away from wine, Li Bai's mood can be remarkably serene and self-sufficient:

山中問答　**Conversation amid the Hills**
問余何意棲碧山　You ask why I lodge in the green hills;
笑而不答心自閑　I smile without replying, the heart at ease by itself.
桃花流水窅然去　Peach blossoms flow on water into the distance;
別有天地非人間　There is another world beyond the realm of man.

Note that the characters for 'naturalness' appear not as one term but as natural components in two lines, perhaps symbolic of the way in which *ziran* has been internalized in the poet's spirit. He feels no need to offer a reply to the enquirer, but does embody it in the second couplet in the image of the flowers flowing silently by. The answer is reminiscent not only of Tao Qian's 'I would explain it, but have forgotten the words' 欲辨已忘言 ('Drinking Wine', No. 5 〈飲酒詩〉其五), but also of Zhuangzi's 'getting the meaning and forgetting the words' 得意忘言 (Ch. 26 'External Things' 外物).[39] Transcendence of the spirit is ultimately independent of any external agent (無所待), and Li Bai's free spirit is certainly not fettered by his favourite beverage.

In fact, even when he writes about wine, Li Bai can do so in a quiet and 'normal' tone.[40] Nevertheless, what is inimitably *sui generis* about his poetry is his 'supra-normal' lens and brush. Witness his exuberant expression of the heroic spirit especially after drinking:

白馬篇　**Poem on the White Horse**

酒後競風采　After drinking, he vies to show his heroic air;
三杯弄寶刀　With three cups he brandishes his precious sword.
……　　　…
叱咤經百戰　Roaring mightily, he goes through a hundred battles,
匈奴盡奔逃　As the Xiongnu troops all flee in disarray.
歸來使酒氣　On return he releases his wine spirit,
未肯拜蕭曹　Refusing to bow to the ministers.

永王東巡歌 其十一　**Songs on the Prince of Yong's Eastward March, No. 11**

試借君王玉馬鞭　Let me borrow my lord's jade horse-whip,
指揮戎虜坐瓊筵　And direct the battles while feasting in the camp.
南風一掃胡塵靜　Our south wind, with a sweep, shall wipe out the barbarian dust,
西入長安到日邊　Breezing west into Chang'an to the fringe of the sun.

Wine makes the warrior invincibly mighty and proudly independent; it makes the strategist relaxed and transcendently self-possessed, able to dust off the enemy effortlessly with a mere 'sweep', and breeze to the 'fringe of the sun' almost in the next instant. Indeed, even when he writes of drinking to dispel melancholy, Li Bai's sentiments are Olympian in scale:

宣州謝朓樓餞別
校書叔雲　**Farewell Dinner to Collator Uncle Yun at Xie Tiao's Tower in Xuanzhou**

抽刀斷水水更流　I draw my sword to stem the water, yet water still flows on;
舉杯消愁愁更愁　I raise my cup to drown my grief, but grief is still more grief.
人生在世不稱意　In life if aspirations cannot be fulfilled,
明朝散髮弄扁舟　Tomorrow let me loosen my hair and set sail in a tiny boat.

將進酒　**Bring the Wine!**

古來聖賢皆寂寞　Sages and worthies since ancient times have all turned silent;
唯有飲者留其名　Only the great drinkers have left behind a name.
……　　　…
五花馬，千金裘　Dappled mount, fur worth a thousand gold—
呼兒將出換美酒　Call the boy to take them and swap for delicious wine,
與爾同銷萬古愁　Together we'll dissolve ten thousand ages of grief!

Ten thousand ages of deepening grief, like gushing water that cannot be stemmed—such is the usual scale and temper of the dynamic sentiments 'let loose' by wine in Li Bai's world. Wine dissolves not only grief, but the distinctions the mind imposes on the world and the frustrations thus generated, so that the self regains its sense of unity with the cosmic order.

That these are more than occasional assertions can be seen in a similar, consistent tone expressing the 'kinetic' way in which wine 'propels' the poet to a union with the Dao:

月下獨酌 四首其二　**Drinking Alone under the Moon, No. 2**
賢聖既已飲　Since I've tasted the sage and the worthy [i.e. clear and muddy wine],
何必求神仙　What need have I to search for immortals?
三杯通大道　Three cups transmit me to the Great Way,
一斗合自然　A measure harmonizes me with naturalness.

月下獨酌 四首其三　**Drinking Alone under the Moon, No. 3**
一樽齊死生　One cup equalizes life and death,
萬事固難審　The myriad matters no longer distinct.
……　. . .
不知有吾身　I do not know my self exists—
此樂最為甚　Such delight is the highest of all!

'Equalizing life and death', readily 'transmitting' him to the Way, wine releases the poet from human distinctions, facilitating a suspension of the self in the 'highest delight' and harmony of cosmic naturalness. Such spiritual transcendence through wine reminds one of Tao Qian, except that Li Bai's spirit is more heroic, and his tone more exuberant. Thus he speaks of the universe on even more intimate and utterly easy terms, at times almost as a master of Nature:

陪侍郎叔遊洞庭　**Accompanying Elder Kinsman, a Former Vice Director, on a**
醉後三首其三　**Tour of Lake Dongting, after Getting Drunk, No. 3**
剗卻君山好　Better shovel away the Junshan islet—
平鋪湘水流　Smooth and even the Xiang waters will flow.
巴陵無限酒　Here in Baling, no end of wine,
醉殺洞庭秋　Thoroughly intoxicating the autumn of Dongting.

陪族叔刑部侍郎　**Accompanying Elder Kinsman Li Ye, Formerly Vice Director**
曄及中書賈舍人　**in the Ministry of Justice, and Jia Zhi, Formerly Drafter in the**
至遊洞庭五首　**Secretariat, on a Tour of Lake Dongting, No. 2**
其二
南湖秋水夜無烟　Autumn waters on the South Lake, a night without mist;
耐可乘流直上天　Would that I could ride the current straight up to the sky!
且就洞庭賒月色　Here on Dongting, let's just borrow some moonlight,
將船買酒白雲邊　And moving the boat, purchase some wine by the white clouds.

Who else but Li Bai could have imagined such an imperial act, shovelling away a whole island on the lake, and turning the latter into a large pool of wine intoxicating both Nature and man? Wine has catalysed the poet's spirit and imagination as a conductor of Nature in the first poem. And any reader who still wonders why Li Bai's wine tastes more delicious than others only needs to read the second quote: purchased with 'borrowed moonlight' (rather than dirty earthly coins) 'by the white clouds' on the grand lake, the poet's wine has all the celestial ingredients and seasoning needed to make for an incomparable quality and flavour. No other Chinese poet can imagine riding straight up to the sky with such natural ease of tone, as if Heaven were simply home. Infected by the poetic spirit, wine has become semi-immortal.

Meanwhile, wine continues to feature in the works of Tang poets within familiar thematic contexts, e.g. in association with personal fortune, friendship, parting, homesickness, reclusion, spiritual freedom, etc.[41] Perhaps only two points need to be briefly mentioned in terms of new thematic associations: the extension of wine as an image of social criticism and as a focal point of romantic feelings. Thus Du Fu uses superfluous rotting wine (and meat) as a contrastive image vis-à-vis exposed human bones by way of social criticism, while Du Mu 杜牧 (803–852) brings out the poignancy of wine as an emotional intensifier in a new context of parting between lovers.[42] Parting of a romantic nature is seldom mentioned in *shi* poetry, and, after the Tang era, is mostly left to expression in the *ci* form. Still, it is indisputably in Li Bai's work that the richest manifestations of wine in classical poetry are to be seen.

The Moderate 'Earthly Immortal': Wine in the Poetry of Su Shi

Human explorations and articulations of any given subject are rarely (if ever) a matter of unlimited originality. By the Song era, it is not easy to find new thematic uses or associations of wine in poetry. Even during the Tang, Li Bai's wine-related poems strike one not so much for their categorical novelty, as for the inimitable dynamism and celestial exuberance of his unique imagination and individual expression. Poets such as Ouyang Xiu 歐陽修 (1007–1072), Su Shi, Lu You 陸游 (1125–1210) and Xin Qiji 辛棄疾 (1140–1207) are all famous for their fondness of wine. The Song masters and their Ming-Qing counterparts continued to write about various mundane as well as more ethereal aspects of drinking. In view of new developments in philosophical thought and painting aesthetics since the Song, a few excerpts from poems that express the supramundane significance of wine may serve as illustration:

醉中遺萬物　In drunkenness I leave all things behind,
豈復記吾年　How then can I remember my age?

....

所以屢攜酒　So it is I often take some wine,
遠步就潺湲　And walk the distance to the purling waters.

(Ouyang Xiu)

卻對酒杯疑是夢　Again facing my wine cup, I wonder if it's a dream;
試拈詩筆已如神　When I pick up my poetry brush, it feels almost divine.

(Su Shi)

朱樓矯首隘八荒　Gazing far on the vermilion tower, the eight directions look
　　　　　　　　cramped;
綠酒一舉累百觴　A round of green wine reaches a hundred cups.
洗我堆阜崢嶸之胸次　It washes clean my lofty and elevated heart,
寫為淋漓放縱之詞章　Expressed as passionate and unbridled verses.

(Lu You)

想當濡毫拂絹素　Imagine him moistening his brush and touching the silk;
酒酣落筆神骨露　Brush strokes in drunkenness reveal his spiritual frame.
萬里青天動海嶽　Under the boundless blue sky, seas and mountains move;
空堂白日流雲霧　Over the empty hall in broad daylight, clouds and mists flow.

(He Jingming 何景明, 1483–1521)[43]

In different ways and on various levels, these poems continue to register the positive effects of wine on spiritual liberation and creative inspiration, whether in poetry or in other art forms like calligraphy and painting: from purifying the heart (Lu) to forgetting the world (Ouyang), from unfettered expression (Lu) to an 'almost divine' brush (Su) enough to activate the seas and mountains, clouds and mists (He).

It is relevant to note that the best Song drinkers are not heavy self-indulgent drinkers. For instance, Ouyang Xiu calls himself an 'old drunkard', yet to him drunkenness is not sensory numbness or loss of consciousness, but a state of spiritual contentment brimming to the point of 'intoxication'. As he indicates clearly in his account of 'Old Drunkard Pavilion' 醉翁亭記, 'the old drunkard's spirit lies not in wine but in the landscape. The delights of the landscape are assimilated in the heart and underpinned by wine' 醉翁之意不在酒，在乎山水之間也。山水之樂，得之心而寓之酒也. As Ouyang's protégé, Su Shi represents this elevated spiritual-aesthetic outlook on wine better than anyone else. One may be surprised to learn that Su Shi cannot take much alcohol: 'I drink no more than half a litre a day. There is no one who cannot drink more than me, but … also no one who likes drinking more than me' 余飲酒終日不過五合，天下之不能飲無在余下者，然……天下之好飲亦無在余上者 ('Postscript to the Biography of Wang Ji' 書東皋子傳後). His couplet 'I drink without draining the cup;/ Half-drunk, the flavour feels especially deep' 我飲不盡器，半酣味尤長 ('Returning from the Lake Late at Night' 湖上夜歸) is perhaps the best guide to understanding his drinking.

The relationship between wine and transcendence in Su Shi's poetry will be explored in a moment. For now, it might be useful to relate Su Shi's poems to two general aspects in the use and expression of wine in Song poetry and beyond, i.e. more frequent snapshots of drinking as a social bond among the common folk (sometimes in the poet's company), and a broader use of the wine image as a means of social criticism. While the former feature is already present in Tao Qian and the latter can be seen in Du Fu, the broader generality of such uses of wine in Song poetry and beyond reflects a deepened social consciousness among the literati poets. Su Shi has also been dubbed an 'immortal' by his admirers, but he is unlike Li Bai in being an 'earthly immortal' who drinks with the common people:

東鄰酒初熟	The eastern neighbour's wine is newly brewed;
西舍豕亦肥	The western neighbour's pigs are fat as well.
且為一日歡	Let's just make a day of merriment,
慰此窮年悲	To soothe the sadness of this closing year.
江城白酒三杯釅	River wall, distilled wine, three cups taste strong;
野老蒼顏一笑溫	Country folk, grey-haired, a smile feels warm.
父老喜雲集	The elders joyously assemble;
簞壺無空攜	Their food and wine vessels come loaded.
三日飲不散	For three days the drinking ceases not;
殺盡西村雞	All the West Village poultry get cooked.[44]

From knowledge of the country folk's working patterns and living conditions to participation in their joy and sympathy for their plight, Su Shi writes with a sure and familiar touch. In his capacity as a caring local official, his bonding with the local populace is clearly closer than Tao Qian's: wine represents a social bond connecting people in joy and hardship alike. While Su Shi does not use wine as a means of direct social criticism through contrasting the wasteful luxury of the rich with the hardship of the poor,[45] his work reflects not only a broader social consciousness among the literati, but a greater readiness to express such subjects in poetry.[46]

What is more, this social consciousness is also manifested in Su Shi's *ci*, and one finds wine functioning in a similar way as well:

浣溪沙 五首	**Tune: 'Sand of Silk-Washing Stream', Five Lyrics**
老幼扶攜收麥社	Bringing the old and young, they come to reap the wheat,
……	. . .

道逢醉叟卧黃昏　On the way I meet a drunk old man lying in the dusk.
（其二）　　　　　　　　　　　　　　　　　　　(No. 2)
垂白杖藜抬醉眼　White-haired, with goosefoot staff, he raises his drunken eyes—
捋青擣麨軟飢腸　Pick greens, grind parched grains to soothe a hungry belly!
（其三）　　　　　　　　　　　　　　　　　　　(No. 3)
酒困路長惟欲睡　Wine-drowsy, long road, I only want to sleep;
日高人渴漫思茶　Sun high, throat parched, in vain I think of tea.
（其四）　　　　　　　　　　　　　　　　　　　(No. 4)

Because of their association with singing girls at the start as well as the basic tone and flavour of the musical tunes which befit their singing voices, most *ci* poems have tended towards a 'feminine' quality of 'delicate restraint' (*wanyue* 婉約) in content and style from the outset. As a result, the lyrical meanings of wine also become more restricted in nature, being largely limited to its associations with such negative feelings as indulgence, sadness, helplessness and frustration.[47] In a *shi* poem cited above, we have already seen Su Shi write about the common folk drinking in festivity on the completion of a bridge. Here in Nos. 2 and 3 of the 'Sand of Silk-Washing Stream' lyrics, the wine is an element in a general reflection of rural life, from joyous harvest, domestic warmth and relaxed drunkenness to a chronic sense of tight livelihood not free from hunger, with the poet himself in the position of an affectionate witness and participant (No. 4).

It will be useful to examine a few more *ci* poems by Su Shi, for the inherited limits of the *ci* form set off the extraordinary range of his lyric expression even more sharply, including multiple senses and rich tones of 'alcoholic vitality':

臨江仙 · 夜歸臨皋 Tune: 'Immortal by the River': Returning to Lin'gao at Night
夜飲東坡醒復醉　Drinking at Eastern Slope at night, sobered then drunk again,
……　　　　　　　. . .
倚仗聽江聲　Leaning on my staff, I listen to the river's sounds.
長恨此身非我有　Always I regret this body is not mine;
何時忘卻營營　When can I forget worldly worries?

水調歌頭　Tune: 'Prelude to Water Melody'
明月幾時有　When did the bright moon come to be?
把酒問青天　Wine in hand, I ask the blue sky.
不知天上宮闕　I know not at the palace in Heaven
今夕是何年　What year it is tonight.

江城子 · 密州出獵　Tune: 'Riverside Town': Hunting at Mizhou
酒酣胸膽尚開張　Drunk to my fill, my heart and valour remain open;
鬢微霜　Hair slightly frosted—
又何妨　What does it matter?

定風波	Tune: 'Calming Wind and Waves'
料峭春風吹酒醒	The chilly vernal wind sobered me up from wine,
……	. . .
歸去	Turn back—
也無風雨也無晴	There is neither wind, rain nor shine.

漁父 四首	Tune: 'The Fisherman', Four Lyrics
漁父醉	The fisherman gets drunk
蓑衣舞	And dances in his straw cloak.
醉裏卻尋歸路	In drunkenness he looks for his way back.
輕舟短棹任橫斜	His light boat and short oars drift aslant at will;
醒後不知何處	Sobered up, he knows not where he is.
（其二）	(No. 2)
漁父醒	The fisherman sobers up
春江午	At noon on the spring river,
夢斷落花飛絮	His dream scattered into falling petals and flying catkins.
酒醒還醉醉還醒	Sobered yet drunk, drunk yet sobered,
一笑人間千古	He laughs at mankind present and past.
（其三）	(No.3)

The scope of lyric expression seen in the excerpts ranges from personal and nationalistic to philosophical sentiments. One finds wine enhancing a spectrum of moods: regret, solitude and agitation in 'Immortal by the River' that long for peace and transcendence of the spirit; a more positive, expansive sense of emotional affinity with the celestial entities (reminiscent of Li Bai) in 'Prelude to Water Melody'; a return to spiritual sobriety and transcendence in 'Calming Wind and Waves'; and a heightened valour of heroic commitment in 'Riverside Town' that aspires to 'hunt down' the alien invaders of the north, not unlike Xin Qiji's patriotic fervour flowing vigorously even in his 'drunken dream':

破陣子 Tune: 'Cavalry Dance'
醉裏挑燈看劍 Drunk, I trim my lamp and survey my sword;
夢回吹角連營 In my dream, I blow the bugle and align the tents.

As noted above, enhancement of patriotic sentiments through wine can be traced back at least to portraits of the assassin Jing Ke, but Su Shi's personal affirmation offered direct inspiration to a long line of patriotic poets in the ensuing eight centuries. In the present emotional context, (red grape) wine became a particularly powerful image in its associative transformation into blood through 'colour migration'. Thus in a direct substitution of blood for wine, the Southern Song general Yue Fei 岳飛 (1103–1142) vows in his 'valiant aspiration' to 'eat the flesh of barbarians in [his] hunger' 壯志飢餐胡虜肉 and 'drink their blood in

[his] thirst' 笑談渴飲匈奴血 (Tune: 'Full River Red' 滿江紅) . The modern female revolutionary Qiu Jin 秋瑾 (1875–1907) does not go quite so far, but also associates wine with her 'heart of ardent blood' 一腔熱血 and her comrades' 'hundred thousand skulls of blood' 十萬頭顱血.[48] What is most noticeable about the wine image in the cited poems is its emotional intensity through co-presence with ardent blood, as though the one imbibed will transform into the other through the heroic spirit. Wine has become the quintessential intensifier of sentiments.

No doubt it is in 'Calming Wind and Waves' and the 'Fisherman' lyrics, the latter based on a tune pattern the poet composed himself, that Su Shi's transcendent spirit can be seen most vividly. It may be noted in passing that a century earlier, Li Yu 李煜 (937–978) also expressed carefree sentiments in a different *ci* tune with an interchangeable title, 'The Fisherman' 漁歌子: 'A jar of wine, an angling rod—how many are there like me in the world?' 一壺酒，一竿身，世上如儂有幾人.[49] But whereas Li Yu's joyous mood exudes from a personal kind of freedom, Su Shi's mood is more universal and philosophical: the elements of a drunk man above rational fetters, dancing, feeling light and drifting at will in oblivion, come close to the images of the true man and the unmoored boat in the *Zhuangzi* (Ch. 6, 32). Even when sobered up, the fisherman's dream is not 'broken' in the usual sense, but transformed into wafting petals and flying catkins in free motion, leaving him in a half-drunk, half-sober state of existence not unlike the awakened Zhuangzi wondering if he is butterfly or man (Ch. 2). Yet in a final twist of insight, Su Shi offers a dual perception of wine as a catalyst of the spirit: he may say 'get drunk here and now, right and wrong, worries and delight are all forgotten' 不如眼前一醉是非憂樂都兩忘, but he also observes 'the transcendent man is so by himself, what merit does wine have? / Right and wrong, worries and delight in the world are empty from the start' 達人自達酒何功，世間是非憂樂本來空 ('Weak, Weak Wine', Two Poems, Nos. 1–2 薄薄酒二首). Here in the work of Su Shi, the association of wine with spiritual transcendence has found its quintessential expression in Chinese poetry.

Closing Remarks

Tao Qian, Li Bai and Su Shi are only the most classic cases of wine-loving poets in China; the story of wine in classical Chinese poetry is a multi-layered narrative that cannot be justly told within the span of an essay. In the brief analysis above, we have seen how wine variously facilitates socializing, numbs the mind, intensifies feelings, releases conceptual fetters, stirs the creative impulse, and transports the spirit to the Way. In general terms, the potential of wine as an element of poetry hinges on a number of factors, including its quality as a stimulating drink, its availability to the literati and its link to a supra-material (philosophical and artistic) plane of experience, along with an awareness of life, death and self-extinction that is well developed within the cultural framework. Such existential awareness reached a high level towards the end of the Han, extended into deepened spiritual and artistic experiences of wine in the Wei-Jin era, and rose to climactic heights in the works of individual Tang and Song poets. One recalls in particular the spirit of Li Bai, who sings of a heroic passion for life and a celestial enjoyment of wine blended into elevated lyric expression, almost beyond the imagination of mortals.

In the long history of classical Chinese poetry, the significance of wine remained constant in some aspects, and became transformed in other aspects in parallel with a sharpened sense of individuality and the enlightening experiences of philosophy and art. Thus the use of wine as social catalyst and as emotional intensifier and anaesthetic is more or less timeless, based on its chemical ability to excite and to numb the mind. On the other hand, wine proved to be a moral degrader in early Chinese political history, which led to a stern sanction within the humanistic framework of Zhou culture. This moral tone became less heavy as experiences and perceptions of wine took on positive elements in time. It took over a millennium of development for the positive uses of wine to be appreciated in full—as liberator of rational constraints on thoughts and feelings, as stimulus to artistic inspiration and transporter of the spirit. But there is little doubt that in the course of time, the semantic gravity of wine moved some distance away from the ritual and social to the individual plane, from moral and political to spiritual and aesthetic dimensions, and from Confucian to quasi-Daoist perceptions.

It should be noted that many drinking literati held an ambivalent attitude to wine. Ruan Ji did not allow his son to follow him in being a drunkard.[50] Xi Kang 嵇康 (224–263), as famous a drunkard as Ruan Ji, admits in his 'Discourse on Nurturing Life' 養生論 that 'wine corrodes one's internal organs' 醴醪鬻其腸胃. Even Lu You, who vows after the manner of Li Bai to 'drink for five hundred years / and stay drunk for three thousand autumns' 一飲五百年，一醉三千秋, is concerned that 'alas, it leaves the body decrepit and ailing' 其如老病身.[51] And since varieties of Chinese wine with a higher alcoholic content probably appeared in the Tang,[52] the constructive and destructive effects of drinking likely intensified as well.

In the final analysis, the topic of this essay is perhaps incapable of yielding conclusive findings, for the simple reason that as a material product, wine has no intrinsic artistic attribute or spiritual orientation. It has been linked to Daoist freedom and artistic creation since Wei-Jin times because, in relaxing mental fetters and shelving worldly concerns, wine did prove to some its efficacy in elevating the creative impulse, stimulating the imagination, and fostering the spirit's return to an original state of unmediated spontaneity and truthfulness. Yet as Su Shi points out, wine, like any passing material agent, cannot fundamentally transform inner human experience or generate anything 'new'. The moralist will still warn against overindulgence in wine as a disruptor of reason and order, while the true philosopher does not rely on anything for inner spiritual transcendence. Nor do art and poetry ultimately depend on the stirring effect of wine. As an element in Chinese food culture, wine will continue to take its changing shape among the hedonist, the moralist, the artist, the philosopher, the average consumer and even the person insensitive to it, now wrapped in guilt, now relished with abandon.

5
The Interplay of Social and Literary History

Tea in the Poetry of the Middle Historical Period

Ronald Egan

This chapter examines the treatment of tea in Tang and Song dynasty poetry. We find a very clear shift in the way poets write about the drink. This shift is more subtle, complicated, and nuanced than the dynastic change from Tang to Song, but it does roughly correspond with that change. The shift is most obvious when comparing poems of the mid-and late Tang periods (roughly 780–900) with those of the mid-eleventh century (the literary 'height' of the Northern Song). These two periods are the focus of this chapter. What we find is that poets adopted distinctly different approaches to the subject of tea and tea drinking during the periods, and these changes reflect in a complex way transformations in the cultural space and economic role of the drink between those eras. Poems about tea reflect conventional and unconventional ways of thinking about the subject, and those ways of thinking are affected by its changing role in Chinese life.

Tea in Tang Poetry

During the Tang dynasty, and certainly from the mid-Tang onward, the consumption of tea was already widespread in the great cities of the empire. Tang poets write about it often. Yet although the drink was widely available, literary treatments of tea tend to handle it rather narrowly, linking it almost always with recluses, immortals, and, especially, Buddhist monasteries, where tea had a long history of consumption by monks who used it to ward off the drowsiness that threatened their long hours of meditation. A poem such as the following by the eighth-century monk-poet Jiaoran 皎然 (730–799) epitomizes the associations of the subject found regularly in Tang poetry:

九日與陸處士	On the Double Ninth Festival, Drinking Tea with Recluse Lu Yu[1]
羽飲茶	
九日山僧院	On the Double Ninth, in a monastery courtyard
東籬菊也黃	Chrysanthemums are yellow by the eastern fence.
俗人多泛酒	Common fellows steep the blossoms in wine,
誰解助茶香	Who knows to be partial to the fragrance of tea?

The contrast constructed here is between ordinary fellows, marked by their lack of refinement, who know only to drink wine, and monks like Jiaoran and his recluse friend Lu Yu 陸羽 (733–804), who are among the elite few who know to appreciate tea and its subtle fragrances. It was Lu Yu who wrote the most important Tang treatise on tea, the *Classic of Tea* 茶經. Although he was not a monk himself, Lu Yu spent periods of his life dwelling in Buddhist monasteries and must have accumulated much of his expertise in tea from the monks he associated with. The chrysanthemums in line two are a conventional motif in Double Ninth Festival poems, and mention of an 'eastern fence' immediately calls to mind the recluse devotee of those blossoms, Tao Qian 陶潛 (365–427). More important to the remainder of the poem is the habit of floating chrysanthemums in wine cups on that festival, mentioned in line three (*fanjiu* 泛酒). That is what common people do on the Double Ninth, while Jiaoran and his friend have a more refined appreciation of tea.

A longer tea poem, also by Jiaoran, provides more detail about the effects of wine and why he was so enamoured with tea. The poem was occasioned by Jiaoran's receipt of a gift of tea from Shan Valley (in modern Shaoxing, Zhejiang):

誚崔石使君	**Poking Fun at Commissioner Cui Shi**[2]
越人遺我剡溪茗	A man of Yue sent me Shan Valley tea
採得金牙爨金鼎	Picking golden leaflets to boil in a golden kettle,
素瓷雪色飄沫香	Plain porcelain like snow, floating bubbles fragrant,
何似諸仙瓊蕊漿	How like the immortals' jewelled flower liquor!
一飲滌昏寐	One sip washes away my drowsy stupor,
情思朗爽滿天地	My thinking is pristine, filling heaven and earth.
再飲清我神	A second sip purifies my soul,
忽如飛雨灑輕塵	Like flying rain suddenly falling on light dust.
三飲便得道	A third sip and I attain the Way,
何須苦心破煩惱	Why vex the mind to break free of life's tribulations?
此物清高世莫知	So pure and lofty it is, yet the world does not know,
世人飲酒多自欺	People deceive themselves by drinking wine.
愁看畢卓甕間夜	How sad to see, Bi Zhuo's night beside the wine vat,
笑向陶潛籬下時	How laughable, Tao Qian beside his fence!
崔侯啜之意不已	Tasting it, Master Cui's appreciation know no end,
狂歌一曲驚人耳	His mad song startled those who heard it.
孰知茶道全爾真	The Way of tea is perfect truth, who understands?
唯有丹丘得如此	Only Danqiu really knows.

This time, Tao Qian is invoked by name, only to be ridiculed for his wine drinking. He is paired with Bi Zhuo, another famous wine drinker who, when he once sneaked into a neighbour's house to steal his wine, was apprehended and tied to the wine vat until dawn.[3] Of interest in this poem is the extreme description it gives of this south-eastern tea's effect upon the poet. The drink does nothing less than bring Jiaoran to an apprehension of the Way. Indeed, in the closing lines, tea is virtually equated with 'perfect truth'. Danqiu is a legendary immortal who was also associated with tea.[4] Jiaoran says that he is 'poking fun' at his friend, Cui Shi, presumably because Jiaoran considered the 'wild song' Cui wrote about tea excessive. But the claims that Jiaoran himself makes for this tea that was given him are hardly modest ones.

So thoroughly is tea associated with monasteries and recluses in Tang poetry that it is spoken of in this way even when transported to the great Tang cities. In the cities, tea is not simply appreciated as tea; it is appreciated as a reminder of the purer and simpler life that is lived in mountain seclusion. While serving in the capital, the powerful Li Deyu 李德裕 (787–850), grand councillor under two emperors (Wenzong and Wuzong), once received a gift of tea from Jiuhua Mountain in the south (modern Chizhou, Anhui). To enhance the experience of drinking it, in the middle of the night he invites an unnamed monk over to drink with him and commemorates the event in this poem:

故人寄茶	**A Friend Sends a Gift of Tea**[5]
劍外九華英	From beyond the southern mountains, sprouts of Jiuhua.
緘題下玉京	Wrapped and addressed, they arrive at the Jade Capital.
開時微月上	As I open them a crescent moon ascends,
4　碾處亂泉聲	Grinding the leaves, a wild mountain spring gurgles.
半夜邀僧至	In the middle of the night I invite a monk to come,
孤吟對竹烹	I recite lines by myself facing the bamboo steamer.
碧沉霞腳碎	The jade sinks, the feet of clouds are shattered.[6]
8　香泛乳花輕	The fragrance floats, milky buds are buoyant.
六腑睡神去	From my six viscera the sleep spirit is driven away,
數朝詩思清	For several mornings my poetry thoughts will be clear.
其餘不敢費	I do not dare to waste the unused part,
12　留伴讀書行	But save the gift for when I am reading.

Line 7: 'Feet of clouds' is a standard term for tea leaves resting on the bottom of the cup.
Line 8: 'Milky buds' refers to the whitish bubbles on the surface of the steeping tea.

Li Deyu, wanting to enjoy his gift from the mountain slopes, invites a monk to come drink with him. His contemporary Liu Yuxi 劉禹錫 (772–842), finding himself drinking tea in a Buddhist monastery in the mountains, goes a step further. When the monks he is drinking with kindly offer to send some tea to him after he returns to his prefectural office, he observes, first, that such an official setting is not conducive to tea consumption and, second, that the act of shipping, though it is widespread, damages the leaves. His conclusion is that one must dwell in the mountains (that is, as a monk or recluse) to truly know the taste of tea. These are the closing lines of his lengthy poem:

西山蘭若試茶歌	A Song on Tasting Tea in a Monastery in the Western Hills[7]
......	. . .
僧言靈味宜幽寂	The monks say the divine flavour befits quiet seclusion.
采采翹英為嘉客	The abundant fluttering leaves become a welcome guest.
不辭緘封寄郡齋	They would send a package to my prefectural office,
4 磚井銅爐損標格	But brick well and copper stove would ruin its character.
何況蒙山顧渚春	Still worse, the spring teas from Meng Mountain and Guzhu
白泥赤印走風塵	Sealed in white clay, stamped in red, they travel dusty roads.
欲知花乳清冷味	If you want to know the pure cooling taste of milky buds,
8 須是眠雲跂石人	You must be one who sleeps in clouds and squats on rocks.

Line 5: Meng Mountain, in Sichuan, was well-known for its tea, as was Guzhu, in Zhejiang.

In what may be the most widely-quoted of all Tang poems on tea—at least a section of it—the early ninth-century poet Lu Tong 盧仝 (790–835) offers a new treatment of the conventional contrast in tea poems between the idyllic mountains where the leaves are grown and the cities where so much of the drink is consumed. Lu Tong retains the juxtaposition, but introduces a new way of developing it:

走筆謝孟諫議寄新茶	Written with a Rapid Brush, Thanking Remonstrator Meng For Sending New Tea[8]
日高丈五睡正濃	The sun was high over the horizon as I slept soundly,
軍將打門驚周公	An officer knocked on my door, startling the Duke of Zhou.
口云諫議送書信	He told me the remonstrator had sent me a package,
4 白絹斜封三道印	Wrapped in white silk, stamped with seals of three circuits.
開緘宛見諫議面	Opening the letter, his face appeared plainly before me,
手閱月團三百片	My fingers counted three hundred round cakes of tea.
聞道新年入山裏	He said when the new year first arrived in the hills,
8 蟄蟲驚動春風起	Hibernating insects began to stir, the spring winds arose.
天子須嘗陽羨茶	The Son of Heaven was intent on tasting Yangxian tea
百草不敢先開花	The other plants did not dare to blossom first.
仁風暗結珠琲瓃	Benevolent winds secretly formed strings of pearls,
12 先春抽出黃金芽	At the start of spring yellow gold buds were put forth.
摘鮮焙芳旋封裹	Picked fresh and dried fragrant, it was wrapped and sealed.
至精至好且不奢	The highest quality, the finest flavour, but not wastefully so.
至尊之餘合王公	His Majesty's surplus could be given to princes and dukes.
16 何事便到山人家	But how could it be sent to a hermit in the mountains?
柴門反關無俗客	My bramble door is kept closed, I have no vulgar guests.

紗帽籠頭自煎喫	A cotton cap covers my head as I brew it myself to drink,
碧雲引風吹不斷	Emerald clouds bring winds that cannot blow them apart,
20 白花浮光凝碗面	White buds and glistening surface are motionless in the cup.
一碗喉吻潤	The first bowl cleanses my throat and lips,
兩碗破孤悶	The second bowl vanquishes my solitary angst.
三碗搜枯腸	The third bowl explores my withered innards,
24 唯有文字五千卷	To find nothing there but five thousand chapters of writing!
四碗發輕汗	The fourth bowl elicits faint perspiration.
平生不平事	The disquieting affairs of my whole life
盡向毛孔散	Are now entirely dispelled through my pores!
28 五碗肌骨清	The fifth bowl purifies my bones and tendons,
六碗通仙靈	The sixth bowl connects me to immortals and divinities.
七碗喫不得也	The seventh bowl I cannot bring myself to drink,
唯覺兩腋習習	Already I sense pure wind gently emanating from under my
清風生	arms.
蓬萊山，在何處	Isles of Penglai, where are you?
30 玉川子，乘此	Master Yuchuan, sit astride this pure wind and let it
清風欲歸去	carry you there!
山上群仙司下土	The immortals on mountain tops govern the world below,
地位清高隔風雨	Their pure and lofty dwelling knows no wind or rain.
安得知百萬億	How could they understand the lot of millions of
蒼生命	commoners?
墮在巔崖受辛苦	Cast down upon rugged cliffs to toil and suffer.
便為諫議問蒼生	Let me ask the remonstrator about the common people—
到頭還得蘇息否	Ultimately, will they ever get to rest or not?

Line 2: 'Duke of Zhou' here refers to dreaming, based on a statement that Confucius makes in the Analects.

Line 9: Yangxian tea, famous at the time, was produced in what is now Yixing, Jiangsu.

Lines 29–30: The Isles of Penglai, in the eastern ocean, are where immortals are said to reside, and Yuchuan is Lu Tong's own name.

Shipments of the finest teas from throughout the empire were, of course, offered as tribute to the emperor each spring. Here Lu Tong imagines that the tea sent to him from his friend, Remonstrator Meng, a court official, had been given to him by the emperor, and that Meng, in turn, sent some of his gift to Lu Tong. In this scenario, the tea that arrived by messenger at Lu's humble dwelling had made a circuit, from the mountains, where it grew, to the capital, and then back again to Lu Tong's rustic dwelling in the hills. The celebrated passage of Lu Tong's poem is the section on the effects that the seven bowls of tea have upon him. Indeed, that section has so overshadowed the rest of the poem that it is often excerpted to stand by itself, and given its own title, 'Song of Seven

Bowls of Tea' 七碗茶歌. In fact, Lu Tong's seven bowls section may be viewed as an expansion of the lines by Jiaoran, quoted earlier, on his own gift of Shan valley tea. What Lu Tong does with the geography of tea is equally interesting, turning the dichotomy between countryside and court into an occasion for social and political commentary. Lu Tong moves from the 'immortality' he achieves from drinking tea, to the immortals' Isles of Penglai, and from there back to the subject of the court, exploiting the long-standing trope of the court and imperial palace as a celestial abode. But Lu Tong, having 'ascended' to divine realms has not forgotten the commoners toiling on mountain slopes who picked the tea in the first place. So he concludes by putting a question to his court official friend that would almost certainly not be very welcome, asking, in effect, if the august officers of the imperial court really have any commiseration for the labouring masses, from whose toil they benefit, and if they really are ever going to give some relief to them. This is an unexpected twist in a poem on a gift of tea.

Tea in Song Poetry

Tea as a commodity

To say that tea had become a commodity by Northern Song times is to dramatically understate its importance. It was not just another commodity. The empire-wide thirst for tea was such that it turned the drink into one of the most important and lucrative of all marketable goods. From its first years, the Song bureaucracy established a monopoly on tea, and this monopoly, at certain times at least, supplied more revenue to the central government than any other source. The history of the Song government's tea monopoly is complex and ever changing. For much of the Northern Song there was not a single tea monopoly but a complicated web of different regional monopolies, alternating with regions exempt from the monopoly. The central government's most important tea monopoly, instituted over the Sichuan tea industry, is the subject of a detailed and probing study by Paul J. Smith.[9] It is clear that government regulation of the tea trade in general was one of the most powerful economic and revenue-generating tools at its disposal. The Song monopoly of south-eastern (Jiangnan) tea production was lifted in 1059. Decades later, in 1102 when Cai Jing 蔡京, as grand councillor under Emperor Huizong 徽宗, proposed reinstituting that regional monopoly, he observed that since that monopoly was dissolved in 1059 the government tea revenues had fallen from over 5,000,000 strings of cash annually to just over 800,000. Within a few years after its re-establishment, the south-eastern monopoly was returning 2,500,000 strings of cash to the government each year.[10]

The new economic role of tea is reflected in an angry poem by Mei Yaochen, reacting to reports that young men of the educated elite were exploiting the restrictions brought about by the government monopoly to make money for themselves:

聞進士販茶	On Hearing of Advanced Scholars Selling Tea for Profit[11]
山園茶盛四五月	Tea grows abundantly in mountain groves in the late spring
江南竊販如豺狼	The illegal traders of Jiangnan are like jackals and wolves.
頑凶少壯冒嶺險	Violent young men brave the mountain heights
夜行作隊如刀鎗	To travel in gangs at night like armed soldiers.
浮浪書生亦貪利	Itinerant students are also greedy for profit
史笥經箱為盜囊	Their book bags are turned into smugglers pouches!
津頭吏卒雖捕獲	The constables at river crossings may arrest them
官司直惜儒衣裳	But the magistrate judges pity their scholars robes.
卻來城中談孔孟	They arrive in the capital prattling about Confucius and Mencius
言語便欲非堯湯	Their speeches find fault with Kings Yao and Tang.
三日夏雨刺昏墊	Three days of summer rain, they complain of a flood.
五日炎熱譏旱傷	Five days of heat, they grumble about a drought.
百端得錢事酒炙	They'll do anything for money to indulge in meat and ale,
屋裏餓婦無糇糧	While back home their wives have no rice to eat.
一身溝壑乃自取	If they end up in a ditch they have only themselves to blame.
將相賢科何爾當	High office and prestigious degree are not what they deserve.

Mei Yaochen's anger is directed at opportunistic students who are abusing their privileged status as having passed the highest level civil service examination, or at least having qualified to take it, by smuggling tea into the capital, where they turn a handsome profit. It was the tea monopoly in the southeast, which ironically was lifted a few years later, which made such smuggling profitable. The monopoly regulated the supply; it was also said to have lowered the quality of tea that was legally available. Higher quality teas, which could command a higher price, were driven underground by the monopoly, and perhaps, as suggested here, into the book bags of opportunistic students.

A poem on tea such as Mei's would be out-of-place in Tang poetic treatments of the drink. It is likely that the commodification of tea had already taken place by the late Tang—at least this is what Paul Smith argues—but such a transformation is not very evident in Tang poems on tea.[12] The drink is still treated by Tang poets as something rare and exotic. It is almost inseparably associated with the quietude and seclusion of Buddhist monasteries. Tang poets do not write about tea as a market commodity, much less as one whose profit potential when sold illegally outside the government monopoly was being exploited by members of the lettered class. The cultural space of tea, if not the economic role as well, changed radically between the ninth and eleventh centuries.

Tea and wit

In contrast with the seriousness of most Tang poems on tea, in which the poet's respect if not reverence for the drink is evident, one often finds among Song period poems on the topic a certain playfulness. Partly this must be a consequence of the light-heartedness so widespread in Song poetry generally, which has often been commented on. But another contributing factor must be the nature of the subject itself. Once the drink moved out of the monastery and its early association with religious meditation—not an activity that lent itself to frivolity—tea consumption was, after all, a mundane pleasure, or a pastime, and often even an indulgence. Tea as a poetic subject, and a relatively new one at that, had none of the lugubrious overtones of so many conventional poetic subjects (e.g. blossoms in spring, moonlit autumn nights). It was quite natural then for Song literati, with their enthusiasm for displays of wit, to adapt the subject of tea to light-hearted verse. Below is an example of this, a tea poem that Huang Tingjian 黃庭堅 sent to Su Shi 蘇軾 in 1087, when the two of them, both returned to imperial favour, were serving together at the court. Su was then a Hanlin academician (the poem's 'Jade Hall' is an alternate name for the Hanlin Academy) and Huang was an editor in the Bureau of History.

雙井茶送自瞻	**Sending Twin Wells Tea to Zizhan**[13]
人間風日不到處	Where the wind and sunshine of the mortal world does not reach,
天上玉堂森寶書	Jade Hall in the heavens is filled with precious books.
想見東坡舊居士	I imagine the former recluse of East Slope there,
揮毫百斛瀉明珠	From his moving brush a hundred bushels of pearls pour forth.
我家江南摘雲腴	Near my home in the Southland they pick these 'fluffy clouds',
落磑霏霏雪不如	The powder falling from the grinder is whiter than snow.
為君喚起黃州夢	May it summon up a Huangzhou dream for you,
獨載扁舟向五湖	Boarding a little skiff alone, you set out for Five Lakes.

Someone must have sent the tea to Huang from Twin Wells, near Huang's hometown in Jiangxi. In the poem the mountain-grown tea, colloquially called the 'succulence of clouds', becomes an attribute of rural seclusion and freedom from the drudgeries of official service. Thus Huang speaks of the drink as inspiring Su with a dream of his Huangzhou exile, which he then further links to the famous withdrawal of Fan Li 范蠡, the Spring and Autumn period minister of Yue, who eventually resigned his post and sailed off to end his days wandering the Five

Lakes region. Of course, neither Su Shi nor, for that matter, Huang Tingjian are really going to resign their recently recovered court posts to become recluses. And Su Shi is glad to have been recalled from his Huangzhou period exile. But in the poetry of the Yuanyou period, Su's Huangzhou exile is remembered nostalgically as a kind of reclusion. In this poem, the Twin Wells tea represents the antithesis to court office and power, and Huang playfully invokes that antithesis as an idyll, even as he and Su labour away in their prestigious posts. Tea is conventionally associated with staving off sleep and drowsiness. But Huang Tingjian, interestingly, often associates the drink with sleep and dreams. In a matching poem accompanying a second gift of Twin Wells tea that he sent to another colleague, Huang imagines another droll effect the gift might have: it should keep Kong Wuzhong's 孔武仲 tongue from drying out as he recites texts day and night. Huang, working in an adjoining office, hears him reciting day after day.[14]

In the following poem, Su Shi shows that he can treat tea in a jocular way even when it is situated in a monastic setting.

遊諸佛舍，一日	Having Visited Several Buddhist Temples, in One Day I Drank
飲釅酒七盞，	Seven Cups of Pungent Tea. In Jest I Wrote this on Master
戲書勤師壁	Qin's Wall[15]
示病維摩元不病	While declaring himself ill, Vimalakīrti was not ill.
在家靈運已忘家	Though living at home, Lingyun had already forgotten home.
何須魏帝一丸藥	What need do I have of the Wei emperor's single immortals pill?
且盡盧仝七碗茶	Let me drink instead Lu Tong's seven bowls of tea!

Su had spent the day, while playing hooky from official responsibilities, visiting various temples on West Lake outside Hangzhou. Realizing that he had consumed 'seven' cups of tea, he naturally thought of Lu Tong's famous tea poem. Su then proceeds to contrast the seven bowls of tea with the single pill that Wendi of the Wei (Cao Pi 曹丕 [187–226]) wrote about receiving from immortals on a mountain top, which allowed him to ascend into the sky and roam about with immortals.[16] With Lu Tong's list of effects in mind, Su suggests that the tea he has consumed renders any such immortality pill unnecessary.

We might not at first understand the relevance of the opening couplet of Su's poem, except that it obviously alludes to famous Buddhists and plays upon the notion of deceptive appearances. But when we notice the poem's alternate title, the point of the opening couplet becomes clear: 'On the sixth day of the sixth month, I requested leave from official duties because of illness, and went by myself to various temples on the lake. In the evening I called upon Sunzhi, and playfully wrote this quatrain to give to him.'[17] Now we understand that Su Shi took the day off on the pretext of illness but he was not really ill, like Vimalakīrti (although the famous lay Buddhist was speaking of another kind of 'illness' altogether). In the second line Su is similarly likening himself to the layman Xie Lingyun 謝靈運 (385–443), who was said to have already 'forgotten' his family and home although he lived among them and did not withdraw to a monastery.

All this is, of course, tongue in cheek. The humour begins with Su Shi, the vice governor of Hangzhou, pretending to be ill that day, when he really was not, and he continues the drollery in the way he characterizes himself in his quatrain. The new role assigned to tea deserves comment. In Lu Tong's poem the effects of the drink upon the poet, bowl by bowl, are described in detail and with seriousness. Lu Tong may change his focus in the concluding lines to the sociology of tea, but in the celebrated 'seven bowls' lines his attitude toward the drink is one of quiet reverence. In Su Shi's poem the focus is not on the tea so much as it is on the wittiness of his lines, as he brings disparate allusions together, culminating in the contrast between Cao Pi's magical pill and Lu Tong's multiple bowls of tea. Tea drinking in Su's poem is not treated seriously. Rather, it is an occasion for the display of his poetic wit and nimble erudition.

Connoisseurship

By Northern Song times, tea drinking had become so widespread that, among the elite at least, a highly self-conscious connoisseurship of the beverage had developed. Expertise was prized in all aspects of preparing tea: choosing the plant whose leaves to pluck, drying and grinding, choosing the water source, the refinement of the cups and utensils, and, finally, the actual process of steeping the ground tea in heated water. The discovery of Fujian teas, which were popularized in the Song capital in mid-eleventh century by the calligrapher Cai Xiang 蔡襄 (1012–67), a Fujian native, and were thereafter prized at the court, ushered in an unprecedented fastidiousness in tea consumption. Writing about brewing a new shipment of Fujian tea he had just received, Mei Yaochen belittles northerners whose drinking habits, stuck in the past, appear crude and outmoded by comparison: 'Do not speak of tea like this to commoners of the north, / All they know about is white clay and mixing in sesame' 此等莫與北俗道，只解白土和脂麻.[18] He is referring to the older practice of flavouring tea with sesame seeds and being content to serve it in plain white cups (as opposed to the dark and variegated southern porcelains that were then in vogue).

We see evidence of the new level of connoisseurship in the proliferation of tea manuals and treatises of various kinds. The number of tea manuals produced during the Northern Song is some three times that produced in earlier times.[19] Several of these were produced at the court of Huizong, including one attributed to the emperor himself.[20] We also see evidence of the increased refinement of tea drinking in the frequent references to 'tea competitions' 鬥茶 in Song texts. These competitions meant different things to different people. It could be the taste or the colour of the tea concerning which aficionados vied. To Cai Xiang, the tea competition was a matter of measuring expertise in the way the tea was mixed with heated water in the cup and focusing on a very specific criterion. When the powdered tea was infused in hot water, tiny bubbles (the 'white buds' we have seen mentioned) rose up to the surface and burst. Attention was paid to whether or not the bubbles that burst along the sides of the teacup left water marks on the cup just above the surface of the tea. A person whose cup showed water marks was the 'loser', a person whose cup had no such marks was the 'winner'.[21]

As we would expect, the new self-consciousness about tea and its preparation is abundantly reflected in Song period poetry on the subject. Below is an example, a poem that Su Shi wrote upon receiving a gift of Jian (i.e. Jianzhou 建州, modern Jian'ou 建甌, Fujian) from a friend while he was serving in Hangzhou.

和錢安道寄惠建茶	Matching a Poem by Qian Andao Accompanying the Kind Gift of Jian Tea that He Sent[22]
我官於南今幾時	For a long time I have served as official in the south
嘗盡溪茶與山茗	I've tasted all the teas of its valleys and its mountains
胸中似似故人面	In my heart I remember them like the faces of my friends.
4 口不能言心自省	My heart knows even those I lack the words to describe.
為君細說我未暇	To give you a detailed account—I have not the time,
試評其略差可聽	But I'll attempt a rough outline for you to hear.
建溪所產雖不同	Although the teas of Jian Creek are not all the same,
8 一一天與君子性	To each one Heaven gave a gentleman's nature.
森然可愛不可慢	They all deserve to be cherished and never slighted.
骨清肉膩和且正	Pure of bone, sleek of flesh, they are harmonious and correct.
雪花雨腳何足道	Are 'snowy buds' and 'rainy legs' worth mentioning?
12 啜過始知真味永	After you drink you know the true flavour that lasts forever.
縱復苦硬終可錄	Even if bitter and inflexible they deserve to be recorded,
汲黯少戇寬饒猛	Ji An was a bit of a simpleton and Kuanrao ferocious.
草茶無賴空有名	Grass teas are undependable and famous for no good reason,
16 高者妖邪次頑懭	The best of them are demonic and the best are perverse.
體輕雖復強浮沉	Light of body, they can float or sink at will,
性滯偏工嘔酸冷	Their nature is crafty and leave a sour and chill aftertaste.
其間絕品豈不佳	The highest quality among them are certainly fine,
20 張禹縱賢非骨鯁	But worthy Zhang Yu failed as a fishbone in the throat.
葵花玉銙不易致	Sunflower blossoms and jade cubes are not easy to obtain,
道路幽險隔雲嶺	The lonely roads are perilous, beyond cloud-shrouded peaks.
誰知使者來自西	Who'd think a messenger would come from the west?
24 開緘磊落收百餅	The opened package clearly revealed a hundred cakes inside.

嗅香嚼味本非別　Their fragrance and their flavour could be from no other,
透紙自覺光炯炯　A gleaming light seemed to show forth through the
　　　　　　　　　wrappers.
秕糠團鳳友小龍　They make Phoenix Cakes husks and befriend Little Dragon,
28 奴隸日注臣雙井　They make Pour Daily slaves and rule over Twin wells.
收藏愛惜待佳客　I'll store them away, treasuring them, to await some
　　　　　　　　　　　distinguished guest,
不敢包裹鑽權幸　Rather than gift-wrapping them to cultivate powerful friends.
此詩有味君勿傳　This poem has its own flavour, please don't circulate it;
32 空使時人怒生瘦　No sense in angering people so they break out in boils!

Lines 11–12: It might be that 'snowy buds' and 'rainy legs' are names of teas from other regions. I suspect, however, that they are visual traits looked for in tea generally: the whitish bubbles on the surface of the liquid, and, perhaps, the gradual sinking of the tea powder in the cup. I think Su means that these qualities, even of Jian teas, are hardly worth talking about: what is truly wonderful about them is their taste.

Lines 13–14: Ji An and Gai Kuanrao 蓋寬饒 were Han dynasty officials, both known for their outspokenness and willingness to criticize even the emperor. It was Emperor Wu, exasperated one day by this trait of Ji An's, who pronounced him to be a 'simpleton'. Despite all the tension occasioned by Kuanrao's outspokenness, he was praised as a 'ferocious beast' by a colleague who admired his daring.[23] Despite their 'shortcomings' (which Su Shi actually views as virtues), these men still warranted 'recording', that is, merited having their biographies included in the Han official history.

Line 15: 'Grass tea' is the term applied in the Song to teas that were not pressed after being dried (and usually ground), to extract the oil. Jian teas were all pressed, because otherwise the oil content was too high, and so 'grass tea' was often used as a general term to refer to non-Jian teas.[24]

Line 20: A minister under Emperor Cheng of the Han, Zhang Yu failed to warn him of the growing threat of Wang Mang, who eventually usurped the throne.[25] 'Fishbone in the throat' is a standard phrase for advisors who speak the truth even when it is awkward and unwelcome (like a fishbone stuck in the throat).

Lines 21–22: This couplet refers to the Jian tea that has been sent to Su. 'Sunflower blossoms' and 'jade cubes' refer to the appearance of the powdered cubes of tea it was formed into.

Line 23: The tea that Qian Andao sent was originally from the southeast (modern Fujian). But Qian Andao himself was not there, he was in Xiuzhou (modern Jiaxing, Zhejiang), close to where Su was stationed in Hangzhou. In fact, Su Shi visited Andao in Xiuzhou around the time of this poem, as he was touring the districts around Hangzhou. To judge from this line, Su was somewhere east of Andao when Andao sent him the gift of tea.

Line 27: Phoenix Cakes (or Dragon Phoenix) was a highly valued type of tea early in the Northern Song, but it was eclipsed by Little Dragon tea, so-called because the cakes were a fraction of the size, sent to the capital by the Fuzhou native Cai Xiang in the mid-eleventh century.[26]

Line 28: Pour Daily was a highly prized Zhejiang region tea, and Twin Wells (which we have seen mentioned earlier) was a famous Jiangxi region tea.[27]

Su Shi may not have been the first poet to liken the character of different teas to the personalities of men, but probably no one before him had developed the analogy so extensively. Beginning with the thought that he recalls the taste of different Jian teas as well as he remembers the faces of his friends, he develops the equivalence to an elaborate set of correspondences between tea and human 'character'. As he does so, he displays not just his wit, but also his considerable knowledge of various teas (both those from Jian and those from outside the region). It is Su's genius not to be content simply to offer generalizations about the 'personality' of tea, but to enhance the specificity of his references with allusions to ministers from the Han dynasty that learned people would be familiar with. Su's mastery of the field of tea is matched by his ability to summon up clever allusions from his knowledge of history. As for his tea expertise itself, Su has clearly moved far beyond generic poetic treatments of tea for its mystique or simplistic contrasts between tea and wine.

Because this is Su Shi, there is more to this poem than just mastery of tea and the ability to connect it with human personalities (and Han history). There is yet another dimension to this poem that surfaces occasionally, then disappears, then surfaces again. Su Shi is thinking about his political enemies in several of his lines about inferior teas, which are 'perverse' or crafty, lack principle, or are used by unscrupulous people to ingratiate them with the high and mighty. Even from the lines themselves (especially 15–20 and 29–30) we might suspect as much. But Su's closing couplet clearly shows that he is thinking of his political opponents and is worried (or feigns worry) about further antagonizing them. If any further indication of this political dimension is required, we have Su Shi's own testimony about the poem, recorded in the affidavit produced as part of the court case against him for defaming the emperor and high ministers, the Poetry Trial at Raven Terrace 烏臺詩案.[28] As Su Shi explains there, the lines about petty and opportunistic men refer to the New Policies adherents he was set against. If this political denunciation of his enemies in a poem about tea strikes us as gratuitous, it is completely in keeping with Su's writings of the time to allow such political commentary occasionally or momentarily to slip into writings on unrelated subjects. So we see that for Su Shi, so thoroughly polarized and politicized was his world during the New Policies era that even while he is displaying his expertise about tea, politics is on his mind.

Parody

Yet there was some ambivalence over connoisseurship in Song times, regardless of the object in question. Carried to an extreme, connoisseurship ran the risk of being viewed as frivolous and snobbish. As much as Song literati clung to what they considered *ya* 雅 'elegant' and sought to distance themselves from the *su* 俗 'common, vulgar', they were conscious that the latter also had its wholesome qualities and the former could become a shallow affectation.

So widespread had not just tea consumption but tea connoisseurship become by the mid-eleventh century that it could occasionally be treated parodically. One could view this development as an indication that, for some, the drink had finally lost its aura as something apart (and above) everyday commercial life. In literary history, such a treatment of tea was probably a Song development. I am not aware of any Tang poem that treats the drink this way, and any that did would be truly exceptional.

We see the parodic impulse, and even impatience with tea connoisseurship, emerge in an exchange of tea poems between Ouyang Xiu and Mei Yaochen, occasioned by Ouyang's receipt of a gift of fresh Jian tea, sent to him by the prefect of Jian'an, a portion of which Ouyang sent, in turn, to Mei Yaochen.[29] Interestingly, the parody and dismissal of the drink is not there at the outset of this exchange. It is something that emerges as the exchange becomes drawn out. In other words, both poets reach a point where the reverence standard in poetic treatments of tea and its connoisseurship can no longer be sustained. Reverence then degenerates into parody.

The shift in attitude occurs in Ouyang's second long poem. The shift does not clearly take place until the final lines of the poem, but there are hints even in earlier lines that Ouyang is finding it more and more difficult to sustain the unqualified enthusiasm for the tea that characterizes the first poem he sent to Mei (along with his gift of the tea) and Mei's first poetic response. This is Ouyang's second poem:[30]

	吾年向老世味薄	As I get older my taste for the worldly things weakens.
	所好未衰惟飲茶	My only fondness left undiminished is for drinking tea.
	建谿苦遠雖不到	Jian Valley is far away, I cannot go there,
4	自少嘗見閩人誇	But since youth I've heard the boasts of natives of Min.
	每嗤江浙凡茗草	I scoff at the common unpressed teas of Jiang and Zhe.
	叢生狼藉惟藏蛇	A confused mass of bushes good only for hiding snakes.
	豈如含膏入香作	How could they compare to golden cakes, so lustrous and
	金餅	fragrant?
8	蜿蜒兩龍戲以呀	Two coiled dragons, their mouths sporting with each other.

其餘品第亦奇絕	The other kinds are likewise marvellous and unmatched,
愈小愈精皆露芽	The smaller and more refined are all Dew Sprouts.
泛之白花如粉乳	When steeped the white buds are like milky powder,
12　乍見紫面生光華	The purple surface, when visible, emits a lustrous glow.
手持心愛不欲碾	Holding it, cherishing it, I'm reluctant to grind it up,
有類弄印幾成瓷	Like fingering the seal of office until it is crushed.
論功可以療百疾	They say it has the power to cure a hundred ailments,
16　輕身久服勝胡麻	Over time it lightens the body, better than sesame.
我謂斯言頗過矣	I say such claims are exaggerated,
其實最能袪睡邪	Isn't its effect, in fact, simply to banish sleep?
茶官貢餘偶分寄	A portion of the surplus of tea office tribute was sent to me,
20　地遠物新來意嘉	Fresh harvest from a distant land, a most generous gift.
親烹屢酌不知厭	I brewed it myself and repeatedly poured, never tiring,
自謂此樂真無涯	Telling myself this pleasure truly knows no bounds.
未言久食成手顫	No one warned me of trembling hands if I drank too much,
24　已覺飢生眼花	My stomach feels hunger pangs, I see spots before my eyes.
客遭水厄疲捧碗	My guests suffer 'water distress', tired of lifting the bowls,
口吻無異蝕月蟆	The mouth feels like the toad that swallowed the moon.
僮奴傍視疑復笑	The servants look on, wondering and laughing,
28　嗜好乖僻誠堪嗟	Such a perverse fondness is truly something to bemoan.
更蒙酬句怪可駭	Matching poetic lines returned to me are strange, frightening,
兒曹助噪聲哇哇	The children add to the ruckus, crying wah-wah!

Line 4: Min is the general name for the south-eastern region of what is today Fujian, where the tea Ouyang received came from.

Lines 5–6: Ouyang's own note on these lines explains that the tea fields of the Jiang and Zhe regions (modern Zhejiang) are said to be full of snakes.

Lines 7–8: Tea from Jian was commonly ground into a powder and then compressed into round or square 'cakes', and the cakes were often stamped with carvings of writhing dragons. See the illustrations of tea cakes in Xiong Fan 熊蕃, 'Xuanhe beiyuan gongcha lu' 宣和北苑貢茶錄, in *Zhongguo lidai chashu huibian* 1: 120–5.

Lines 9–10: In these lines it begins to sound like Ouyang's gift of tea included a variety of Jian teas. Dew Sprouts is known as one of the famous teas from that region.

Lines 13–14: The tea cakes were reground into powder for brewing. Line 14 probably alludes to the famous reluctance of Xiang Yu 項羽 to reward meritorious leaders under him with enfeoffment (as described by Han Xin 韓信), which made him hold seals of appointment in his hands, unwilling to confer them, until they were ruined.[31]

Lines 15–16: Various parts of the sesame plant (the seeds, the oil extracted from them, the leaves, the fruit) had long been ingested for their medicinal properties as well as taken in Daoist regimens, where they were believed to purify and 'lighten' the body.

Line 26: Eclipses of the moon were explained, in popular lore, as resulting from the moon being swallowed by the toad that lives there. It's not clear exactly what tea-induced sensation in the mouth Ouyang is referring to. Of course, he inherited this difficult rhyme word from the earlier poem he wrote.

Line 29: This refers to the matching poem that Mei Yaochen wrote in response to Ouyang's first poem. To understand this line, we should bear in mind that several of the rhyme words, which Ouyang had first chosen, are odd and unusual in poetic diction.

A parodic tone begins to appear already in lines 13–14: Ouyang is poking fun at himself by comparing his attachment to the tea cakes to Xiang Yu's reluctance to confer seals of enfeoffment on deserving ministers. Next, Ouyang questions claims about the marvellous effects the drink is supposed to have upon the body (lines 15–18), deflating them. The poem becomes openly parodic from line 23 on, as Ouyang describes the adverse effects that too much of the caffeinated drink can have.

Mei Yaochen's response to this poem goes even further, quite openly rejecting the drink and its connoisseurship as something that has become an impediment to quiet sitting and the friends' enjoyment of each other's company: 'I don't want "pure wind emanating from my armpits" / All I want is to sit facing bamboo and to face flowers' 不願清風生兩腋，但願對竹兼對花.[32] The first line explicitly rejects what Lu Tong had listed as one of the beneficial effects of tea (seen earlier), and does so in a way that makes it sound ridiculous.

The shifts we have noticed in the poetic treatment of tea from Tang to Song reflect changes, first, in the social context of tea consumption and, second, in the way the drink was thought about owing to the new roles it came to fulfil in Chinese society. The literary progression may not, strictly speaking, exactly coincide chronologically with the social movement of tea from mountains and monasteries to urban centres. There is reason to think, as noted earlier, that the literary progression lags behind what was actually happening to the drink in society, that is, that Tang poets who nearly always associated the drink with recluses and monks were writing conservatively about a stage in the history of tea consumption that had already given way to a new reality. It should not surprise us that there would be such a chronological discrepancy. We could surely find other examples of elite poetry being less than perfectly synchronized with developments in popular culture. What is interesting, nevertheless, is how dramatic and clear-cut the change in poetic treatments is, once it takes place. In this instance, then, we see how literary production is affected by social change and developments in economic history and material culture. That is not to say that literary production is merely and simply reflective of social change. The transformation in poetic treatments of tea is clear-cut without being universal. No doubt some poets even after Ouyang Xiu, Mei Yaochen, and Su Shi, continued to write about tea in the earlier way, invoking again its unworldly mystique. But to do so, say, in the Southern Song period, would be a conscious return to an earlier mode of writing about the drink.

6
The Obsessive Gourmet

Zhang Dai on Food and Drink[1]

Duncan Campbell

[F]or the people, food is Heaven (民以食為天)[2]
A greedy Dongpo,
Starving at Solitary Bamboo.
饞東坡餓孤竹

—Zhang Dai 張岱,
'Inscription for My Own Tomb' (Zi wei muzhiming 自為墓誌銘)[3]

A dandy in white silk breeches will never starve.
紈褲不餓死

—Du Fu 杜甫 (712–770), 'Twenty-two Rhymes Presented to Wei Ji,
Assistant Director of the Left in the Department of State Affairs'
(Fengzeng Wei zuocheng zhang ershier yun 奉贈韋左丞丈二十二韻)

Among the rich, frugality is considered to be a virtue, but one that is observed intermittently, as periods of fast alternate with those of feast; at this level a frugal diet is associated more with fasting and voluntary denial than with famine and the ineluctable elements; abstinence was internalized as a way to grace rather than the result of external pressures that heralded starvation.

—Jack Goody, *Cooking, Cuisine and Class: A Study in Comparative Sociology*[4]

Of the various books that the late Ming dynasty historian and essayist Zhang Dai 張岱 (1597–1684?)[5] either wrote or compiled over the course of the long and prolific second half of his life, many did not safely negotiate that passage from manuscript to imprint that so often spelled the difference between survival and loss of text in China.[6] Although, somewhat unusually in this respect, the late 1980s and 1990s saw the first publication of a number of his manuscripts, found preserved in various libraries,[7] sadly, given both Zhang Dai's privileged upbringing and his finely-honed instincts for fine living, one work that now seems lost forever is his book of recipes, entitled the *Old Glutton's Collection* (*Laotao ji* 老饕集), which was based on an earlier compilation put together by his grandfather. Fortunately, however, Zhang Dai's preface (*xu* 序) to this work, translated below, was included in the major collection of Zhang Dai's prose writings, his *Paradise Collection* (*Langhuan wenji* 琅嬛文集), and has thus survived.[8]

It is a preface of some considerable interest, quite apart from the insights it provides into Zhang Dai's own life and preoccupations. In his preface, Zhang Dai provides something of an insider's digest history of the traditional Chinese discourse on food and cooking, a tradition that, in the opinion of the anthropologist Jack Goody, represents one of the world's most complex of cuisines and associated culinary discourses. Goody speaks of the culinary differentiation of culture (between private and public, and along regional and hierarchical lines) which, in China, as much as in the classical world, was 'linked to a particular kind of hierarchy, with distinct "styles of life", a hierarchy that is in turn based upon a certain type of agricultural system', and which engendered opposition at both the conceptual and the political levels.[9] Goody notes a set of specific characteristics of such cuisines: the link between cuisine and class; contradictions, tensions and conflicts connected with this differentiation; an increased range of ingredients and menus resulting from exchange, tribute and commerce; the specialization of cuisine encouraged by the collection and publication of recipes; an elaboration of the gendered division of culinary labour with high-status tasks often being transferred from women to men; a close and long-standing link between food and sex; and finally, a link between eating and health.[10] We can observe many of these characteristics at work in Zhang Dai's preface.

K. C. Chang has argued that 'perhaps one of the most important qualifications of a Chinese gentleman was his knowledge and skill pertaining to food and drink'.[11] In these terms, Zhang Dai seems splendidly qualified. He was a man of many and varied obsessions: rocks and gardens, actors and operas, books, handicrafts, painting and calligraphy, friends and flowers, birds, dreams, tea and medicine and, perhaps above all else, the West Lake of Hangzhou. Eating was one of his abiding preoccupations as well, and his voluminous writings are studded with memories of eating and of food, all of them recalled to mind and recorded at a time when Zhang Dai was suffering, by his own account, from extreme privation: 'If starvation too is such a common-place affair, / Then how marked a feature of my life it has now become!' 餓亦尋常事尤於是日奇, read the first two lines of a set of two poems entitled 'Birthday of the Jiawu Year: On this Day, I Starve' (Jiawu chudu shi ri e 甲午初度是日餓) written in 1654, a decade after the fall of Beijing, the northern capital of the Ming.[12] He ends this poem with the lines: 'When poverty becomes as real as this, / Recalling the past, oddly, affords a modicum of joy' 一貧真至此回想反開頤.

Here, before I turn to Zhang Dai's preface, for instance, is an item from his *Dream Memories of Taoan* 陶庵夢憶 that reveals the extent to which his own obsession with food was one that was very much a function of the circumstances of his gilded upbringing.

Zhang Donggu's Addiction to Wine 張東谷好酒

Ever since the time of my great-great-grandfather, Zhang Tianfu [1513–1578], my family had been renowned as great drinkers; over the generations, however, this ability has been lost.

Neither my father nor his brothers could drink much more than a single goblet of wine, accompanied by a plate of pickled eggplant, before their faces would turn a bright red. At family meals and banquets they paid attention solely to the food. As a consequence, the fare of our kitchen was the best to be had throughout the region east of the Yangzi River. As soon as a platter of food appeared on the table my uncles would tuck in. In an instant the food would disappear, and my uncles, their bellies now bulging, would get up and wander off on their own various pursuits, having not raised a cup to their lips throughout the entire meal. Even when guests happened to be present, my uncles would quit the table before they had a chance to bid their hosts goodbye.

That man of the mountains, Zhang Donggu, was a great drinker who was often left most frustrated by this habit of my family. On one occasion he rose to his feet and, exasperated, exclaimed to my father: 'You brothers really are most eccentric! The meat you eat, regardless of whether it is good or not; the wine you don't drink, without even knowing if it is worth drinking or not.' His was a finely turned sentence or two, embodying all the refined and insouciant air of the men of the Jin dynasty. More recently, however, some reprobate included Zhang's bon mot in a work entitled *A Record of the Glories of the Tongue* but so mangled is it in the retelling that it becomes the stiff and lifeless: 'The brothers Zhang are eccentric in the extreme by nature! Regardless of whether or not the meat is good to eat, they will not eat it, and regardless of whether or not the wine is good to drink, they will not drink it.' So many there are in this age of ours who seem to have at their disposal a reverse version of the Midas Touch, invariably turning whatever they touch into stone!

Zhang Donggu was a most jocular figure, but he happened also to be desperately poor with, in the saying of old, 'not the ground to stick an awl'. On one occasion he took a case against a local young good-for-nothing who accused him of being an old moneybags. Zhang Donggu rushed off to see my grandfather, complaining: 'Shaoxingers are such a hateful lot—lying to my very face, calling me a moneybags!' My grandfather would always laugh out loud whenever he retold this story.

余家自太僕公稱豪飲，後竟失傳。余父余叔不能飲一蠡殼，食糟茄，面即發頳，家常宴會，但留心烹飪，庖廚之精，遂甲江左。一簋進，兄弟爭啖之立盡，飽即自去，終席未嘗舉杯。有客在，不待客辭，亦即自去。山人張東谷，酒徒也，每悒悒不自得。一日，起謂家君曰：「爾兄弟奇矣！肉只是吃，不管好吃不好吃；酒只是不吃，不知會吃不會吃。」二語頗韻，有晉人風味。而近有儈父載之《舌華錄》，曰：「張氏兄弟賦性奇哉！肉不論美惡，只是吃；酒不論美惡，只是不吃。」字字板實，一去十里，世上真不少點金成鐵手也。東谷善滑稽，貧無立錐，與惡少訟，指東谷為萬金豪富，東谷忙忙走愬大父曰：「紹興人可惡，對半說謊，便說我是萬金豪富！」大父常舉以為笑。[13]

After the fall of his dynasty, however, recalling to mind such memories also induced in Zhang Dai an intense and, one assumes, not entirely insincere sense of guilt, as can be seen in the following item from the same work: [14]

Crab Society 蟹會

Of all the various foods, only the clam and the river crab embody, in and of themselves, the Five Flavours,[15] requiring the addition of neither salt nor of vinegar.

In the tenth month the river crabs grow fat, as do the grains of the paddy rice, and their shells become as large as dishes as they pile up, one on top of another. The purple ones are as huge as a clenched fist, their little claws bursting with flesh and as oily as those of the millipede. Lifting their shells exposes layers of congealed fat, in appearance like jade lard or powdered amber, in taste sweeter even than the Eight Treasures of the kitchen.[16]

As soon as the tenth month had arrived, then, I would form a Crab Society with a group of my friends and we would arrange to meet up shortly after noon, boil up the crabs and eat them, each person having been allocated six crabs. Fearing that the crabs would become cold before we ate them, we would cook them one by one in turn. For accompaniment, we would prepare a fatty salted duck and red curds. The drunken clams would be like amber and vegetables such as bamboo shoots would be boiled in duck stock. For fruit we would have Xie's tangerines[17] and wind-dried chestnuts and water chestnuts. To drink, we would have Jade Pot Ice and our vegetables would consist of bamboo shoots from Bingkeng, our rice would be the whitest of White Yuhang, newly harvested, and we would rinse our months with Orchid Snow tea.[18]

Thinking back on this today, it is as if we had supped upon the immortal provisions of the Kitchen of Heaven, filling our bellies and befuddling our heads; how shameful, how very shameful!

食品不加鹽醋而五味全者，為蚶、為河蟹。河蟹至十月與稻粱俱肥，殼如盤大，墳起，而紫螯巨如拳，小腳肉出，油油如蟆蛋。掀其殼，膏膩堆積如玉脂珀屑，團結不散，甘腴雖八珍不及。一到十月，余與友人兄弟輩立蟹會，期於午後至，煮蟹食之，人六隻，恐冷腥，迭番煮之。從以肥臘鴨、牛乳酪。醉蚶如琥珀，以鴨汁煮白菜如玉版。果蔬以謝橘、以風栗、以風菱。飲以玉壺冰，蔬以兵坑笋，飯以新餘杭白，漱以蘭雪茶。繇今思之，真如天廚仙供，酒醉飯飽，慚愧慚愧。[19]

Zhang Dai's engagement in this discourse of food and eating, and his compilation of his book of recipes should best be understood in terms of a specific moment in time, the late Ming dynasty. This period (conventionally dated from the middle of the sixteenth century until the middle of the seventeenth) proved a most unsettling time for China's ruling elites. Rapid economic development, fuelled by the growth of commodity markets and the monetization of silver, served to undermine existing status relationships and led to higher levels of urbanization and social mobility. A commercialized publishing industry fed off of and into an expansion of literacy and educational opportunity and a flourishing popular culture that displayed a greater willingness to question Neo-Confucian orthodoxies. In the eyes of contemporaries, accompanying such socioeconomic changes were those age-old and unmistakable tokens of dynastic decline; at the upper levels, incompetent and extravagant emperors, the expansion of eunuch power, factionalism and corruption at court, and the empire's increasingly obvious inability to deal effectively with threats, both internal and external, to the political order; at the local level, ever increasing conspicuous consumption. The collapse, when it finally came in the form of peasant rebellion followed by 'barbarian' invasion, proved one of the most dramatic and cataclysmic in Chinese history.[20]

Before the collapse, the disordered circumstances of the times induced among the Chinese literati intense anxieties about self-definition and worth, status, learning and money. After the collapse and the establishment of Manchu authority, Chinese men-of-letters were faced with more acute choices concerning those most important of Confucian virtues, loyalty and righteousness.

The economic boom of this period, especially in the lower Yangtze region, made it possible for rich merchants, traditionally a most despised class of people, to buy themselves the trappings of culture and fine living. This spurt in conspicuous consumption, and the consequent breakdown of the hitherto strictly enforced sumptuary laws, seems to have become particularly evident after the 1550s, and, in the minds of contemporaries, provided stark contrast to the simplicity and austerity of early Ming food culture.[21]

To contemporary men of letters such as Zhang Dai, it was good taste and good taste alone that could buttress their status as self-declared defenders of culture and tradition. What exactly constituted good taste was something that they sought to define in countless handbooks of refined living in which they categorized, listed, ranked, praised and blamed the commodities that seemed now so much more available to everyone. Critical to this enterprise were the issues of artificiality and authenticity that Zhang Dai highlights in his preface.[22] As Craig Clunas has argued in his analysis of such handbooks, they must be understood as 'consciously constructed attempts to reduce the confusion of the Ming world of goods to order',[23] and the unprecedented number produced in this period 'points to a heightened awareness of the production and consumption of luxury goods as an arena for potential social conflict, if not correctly handled'.[24] The handbooks sought to differentiate between people on the basis of what and how they consumed, and as such they serve to engender in their contemporary readers a sense of reassurance in an otherwise rapidly changing world, whilst for us they betray the social anxieties and political insecurities of a male elite threatened by new sources of wealth and power.[25] The discourse on food, in the hands of men such as Zhang Dai, was a highly moralized one that had implications of the most serious kind about political legitimacy and historical continuity.

Preface 自序, *The Old Glutton's Collection* 老饕集

The various flavours of the fowl and the beast, the insect and the fish, the plants and the trees were only differentiated, the one from the other and throughout the empire, during the age of Shennong.[26] Thus it is that our mouths can now distinguish immediately the salty from the sour, the bitter from the pungent. As to such flavours as the sourness of chicken, the pungency of the goat, the saltiness of the cow's curd and of grain, however, these the sage alone can distinguish. During the middle age of antiquity, then, only Confucius truly understood flavour, and the two words 'finest' and 'finely' from the line in his Analects [X.8] that goes: 'Even if his rice is of the finest quality, he does not gorge himself; even if his meat is finely minced, he does not gorge himself'[27] serve to encapsulate the profundities of food and drink. In terms of the eating of cooked food, Confucius' own behaviour served to sum things up for, after all, we are told that: 'If it is badly cooked, he does not eat it', whilst the same is true of raw food for we are also told that: 'If it is not served at the right time, he does not eat it', these sentences constituting a veritable Classic of Food and Eating, being also therefore a theory about the nourishing of life.

With the death of Confucius, however, schisms developed, resulting in the production of works such as He Zeng's *Menus*,[28] Wei Juyuan's *Classic of Food*,[29] Duan Wenchang's *Food Regulations*[30] in 50 *juan*, Yu Cong's *Recipes*[31] in 10 *juan*, Xie Feng's *History of Food* also in 10 *juan*, and Meng Shu's *Food Statutes* in 100 *juan*. In the processes of frying and boiling, roasting and broiling, food becomes adulterated with the blood of sacrificial animals, with intestinal fat, with the odour of the goat and with fragrant herbs, and the basic tastes of the various foods are lost completely. Nowadays the Grand Provisioners to the Court use sugar to mask the proper taste of imperial meals and this has given rise to all sorts of artificiality and affectation, their crime in this respect being as heinous as that of those who eat their food raw and unprepared.

In later ages, it was only the Song dynasty scholar Su Shi who understood such matters. Both his 'Prose-poem on the Old Gourmand'[32] and his 'Song of Pork' so comprehend the delights of gluttony that they set the mouths of readers watering. To understand the single word 'cooked', as found in both these pieces, is already to apprehend more than half the story. Towards the end of the Song dynasty, however, when the Learning of the Way began to prevail and scholars did not want the mouth and the stomach to overburden their understanding of the Nature of Man and his Destiny, this art was discarded and little discussed, even common folk having a laugh at Su Shi's expense for his practice of marinating his meat with a pinch of tea. By the time of the Yuan dynasty with their habit of eating their game unskinned and still bloody, food was eaten almost uncooked. With the flourishing of our present dynasty, it was only with the advent of the reign of the Xuanzong Emperor [1426–35] that the usages of the various eating and drinking vessels were again fully understood, hence the saying: 'The third generation of officials wore clothes and ate cooked rice.' Although the discourse of the age refers to the common people, in essence the family habits of the Imperial Household are no different.

My grandfather Zhang Rulin formed an Eating and Drinking Society with Bao Yingdeng[33] and Huang Ruheng [1558–1626] of Wulin[34] in order to investigate the proper tastes of things. He compiled the *History of Cooked Food* in 4 *juan*, taking much of his content from Gao Lian's *Eight Treatises on the Art of Living*, but without, it seems, neglecting the peppers, the ginger, the shallots and the onions.

I, for my part, am dissatisfied with the cooking methods of the Grand Provisioners and so I have edited and supplemented the text of my grandfather's work, and have thus corrected its faults. How can a poor pedant such as myself ever hope to surpass the efforts of my forefathers? It is just that I have been blessed with the ability to distinguish between the taste of the water of the Sheng and of the Zi rivers,[35] to tell when the flesh of the goose is that of a black or a white one, know whether the chicken has perched in the open air[36] or when the meat has been cooked over firewood that is already worn-out,[37] and have become so besotted with such things that I could not resist this editing task. Thus it is that I have taken up his book and rearranged it, ensuring that it is 'properly cut',[38] retaining what is fresh in taste and deleting all the artificiality of the methods of seeping and broiling. Although this present work has none of the exhaustiveness and refinement of either the *History of Food* or *Food Statutes*, a troop of three thousand hand-picked mounted cavalry may nonetheless occasionally defeat an exhausted army of ten thousand men. It is only in the mouths of those who eat it, after all, that the excellence or otherwise of the entire meal may be understood at the first bite.

世有神農氏，而天下鳥獸虫魚草木之滋味始出。蓋鹹酸苦辣，着口即知。至若雞味酸，羊味辣，牛酪與栗之味鹹，非聖人不能辨也。中古之世，知味惟孔子。「食不厭精，膾不厭細」。「精細」二字，已得飲食之徵。至熟食則概之失飪不食，蔬食則概之不時不食。四言者，食經也，亦即養生論也。

孔子之後，分門立戶，何曾有單？韋巨源有《食經》，段文昌有《食憲章》五十.卷，虞宗有《食方》十卷，謝諷有《食史》十卷，孟蜀有《食典》百卷。煎熬燔炙，雜以膵膓薑薤，食之本味盡失。於今之大官法膳，純用蔗霜亂其正味，則彼矯強造作，罪且與生吞活剝者等矣。

後來解事，只有東坡。《老饕賦》與《豬肉頌》，清饞領略，口口流涎。但知有「熟」之一字，則思過半矣。嗣後宋末道學盛行，不欲以口腹累性命，此道置之不講，民間遂有東坡茶撮泡肉之消。循至元人之茹毛飲血，則幾不火食矣。我興，至宣廟，始知有飲食器皿之事。語云：「三代仕宦，著衣食飯。」世雖概論平民，要知帝王家法亦不能外也。

余大父與武林涵所包先生、貞父黃先生為飲食社，講求正味，著《饗史》四卷，然多取養生八箋，猶不失椒薑葱。用大官炮法，余多不喜，因為搜輯訂正之。窮措大亦何能有加先輩！第水辨澠淄，鵝分蒼白，食雞而知其栖恒半露，咬肉而識其炊有勞新，一往情深，余何多讓？遂取其書而銓次之，割歸於正，味取其鮮，一切矯

揉泡炙之制不存焉。雖無《食史》、《食典》之博洽精腆，精騎三千，亦足以勝彼
羸師十萬矣。鼎味一臠，則在嘗之者之舌下討取消息也。

Just as Zhang Dai's excursion into the discourse on cuisine can be understood to have the general and theoretical levels of meaning that I have argued for them above, food (or, more particularly, its absence) can also be said to have had a specific, and painful, significance for him as a 'remnant subject' (*yimin* 遺民) over the course of the second half of his long life.

Zhang Dai had been born to a family of immense wealth, prestige and scholarly achievement, and had grown up in the very lap of late Ming luxury and extravagance, within splendid gardens and surrounded by antiques, a book collection of over 30,000 volumes, family opera troupes and singing girls. We gain glimpses of him and his world in the diaries of his friend Qi Biaojia, and the following entry, dated the 24th day of the 5th month of the Dingchou year (1637), captures the extent to which this world was one of travel and of gardens, of music, poetry, opera and singing girls, of fine food and drink shared with good companions under increasingly difficult circumstances:

> We set off by boat and whilst on board I worked upon my 'Record of the Famous Gardens of Zhejiang'. When we reached Pian Gate, Qi Qizhi paid a call upon me, and we set off together to visit Zhang E. Before long, Zhang Dai turned up and pressed us to join him in attending a meeting of the Maple Poetry Society. Our friends had already gathered in the No-Two Studio[39] by the time we arrived and the meeting was being held in Cloudy Forest Autumn Pavilion that Zhang Dai had recently had constructed and where our friends now often met to talk. Ni Yuanlu[40] was the last to turn up. After our meal, Zhang Dai brought out his lute and began to play, accompanied by the actors with their drums and flutes. At dusk we watched a performance of the *Story of the Red Silk*.[41] Once the party had broken up, I stayed the night on board my boat.
>
> 發棹，舟中作《越中名園記》。抵偏門，齊企之來晤，與之訪張介子。頃之，張宗子來，促遂赴其酌楓社。諸友已集於不二齋，宗子新構雲林秘閣，諸友多晤談於此。倪鴻寶最後至，飯後宗子彈琴，優人以鼓吹佐之。及暮，觀演《紅絲記》。席散宿舟中。[42]

From midlife onwards, however, with the collapse of the Ming dynasty and by his own account, Zhang Dai's life was eked out in arrant poverty, 'his state fallen, his family destroyed' (*guo po jia wang* 國破家亡),[43] shunned by friends and the books he had so loved used to stoke the cooking fires of the marauding troops who had brought such destruction to his world.[44] After the fall, he had only his memories to live off, as he makes clear in a tomb inscription that he writes for himself and in which he speaks of himself in the third person:

In his youth, he was a dandy in white silk breeches, addicted to luxury and extravagant display, to monasteries, to beautiful maids and seductive serving boys, to gaudy clothes and fine food, stallions, lanterns, fireworks, actors and music, to antiques and flowers and birds. He craved good tea and a game of chess, was afflicted by the love of books and the demons of poetry.

Having expended the energies of half his lifetime on such things, they all became but a dream when, in his fiftieth year, his state fell and his family was destroyed. He fled the chaos to live amidst the mountains, all that remained to him being a dilapidated bed and a rickety teapoy, some chipped antiques and a cracked lute, a few tattered volumes and a broken ink stone. He dressed now in coarse linen and dined off plain vegetables, with often not enough for the next meal. Reflecting on his life twenty years earlier, he seemed now to belong to another world altogether.

蜀人張岱，陶庵其號也。少為紈褲子弟，極愛繁華，好精舍，好美婢，好孌童，好鮮衣，好美食，好駿馬，好華燈，好煙火，好梨園，好鼓吹，好古董，好花鳥，兼以茶淫橘虐，書蠹詩魔。

勞碌半生，皆成夢幻。年至五十，國破家亡，避跡山居。所存者，破床碎几，折鼎病琴與殘書數帙，缺硯一方而已。布衣疏莨，常至斷炊。回首二十年前，真如隔世。[45]

Zhang Dai's celebrated and moving author's preface to his *Dream Memories of Taoan* makes it clear the extent to which his memories of past pleasures were now most uncomfortable ones:

He wrote his own elegy and frequently found himself on the verge of suicide; but because his *Book of the Stone Casket* was as yet not complete, he continued to gaze upon and breathe within the world of man. But his bin was often empty of grain; he had no firewood for a cooking fire. It was only then that he understood that the story about the two old men of Mount Shouyang, Boyi and Shuqi, and how they determined to starve themselves to death, unwilling to eat the rice of Zhou, was simply the humbug of those who lived after them. For his part, with whatever vigour was left him through his pangs of hunger, he was wont to amuse himself with brush and ink.

作自挽詩，每欲引決，因《石匱書》未成，尚視息人世。然瓶粟屢罄，不能舉火，始知首陽二老，直頭餓死，不食周粟，還是後人妝點語也。饑餓之餘，好弄筆墨。[46]

Just as the especial importance of Zhang Dai's obsession with food can be readily observed in the ease with which he moves, in his preface to *The Old Glutton's Collection*, from a generalized and moralized history of cuisine to a history of his own family's involvement with food and then on to the nature of his own 'besottedness' (*yiwang shenqing*) with it, it can be seen also in his close juxtaposition, in his author's preface to *Dream Memories of Taoan* and elsewhere, of the processes of eating and those of living and writing.

There is one final and marvellous illustration of my point. Suddenly, towards the end of his 'Inscription for My Own Tomb', Zhang Dai finally introduces himself into his own text in the first person for the first time, in the following manner:

> He was born during the Mao hour [5–7am] of the 25th day of the 8th month of the Dingyou year [1597], this being the 25th year of the reign of the Wanli Emperor of the Great Ming dynasty, the first son of Master Zhang Yaofang [1572–1633], minister of the State of Lu, and his wife, née Tao 陶. As a child, he suffered frequently from asthma and for his first decade he was raised in the household of his maternal grandmother, née Ma [1559–1620]. His great-grandfather on his maternal side, Tao Yunjia [1556–1632], had once served in office in the combined Province of Guangdong and Guangxi and whilst there had stored up enough Bovine Yellow Pills to fill several boxes, and for the first sixteen years of my life I ate my way through this supply of medicine until my condition was completely cured.
>
> 生於萬曆丁酉八月二十五日卯時，魯國相大滌翁之樹子也，母曰陶宜人。幼多痰疾，養於外大母馬太夫人者十年。外太祖雲谷公宦兩廣，藏生牛黃丸盈數籠，自余因地以至十有六歲，食盡之而厥疾始廖。[47]

In a sense, then, and particularly in terms of his own representation of himself, Zhang Dai was, quite literally, what he ate, for it was only in the process of eating that his 'self' was born as a subject within his autobiographical text. And, as embodied in the second of my epigraphs for this chapter, Zhang Dai's explicitly final textual representation of himself ('A greedy Dongbo, / Starving at Solitary Bamboo') is as a gourmet transfixed by the moral imperative to starve himself. Fortunately for us all, however, 'he continued to gaze upon and breathe within the world of man' and to 'amuse himself with brush and ink'.

7
Tasting the Lotus

Food, Drink and the Objectification
of the Female Body in Gold, Vase, and Plum Blossom

Isaac Yue

Food and sex are commonly perceived as two of the most dominant neurotic compulsions in any living creature—a phenomenon that is substantiated by different disciplinary investigations. The anthropologist Richard Leakey, for example, acknowledges the importance of such compulsions and comments that '[i]f our ancestors had not invented the food-sharing economy of gathering and hunting around three or so million years ago, we would be neither as intelligent as we are today, nor so interested in each other's sexuality.'[1] In psychology, the significance of these two compulsions is similarly recognized as libidinal drives. In China, the association of food with sex was recognized at an early historical stage, and carries with it distinctive imprints of a patriarchal culture that reflect the development of the Chinese civilization. For instance, in 'Summoning Back the Soul' 招魂 from the *Songs of the South* 楚辭, the deliberate parallelization of food with women (as sexual objects) is unmistakable in the poet's identification of the two 'items' as equally instrumental to the return of the spirit. That beautiful women are presented alongside a range of delicacies, including the 'aromatic stew of fatty beef tendon' 肥牛之腱臑若芳些 and the 'braised turtle and roast lamb with sugar cane syrup' 覷鱉炮羔有柘漿些, not only reveals the way society perceived women and food as of parallel importance, but helps establish the tradition of chauvinistic hedonism in China, in which women are delegated to the same level of food and objectified by men during the rite of supplication. It is an ideology that endured and intensified through many of the Chinese imperial dynasties.

This chapter examines the legacy of this social gender ideology as reflected in the literary 'tradition' of late Ming society and considers its implementation, and thereby implications, in one of the most representative literary texts of the era—*Gold, Vase, and Plum Blossom* (*Jinpingmei cihua* 金瓶梅詞話, hereafter referred to as *GVP*).[2] As a text that is intended first and foremost to be a piece of social criticism, *GVP* is widely appreciated by today's critics for its critique of a society 'mainly driven by lust, greed, and vanity'.[3] Compared to the powerful discourse evoked by the text with regard to the tension between eroticism and religious moralism, which has received a significant bulk of scholarly attention, the theme of food has only emerged as a topic of academic interest in recent years, capturing the attention of such critics as Dai Hongsen 戴鴻森,[4] Zheng Peikai 鄭培凱,[5] Huang Lin 黃霖,[6] Zhao Jianmin 趙建民, and Li Zhigang 李志剛.[7] However, in spite of the contributions of their studies to the understanding of the novel's representation and treatment of the topic of food, their tendency to consider this subject from a socio-historical perspective, and to contextualize the descriptions of food within the history of Chinese gastronomic culture, means that one of the most important aspects about food in the work, which concerns its relationship to women (sexuality), is vastly overlooked. The intention of this study is therefore not only to demonstrate the theme of food as a literary motif of cultural significance, but also to consider the way it is evoked throughout the novel to complement its sexual politics and reflect the mentality of the Mings concerning gender roles. This chapter will begin with the examination of the author's usage of the trope of food in the text and the meticulousness of its staging, in which I consider the parallel evocation of food and the presentation of sexual scenes as denotative of an inseparable relationship between the two subjects. Then I turn to specific examples of female characters who are portrayed in relation to food, and discuss how the objectification of women is achieved through the strategic association of their sexuality with food. Finally, I analyse the names of the female characters in food terms and discuss how their names aptly reflect individual character traits and contribute to the formulation of a specific gender politics in the novel. Through these analyses, I hope to offer a more complete reading, and to arrive at a better understanding, of the novel's position regarding the gender dynamics of patriarchal power and female subjugation, and the way the literary presentation of this topic can be considered reflective of the mentality of Ming society concerning gender roles.

Food and Sex: An Interrelationship

More often than not, *GVP* is considered by readers to be primarily a work of eroticism, if not pornography. For this reason, in both the public and academic spheres, the depiction of various sexual acts tends to draw the bulk of readers' attention, to the point that other themes in the novel are overshadowed. One of the major themes that is often overlooked is that of food. This is lamentable given the fact that, apart from the ubiquitous sexual scenes, not only does gastronomy represent one of the most frequently occurring themes in the novel, but there are also patent signs that the author intended it to play a crucial role in the overall sexual dichotomy of the narrative. In recognition of the relationship between food and sex in *GVP*, Hu Yannan 胡衍南 writes:

Every sexual scene appears together with the portrayal of a variety of food and drinks. The evocation of food and drink has different purposes, but tea and wine are certainly the media that lead to the sexual acts between men and women. Thus, drink is utilized as an aphrodisiacal agent, the appearance of which clearly hints of the acts between the men and women that are to follow.

伴隨着每一場性交的發生，其中必然有各式的茶酒和美食，雖然在不同的狀況下，這些飲食的取用各有它的功效，但是茶與酒確是小說裡男女風流韻事的首要媒介，發揮着「催情」效果，而茶與酒的出場也多半對接下來的男女互動，提供一個大致不差的暗示。[8]

Despite such keen awareness of the authorial intention to connect food to sex, Hu's perception of the former as prelude to the latter fails to take into account the existence of an interrelationship between the two, and the deliberate setting of one as the natural extension of another. For example, when Li Pinger 李瓶兒 finally succumbs to the seduction of Ximen Qing 西門慶 and invites him to climb over the wall to visit her in her chamber, waiting for him is 'an assortment of food and wine, neatly laid-out on a table' 一桌齊齊整整酒肴菓醪 (177). Although sexual intercourse does in fact occur after the couple has consumed some wine, the blatant intention of both parties to participate in the sexual act demonstrates the presentation of food to be a premeditated preparation for copulation, instead of the latter occurring as an accidental consequence of the former. This interpretation is further substantiated by one of Pan Jinlian's 潘金蓮 attempts to seduce Wu Song 武松, during which her sexual advances are symbolically prefigured by the purchase of 'wine and meat' 酒肉 (17) and her presentation of them to Wu in his room. The fact that the outcomes of these two episodes differ (in that Pan's advances are rejected while Li and Ximen end up indulging in sexual amorousness) further refutes the proposition that food is an antecedent to sex, since Pan's failure does not diminish the sexual intent in her presentation of the food to Wu.

It is in this context that the themes of food and sex are set up by the novel as interrelated—that not only is food (regardless of type) conceived of as inherently sexual, but sex is also recurrently invoked in blatant gastronomic terms. The recognition of this interrelationship as non-causal represents an important key to the understanding of the cultural ideology behind the novel's interpretation of the similarities between food and women in a predominantly male-dominant society. In order to fully understand this dynamics, let us first consider the novel's construction of a parallel between food and sex, which is achieved in both linguistic and physical terms. During one of the early encounters between Ximen and Pan, the following occurs:

[Ximen Qing] produced from his sleeve a golden gilded box painted silver inside, containing breath-freshening aromatic teacakes. With the tip of his tongue, he delivered the cakes into the woman's mouth one by one. They embraced and enjoyed each other's tongue, loud as two slithering snakes. Old woman Wang paid them no attention and tended to her own business. She continued to serve them food and wine and the couple remained at their amorous game until they had consumed sufficient alcohol, at which point the flame of passion engulfed them …

〔西門慶〕向袖中取出銀穿心、金裏面，盛著香茶木樨餅兒來，用舌尖遞送與婦人。兩個相摟相抱，如蛇吐信子一般，嗚咂有聲。那王婆子只管往來拿菜篩酒，那裡去管他閑事，由著二人在房內做一處取樂玩耍。少頃，吃得酒濃，不覺烘動春心……(57)

In this episode, besides the obvious corresponding comparison to previous examples of the offering of food as a means through which sexual intercourse is initiated, the interrelationship between food and sex is further substantiated, this time through the deliberate linguistic contextualization of eating as a sexual event. This is achieved through the attribution of such overt sexual descriptors of the couple as 'two slithering snakes' during an event that is technically more about feasting (the exchange of tea-cakes between the couple via their tongues). The fact that the moment of copulation is made explicit in the last sentence of the quotation—when the couple is finally engulfed by 'the flame of passion'—further pinpoints the author's intention to maintain focus on the act of feasting up to this point. It is, however, important for us to recognize the overt implementation of such sexual language on eating, which not only discombobulates the distinction between feasting and copulation, but effectively establishes the conception of the idea of gastronomic fulfilment and sexual satisfaction as a transferrable experience. In other words, through the complementary sexual language, the insertion of Ximen's tongue into Pan's mouth takes on metaphoric implications and becomes denotative of the male's penetration of the female genitals. It is an idea that reveals the novelist's awareness of the underlying and subconscious interconnectivity between food and sex. According to Freud:

The normal sexual aim is regarded as being the union of the genitals in the act known as copulation, which leads to a release of the sexual tension and a temporary extinction of the sexual instinct—a satisfaction analogous to the sating of hunger … Moreover, the kiss, one particular contact of this kind, between the mucous membrane of the lips of the two people concerned, is held in high sexual esteem among many nations (including the most highly civilized ones), in spite of the fact that the parts of the body involved do not form part of the sexual apparatus but constitute the entrance to the digestive tract.[9]

If we consider Freud's observation in the context of the above-cited scene in *GVP*, we see that the novel demonstrates an apparent and acute awareness of such primeval connection between gastronomy and sexuality. Moreover, we see also a conscious desire to incorporate a physical element into this predominantly cognitive analogy. Indeed, whereas according to Freud, the exchangeable parameter between food and sex is mostly confined to the sense of satisfaction one gains from feasting and copulation, the above example from *GVP* displays an intent to develop this idea in the 'physical' sense by suggesting the interchangeability of the very orifices (the mouth and the genitals) to which the senses are allied. It is an endeavour that is further demonstrated in the famous grape arbour scene, in which:

> Having inserted a plum into the woman's vagina, Ximen neither removed it nor followed up with further action. The impasse made Pan all the more agitated and fluids flowed wildly from her vagina . . .
>
> 又把一個李子放在牝內，不取出來，又不行事。急的婦人春心沒亂，淫水直流……
>
> (392)

Ximen then leaves Pan in this condition and falls asleep. When he reawakens:

> He plucked the plum from the woman's vagina and fed it to her. Then, sitting himself on top of a pillow, he took out his bag of sex toys from the folds of his silk coat, mounted a silver clasp and a ring of sulphur onto himself, and proceeded to dally at the entrance of her vagina without penetrating. The woman's frustration grew to the point that her entire body began to arch toward Ximen. 'Daddy,' she screamed, 'hurry up and enter me. You are driving your whore crazy! I know you're mad at me for what I did to Li Pinger, but after what you've done to me today, I dare not ever cross you again!'
>
> 於是先摳出牝中李子，教婦人吃了。坐在一隻枕頭上，向紗褵子順袋內取出淫器包兒來，先以徵使上銀托子，次用硫黃圈束著；初時不停只在牝口子來回播揾，不肯深入。急的婦人仰身迎播，口中不住聲叫：「達達，快些進去罷，急壞了淫婦了。我曉的你惱我，為李瓶兒故意使這促恰來奈何我！今日經着你手段，再不敢惹你了。」
>
> (392)

If, in the earlier teacake feeding episode, the interrelationship between food and sex is achieved mainly through linguistic means (through the attribution of sexual language to the act of feasting in which sex is displaced through eating), then the above scene serves to consolidate this idea through the physical manifestation of the analogy. When Ximen first inserts the plum into Pan's genitals, the narration makes it clear that his intention is to punish her by denying her the opportunity to copulate. This is interesting because the insertion of the male genitals into the female's is one of the most universally-recognized and fundamental process in the act of sexual union. The utilization of the plum, rather than the male genitals, therefore symbolizes an antithesis to the 'natural' way and represents an unorthodox manoeuvre which, when considered along-side the previous example of the tea-cake episode, suggests the possibility of the physical displacement of the two relevant orifices—the mouth and the genital. This interpretation is further confirmed when Ximen removes the plum from Pan's vagina and inserts it her mouth, at which point he consents to copulate with her. The depiction of the act of inserting food into the mouth as symbolic of copulation and that of food into the genitals as its opposite underlines a deliber-ate reversal of the functions of the orifices. Besides posing a challenge to the convention of perceiving the concepts of food and sex as independent of each other, it also reinforces the notion that the novel sees the roles of the two orifices as exchangeable in function.

Food, Herbal Medicine, and the Conception of Sexuality

The presentation of the servitude of women, through the perceived paral-lels between their sexuality and food, is an ancient idea that is reflected in such pre-Qin classics as 'Summoning'. It is a tradition that *GVP* not only acknowledges, but sustains through its subjugation of the female characters in a food-related context. However, whereas the connection of women to food in 'Summoning' sets up a somewhat superficial view of women as inanimate objects, *GVP*, through its depiction of the ability of men to activate or deactivate the sexuality of women, demonstrates an endeavour to dehumanize the female body through the concept of food, which is achieved in spite of its awareness of the sexual urge of women (such as in the previously discussed plum scene). In other words, the usage of the food motif in *GVP* illustrates a conscious process of the objectification of the female body that importantly informs the overall sexual discourse of the novel.

In her reading of *GVP*, Ding Naifei juxtaposes the grape arbour sexual play with the eventual killing of Pan by Wu Song and identifies a deliberate intention to objectify the female body into 'a thing/body: to be punished and reformed by playing with its apertures and extremities'.[10] She considers the theme of the subjugation of women crucial to the expostulation of the gender dynamics in the text as a whole. Such a reading is consonant with our observation of the role of food in *GVP*, but whereas Ding's concern is primarily with the dehumanization of women, our reading uncovers the strategic importance of food as a means to achieve such objectification. Through the conception of the interchangeability between eating and copulation, *GVP* not only presents food as the key which, when inserted into the orifices, makes possible such interchangeability, but importantly sets food up as a sort of weapon, through which men come to wield control over a woman's sexuality. The novel, in this sense, not only draws an interconnection between food and sex, but considers food an important symbol that reflects society's tendency to subjugate and objectify women. As Carol J. Adams proposes, in most patriarchal societies there exists an inherent connection between women and food (in particular, meat). She describes it as a 'cycle of objectification, fragmentation, and consumption'[11] in which:

> Objectification permits an oppressor to view another being as an object. The oppressor then violates this being by object-like treatment: e.g., the rape of women that denies women freedom to say no, or the butchering of animals that converts animals from living breathing beings into dead objects … Consumption is the fulfilment of oppression, the annihilation of will, of separate identity. (47)

By considering the way society 'renames' cattle as beef and the way it is fragmentized into parts (such as sirloin and rib-eye) before its eventual consumption, Adams traces a similarity between this process and the manner in which women are treated in western societies, specifically the way the female body is objectified, fragmentized and finally 'consumed' by men. Although the fragmentation aspect of the theory, based distinctly on the western system of ontology, does not necessarily apply to *GVP* and its Chinese lexicological context, its general premise of how women are treated as objects and consumables provides a useful framework for us to conceptualize the way such gender dynamics—man as the empowered and woman as the passive beings—are sustained in *GVP* through the concept of food.

To illustrate this, let us consider the way the female genitals are frequently termed lexically as *pin* 牝 (a female consumable animal [*xumu* 畜母]),[12] while in contrast, the preferred terminology for the phallus—*chenbing* 麈柄—does not carry any food-related connotation. In addition, the female characters of *GVP* are commonly described in terms that are evocative of food or dining: such as when Yuzaner 玉簪兒, in her endeavour to attract the attention of her master, wears a peculiar style of makeup that resembles 'a pale winter melon' (*qing donggua* 青冬瓜) (1553); or during Ximen's initial meeting with Shen Erjie 申二姐, when he finds himself captivated by her 'silvery teeth that resemble glutinous rice in her mouth 糯米銀牙噙口內' (949). The application of such food-related linguistic descriptions fits well with Adams's theory: that before women's eventual consumption by men as passive recipients in the sexual act, they are first depersonified and conceived of as consumable objects. It is a concept that is further supported by the strategy in *GVP* to situate women within the domain of food through the concept of herbal medicine. For example, shortly after the death of Ximen, Pan chances to meet Chen Jingji 陳經濟 in the storage and indulges in sexual intercourse with him. The narration of this scene is supplemented by the following verse:

浪蕩根插入蓖麻內	The root of philander is inserted into the *ricinus communis*,
母丁香左右偎	Flanked by the *fructus caryophylli* on either side,
大麻花一陣昏迷	The cannabis flower loses consciousness.
白水銀撲簌簌下	Flowing freely is the mercury,
紅娘子心內喜	Happy inside is the red moth,
快活殺兩片陳皮	The two slices of dried tangerine peel erupt in ecstasy.
(1426)	

By devoting this entire poem to the contextualization of the female body in medicinal terms, such as linking the *fructus caryophylli* and dried tangerine peels to the vulva and mercury to the vaginal secretions, the author's intention to further bring attention to the interrelationship between gastronomy and the female body is evident. While this may be unsurprising given the inherent connection between food and Chinese herbal medicine, of significant interest is the fact that many of the medicines cited in the poem, including the *ricinus communis*, cannabis flower, mercury, and the red moth, were as well-known during the Ming dynasty for their potent poisonous nature as for their medicinal benefits. This suggests a deliberation on the part of the author to imply that, like medicine, the sexual act can be beneficial to one's health but also lethal once it becomes inordinate gratification. Besides matching the centrality of the novel's criticism against 'excessiveness',[13] such a reading is further affirmed by Li's proclamation that 'you [Ximen] are like the medicine that cures me. Having been touched by your hands, I can only think of you day and night' 你是醫奴 的藥一般，一經你手，教奴沒日沒夜只是想你 (268). Li's inability to suppress her desire for Ximen and her obsession with thoughts of him reflect the fact that to her, sex with Ximen is more of an addiction than a beneficial herb. By considering the way the novel contextualizes the female body in such medicinal terms, we find once more evident of the author's perceived parallel between food and the female sex and the intention to evoke this relationship to establish a specific sexual discourse in the novel—an aspect which warns against the indulgence of excessiveness in both sexual and gastronomic satisfaction. It is a strategic subjugation of women as food-related objects that is further evidence in the nomenclature of the main female protagonists.

Character Names and the Objectification of the Female Body

The title of *Gold, Vase, and Plum Blossom*, beyond reflecting the novel's warning against excessiveness (specifically capitalism), which is deliberately echoed by the story's evocation of the 'flower in the golden vase' 花插金瓶 (132) motif, is also highly suggestive of sexuality and lovemaking. As André Lévy points out:

> Gold (*jin*) is also metal in general, an element associated with the west, autumn and death; ping, a narrow necked vase, recalls the receptacle of fecundity; and mei, the plum tree blossoming in winter or early spring, is obviously 'steadfastness' but also sexuality out of season.[14]

Given the significance of the theme of sexuality in the text's overall plot, Lévy's interpretation is obviously apt. What has not been analysed but is of equal significance is the way the novel's discourse on the subjugation of women is supported through a gastronomical context, and how this strategy is present in the names of the individual characters (of which the title of the novel is eponymous). Given what we have learned in respect to the recurrent objectification of women within the sexual discourse of the text, as well as to the evocation of the theme of food to complement this discourse, it would not be unrewarding to consider the names of the characters in relation to gastronomy and the way this, too, provides an effective strategy to objectify women and thereby enables the formulation of the text's patriarchal cultural politics.

We begin our investigation with the most complicated character of the novel— Pan Jinlian. Because the word *jin* (gold) in Pan's name carries a distinctive implication of capitalism, it is conventionally interpreted this way for it echoes the plot of the novel. However, it should be noted that in the early Daoist tradition, gold is also thought of as a substance that is medicinal and edible. Citing the *Book of Jade* (*Yu jing* 玉經), *Baopuzi* 抱朴子 states that 'he who eats gold shall live as long as gold; he who eats jade shall live as long as jade' 服金者壽如金，服玉者 壽如玉.[15] During the Ming dynasty, although the conception of gold as medicinal is not yet widely disputed, contemporary medical texts such as *Bencao mengquan* 本草蒙筌 and *Bencao gangmu* 本草綱目 warn users of the poisonous nature of the metal.[16] The conception of gold in an edible context thus resonates with the text's conception of the relationship between medicine/poison and sexuality, which appropriately sums up Pan's character. In other words, by focusing on the gastronomic theme, what is revealed is that the connotation of 'poison' that can be found in the word 'gold' provides a subtle reference to Pan's character traits of a sexually immoral woman (*yinfu* 淫婦)—a reading which is as relevant, if not more revealing, than the reading of gold as simply a metal.[17]

Of the two words that make up the name Jinlian, *jin* is not problematic because whether it is interpreted as metal (in capitalistic terms) or a type of food, it matches the character of Pan and does not contradict the overall theme of the novel. The same cannot be said for the word *lian*. In conventional scholarship, *lian* is often conceived of as a flower that mimics Pan's bounded, or lotus, feet which measure under three inches (*sancun jinlian* 三寸金蓮). It is, however, a conception that is contradictory to the characterization of Pan. As a flower, the lotus is one of the most culturally esteemed plants in imperial China and immediately conjures not only beauty, but, more importantly, purity. In 'The Love of the Lotus' (Ailian shuo 愛蓮說), Zhou Dunyi 周敦頤 (1017–1073) extols:

> My sole love is the lotus, for it remains untainted in spite of the muddy soil it springs from, unpretentious in spite of the translucent water it bathes in; it is hollow but stands upright and has neither branches nor vines; its aroma travels far but does not overwhelm; its figure grows tall and elegant; it is to be admired from afar but not sullied in play.
>
> 余獨愛蓮之出淤泥而不染，濯清漣而不妖，中通外直，不蔓不枝，香遠益清，亭亭淨植，可遠觀而不可褻玩焉。

As Pan is a character who is considered by Victoria Baldwin Cass to have a three-fold identity: the 'evil consort' that bewitches people, the 'matchmaker' that is reminiscent of the lascivious 'old hag' of traditional European literature, and the 'demon-judge' who annihilates,[18] it is difficult to see how she can be associated with the lotus, a plant that is synonymous with incorruptible chastity and virtue. What is often overlooked, however, is the fact that *lian* not only refers to the flower, but also to the food—the lotus seed. The following scene from Chapter 19 offers credibility to an interpretation of the novelist's usage of the word *lian* in connection with the lotus seed rather than the flower:

> The woman [Pan] pulled up her dress and sat on top of his body. Having fed him wine, which was transferred from her own mouth to his, she reached out with her delicate hand and lifted a lotus pod from the table, and offered him a lotus seed.
>
> 'Why on earth would I want to eat that,' said Ximen Qing, 'it's unappetizingly bitter.'
>
> 'My boy,' said the woman, 'you're tempting fate by refusing food from your mother's hands.'
>
> 婦人一面摟起裙子，坐在身上，噙酒哺在他口裡，然後在桌上纖手拈了一個鮮蓮蓬子，與他吃。
>
> 西門慶道：「澀剌剌的，吃他做甚麼？」
>
> 婦人道：「我的兒，你就掉了造化了，娘手裡拿的東西兒你不吃。」(257)

Given Pan's incontestable affiliation with the lotus, her decision to pluck the lotus seed from the pod and feed it to Ximen during sex is of immense significance in that it not only suggests the idea of Pan offering herself to Ximen in both the sexual and gastronomic sense, but further supports the implication that Pan perceives herself more as a lotus seed than a lotus flower. There are also other indications in this passage to suggest this gastronomic interpretation of the word *lian* as more proper than the traditional floral association. Initially, Ximen resists the offer of the lotus seed because he considers it to be 'unappetizingly bitter' 澀剌剌. Compared to the image of the lotus as incorruptibly pure, the idea of Pan as a 'bitter' lotus seed is not only appropriate, but more crucially foreshadows the eventual death of Ximen during sexual intercourse with Pan. The obvious similarities between the bitterness of the lotus seed and the 'poisonous' nature of Pan, with both being insinuative of the character of Pan and the unfolding of the plot, also substantiate this interpretation.

In the discussion of Pan's name up to this point, we have overlooked one important question—that the author of *GVP* did not name Pan but instead 'borrowed' her from *The Story of the Water Margin* (*Shuihu zhuan* 水滸傳). As such, whether we interpret her name as an allusion to gold, medicine, flower, or a type of food, it should not and could not have any bearings to the overall theme of the *GVP*. There are, however, two additional factors that support our reading. Firstly, given the metaphorical richness (including gastronomic references) found in the title of the novel as well as its three eponymous characters, it is entirely plausible that the author perceived potential in Pan's name in the first place and decided on the names of Li and Pang to complement Pan. Secondly, and perhaps more importantly, there is the possibility that Pan is not originally a character in the novel, and that the leading role previously belonged to Song Huilian 宋惠蓮. I base this speculation on the close reading of the plot discrepancies found in chapters seventeen and eighteen by Wei Ziyun 魏子雲, who surmises that the original role of the protagonist belonged not to Ximen but someone named Jia Qing 賈慶, and that it was only later when the novel was being rewritten that, perhaps due to the similar brushstrokes in which the two names are written, the decision was made to import Ximen from *Water Margin* and alter the structure of the original story. Following this argument, it would be logical to deduce that Pan was most certainly only introduced at this stage of the revision, which means the original female protagonist was someone other than Pan. The only obvious candidate is Song. Aside from the fact that the two characters originally share the same name—an extemporaneous revelation that does not serve any specific purpose in the novel—critics such as Robert Yi Yang rightly point out the extent to which the two 'lotuses' overlap: that Song is not only commonly perceived as the 'replacement' of Pan, but in terms of personality, the former is almost the 'shadow' of the latter. Thus, following Wei's speculation, it does not seem farfetched to consider Song to be the original representation of gold (*jin*) in *GVP* and that many of the episodes featuring Pan may have originally belonged to Song. If this is the case, then it would help explain the deliberate connotations that we are able to observe in the name Jinlian.[19]

To further substantiate our reading of Pan's name in food terms, we note a similar pattern in the name of Pang Chunmei, in which the word 'mei' can reference either the plant (the plum blossom) or the food (the plum). Although as a flower, Lévy's interpretation of the plum blossom as 'sexuality out of season' is a fitting summary of the theme of the novel, as a character whose sexual ambition is unmistakably and constantly overshadowed by Pan, Pang is apparently the least likely of the three female protagonists to have this name bestowed upon her. Moreover, in the context of Ming dynasty literature, the plum blossom is actually widely appreciated by the contemporary public for its virtue and dignity and eulogized in this context by poets such as Tao Zongyi 陶宗儀 (1329–1410), Gao Qi 高啟 (1336–1373) and Wen Zhengming 文徵明 (1470–1559). We are, therefore, confronted by the same problem that we experienced with Pan's name in terms of our inability to explain the application of the floral sense of the name to the character of Pang.

By contrast, when viewed in its context as a type of nourishment, the plum was not only immensely popular with the Ming public, with contemporary culinary texts such as *Simple Dishes of the Mountain* (*Shanjia qinggong* 山家清供) offering at least six unique recipes for the plum, including teacakes and congees, but the novel also contains crucial reference to the interpretation of the plum as a type of food that represents the character traits of Pang. Toward the end of the novel, readers are introduced to a type of food called the 'sour plum bolus' (*mei suan wan* 梅酸丸)—the nature of which is explained by Ximen to Ying Bojue 應伯爵 as follows:

> You'll never dream what this is. It was brought to me yesterday by one of my people, from one of the boats that arrived from Hangzhou. It is called 'coated plum'. It is a mixture of an assortment of herbs, treated in honey and then coated on top of the plum. It is then wrapped inside a layer of minty orange leaves. Only then can you create a taste as marvellous as this.
>
> 你做夢也夢不着，是昨日小價杭州船上捎來，名喚做衣梅。都是各樣藥料，用蜜煉製過，滾在楊梅上，外用薄荷橘葉包裹，才有這般美味。(1079)

As can be deduced, the procedures that go into creating the 'sour plum bolus' are both laborious and time-consuming. Through this extended process, the plum—a rather ordinary and easily accessible type of food—is transformed into a rare delicacy that no longer tastes like the plum, to the extent that Ying is unable to determine what it is. It is a process of transformation that parallels Pang's career from a lowly servant girl to the matron of the Zhou household. Indeed, as someone who is originally purchased by Wu Yueniang 吳月娘 for 'sixteen taels of silver' 十六兩銀子 (1468) and 'a few bolts of cloth' 幾匹大布 (90), Pang's rise to her eventual position closely mirrors that of the sour plum bolus, in the sense that her origin is masked by layers of expensive garments and trinkets, which are to be treated as the equivalent of the honey and herbs used to coat the sour plum bolus. Of her ultimate metamorphosis, during her returning visit to the Ximen household near the end of the novel, her appearance is described in the following manner, with great attention to detail:

> Pang did not arrive until midday. Her hair, adorned with many pearls and rings made of foreign beads, was held in place by golden combs of the design of the phoenix head. She wore a bright red robe with broad sleeves, embroidered with four beasts facing a *qilin*, an azure skirt of the pattern of one hundred flowers, and a golden girdle. Her flower-embroidered shoes were bright red with white silk embellishment and thick soles. Her four-man sedan chair with golden ornaments and a silk cover was preceded by order-barking soldiers carrying staves. Servants followed with trunks and cases, with two smaller sedan chairs for the maids scurrying after them.
>
> 春梅看了，到日中纔來。戴着滿頭珠翠，金鳳頭面釵梳，胡珠環子。身穿大紅通袖四獸朝麒麟袍兒，翠藍十樣錦百花裙，玉玎當禁步，束著金帶；腳下大紅綉花白綾高底鞋兒。坐着四人大轎，青段銷金轎衣。軍牢執藤棍喝道，家人伴當跟隨，抬着衣匣；後邊兩頂家人媳婦小轎兒，緊緊跟着大轎。(1624)

Such a grand entrance not only prompts Wu's sister-in-law to observe that Pang is 'no longer what she used to be' 今非昔比 (1624), which acutely summarizes the extent of her transformation, but more importantly sets up a stark contrast to her actions that follow. These include sentimental conversations with remaining family members and visits to locations that she used to frequent. The fact that her death is brought about by her continuation of a promiscuous lifestyle further mirrors the fundamental nature of the sour plum bolus, in the sense that both the character and the food remain the same in name and essence despite the dramatic changes in appearance. Thus, like Pan and the lotus seed, the consideration of the plum as a type of food provides a much more fitting way to view Pang than the plum blossom.

Although not as prominent or suggestive as the case of Pan and Pang, the strategy of naming a character according to gastronomic symbols is also present with Li. Although the word *ping* 瓶 is popularly conceived of by critics in terms of a flower vase—a sensible connection given the 'flower' character in the name of her first husband, Hua Zixu 花子虛,[20] it should be pointed out that the term can equally be interpreted as a container for drinks like tea and wine. The fact that such containers were commonly made of ceramic at the time further means the possible attribution of the quality of the material onto the character. That ceramic is commonly considered as fragile, delicate, and beautiful certainly provides another set of appropriate descriptors for Li. Thus, instead of persisting to understand Li as a 'vase' and an extension of her former husband, who dies very early in the novel, as in the case of Pan and Pang, we are able to derive a much more appropriate reading of the name of the character through a gastronomic perspective.

To conclude, in all three cases—Pan, Li and Pang—the deliberate gastronomic association found in their names not only reveals a conscious desire on the part of the author of *GVP* to consider women in food terms, but also demonstrates a high degree of meticulousness in matching the personalities of the characters with specific food-types. It is a strategy that, besides offering insights into this mentality of the Mings concerning this topic, more importantly consolidates our reading of the authorial intention of setting up a distinct gender politics in the novel through gastronomic contextualization. Food, in other words, represents an important theme in the novel without which the impact of its sexual discourse would be weakened.

Conclusion

Few would object to the reading of the sexual discourse of *GVP* in terms of the subjugation of women. Indeed, women's powerlessness is blatantly expounded again and again in the novel through the overwhelming number of episodes that are deliberately set up to emphasize this issue—episodes which include the drinking of the man's urine by Pan (1185) and Ruyier 如意兒 (1255) and the scarring of the body by incense performed on Wang Liuer 王六兒 (592), Mrs Lin 林太太 (1347) and Ruyier (1352). However, in this study, by drawing attention to the topic of food, I not only demonstrate gastronomy to be of as much significance as the sexual denigration of women, but argue that the two themes are interrelated in multifarious ways—in linguistic as well as thematic terms. By arguing for the importance of reading the sexual theme alongside the gastronomic one, I show the extent to which *GVP* (and by extension the late-Ming social milieu that it reflects), despite its recognition of feminine sexual desires, is a participant in the patriarchal tradition established in ancient literature like 'Summoning' (through its evocation of the concept of gastronomy to subordinate the female body). Moreover, the sexual discourse of the novel is also revealed in that while its theme cautions readers against the excessiveness of sex in general, it does so through a patriarchal perspective in which women continue to exist in servitude. The exploration of the way the female body is objectified in food terms sheds light on the novel's consideration of the social position of women in late Ming society and the way such a view informs the overall gender dynamics of the text.

8

Eating and Drinking in a Red Chambered Dream

Louise Edwards

Cao Xueqin's 曹雪芹 mid-Qing masterpiece, *The Story of the Stone* or *The Red Chamber Dream* (*Honglou meng* 紅樓夢), is frequently referred to as a treasure of China's 'food and drink culture' 飲食文化.[1] Celebrated as the great classic Chinese novel of manners, *Honglou meng* provides readers a rich scope in which to appreciate the culinary luxuries of mid-Qing aristocratic life. Throughout the novel's 120 chapters readers are introduced to over 180 different types of food-stuffs and beverages described through dozens of meals and banquets ranging from simple snacks and invalid meals to elaborate banquets. Previous scholar-ship has celebrated Cao Xueqin's skill in capturing the glory of mid-Qing China's cuisine and his remarkable talent for describing elite class rituals and manners relating to food and wine but failed to do justice to the deeper, symbolic role that food and drink perform in the novel. *Honglou meng*'s intricate descriptions of food and drink are more than mere decorative details that confirm the opulence of the Jia mansions and the privilege of its residents.[2] Kam-ming Wong reminds us that in the first chapter of the novel Cao challenges readers to analyse his 'idle words' with a gourmet's metaphor: 'Who can fathom their taste?' 誰解其中味?[3]

This chapter shows how Cao Xueqin used food and beverages to mark boundaries between the pure and the profane in the Jia mansions' key symbolic space—Prospect Garden 大觀園. The temporal and unstable division between purity and profanity stands at the core of the novel's moral message as the garden, created as a realm of youthful, feminine purity, is penetrated by the pol-lution of the adult world's masculine dominance.[4] The corruption of the garden sanctuary is inevitable as Keith McMahon explains in his work on Qing fiction 'the excess of purity or insularity invites an opposite excess of transgression'.[5] In previous research I have outlined the roles sex, age, space, and art play in the novel in signalling shifts in the distinction between purity and profanity.[6] This chapter extends that framework to examine the mechanisms by which food and drink mark the pollution of the protected world of Prospect Garden. It argues that Cao Xueqin provided readers with keys presaging the dismantling of the garden sanctuary and the decline of the Jia family through his depiction of food and drink and in his discussions about their exchange and consumption.[7]

Building the Moral Boundaries of the Jia Mansions through Food and Drink

In Chapter 16, the Rong branch of the Jia clan receives word from the Palace that their eldest daughter, Jia Yuanchun 賈元春, earlier elevated to the status of Imperial Concubine, will be making a rare, indeed unprecedented, visit home to see her family. The entire Jia clan is immediately mobilized to prepare for the visitation. A section of land adjoining the Rong mansions and those of the senior branch, the Ning mansions, is set aside for the construction of an elaborate garden that will house Yuanchun during her single evening visit home. After her visit, she sends word that the novel's young male protagonist, Jia Baoyu 賈寶玉, and his female cousins are to live in the garden and, accordingly, a new structure of household organization forms around this relocation from Chapter 23 onwards. In the process Cao Xueqin establishes the division between femininity, youth and purity and masculinity, age and pollution that will frame the moral order of his novel. As the designated residence of the unmarried girls and Jia Baoyu, Prospect Garden is to be protected from the impurities of the outside world. Older women household employees serve as gatekeepers monitoring people entering and exiting the garden. Baoyu, an effeminate and gentle boy known for his reverence of girls and loathing of men and married women, is the only male allowed into the garden. If workmen are required to enter this place of purity, the resident girls are reminded to stay indoors and, should they need to move between buildings, to use the specially screened walkways designed to protect the girls' modesty. The garden is a world of youthful, feminine purity in keeping with Baoyu's philosophy of life that 'the pure essence of humanity was all concentrated in the female of the species and that males were its mere dregs and off-scourings' (1.20.407–8) and that once married, women can become 'worse than the men' on the basis that 'it must be something in the male that infects them' (3.77.134).

> 他便料定，天地靈淑之氣只鍾於女子，男兒們不過是些渣滓濁沫而已 (1.20.452)
>
> 奇怪，奇怪！怎麼這些人只一嫁了漢子，染了男人的氣味， 就這樣混賬起來，比男人更可殺了！(2.77.1884)

Baoyu's philosophy of the nexus between sex and age is addressed to the women gatekeepers, one of whom replies in a rather bemused tone saying, 'In that case, all girls must be good and all women must be bad.' Baoyu confirms this analysis with 'That is precisely what I *do* believe' (3.77.134).

> 守園門的婆子聽了，也不禁好笑起來，因問道：「這樣說，凡女兒個個是好的了，女人個個是壞的了？」寶玉點頭道：「不錯，不錯！」(2.77.1884)

Prospect Garden is a girl's kingdom of purity protected, albeit temporarily, from the pollution of the outside world. The movement of objects in and out of the garden mark the distinction between its feminine purity and the masculine pollution of the outside world and reminds readers of the threat that the outside world poses to its sanctity and security. Maram Epstein explains that Cao Xueqin 'simultaneously destabilized and subverted the social and physical boundaries which separate masculine from feminine even while he used them as categories'.[8] For example, soon after the garden is occupied, in Chapter 24, Baoyu's page, Tea Leaf 茗煙, provides Baoyu with some romantic fiction but warns him not to take the books into the garden, but rather, to read them in his outside study—the tawdry world of sexual desire should remain outside the walls of Prospect Garden. Similarly, in Chapter 74, the entire garden, including all the young mistresses' individual quarters are searched in order to identify which of the garden's residents is responsible for bringing a small purse embroidered with erotic images into the grounds. During the search they find that one young maid, Picture 入畫, has been storing her brother's clothing in her quarters—she is summarily punished for bringing polluting objects into the sanctity of the garden.[9] The source of the erotic purse remains a mystery but the panic at the event and the subsequent disclosure of masculine profanity signals the impending tragedy awaiting each of the young women in the garden.

Cao Xueqin similarly used the provision of food for the garden's residents as a device to mark the insecurity of the boundaries of this safe haven from worldly pollution—and the futility of attempting to prevent this pollution from entering. In the winter after the young girls and Baoyu have moved into Prospect Garden, a special system of food preparation is established to protect them from the winter cold. Prior to this time they had been leaving the garden to eat with their elders, but as the temperature drops and the days grow shorter the older women decide that the extensive exposure to cold is detrimental to the youngsters' health. According to Baoyu's mother, Lady Wang:

> It's so bad for one to be exposed to the cold immediately after eating. It's also not good to eat food after being out in the cold with an empty stomach. The empty parts fill up with cold air and then the food presses it down inside one. (2.51.530)
> 喫些東西受了冷氣也不好，空心走來，一肚子冷氣，壓上些東西也不好 (2.51.1245)

With a rearrangement of domestic finances and the redeployment of existing staff, a separate kitchen in a large five-roomed building just inside the back wall of Prospect Garden is established as the site for all food preparation destined for the garden. Originally intended for use only during the winter, the kitchen becomes a permanent feature of the garden's operations. A Mrs Liu 柳氏, who had previously worked as supervisor to the household's young actresses, is appointed head cook. The new kitchen became the location for all food preparation for all garden residents—Baoyu and the young mistresses as well as their maids and servants. This task increases in complexity as the number and range of individuals living in the Garden expands to include a host of young actresses as maids. Food supplies carried into the garden have to pass by the various gatekeepers and runners who monitor all movement in and out of the garden. Once each meal is prepared, women servants and maids carry the meals from the kitchen to each household in the garden.

Cook Liu's travails in supplying sufficient food within a fixed budget to Baoyu and the girls, with their various personal food preferences, occupy the middle sections of the novel. In Chapter 61 we learn from Cook Liu that she is responsible for cooking meals for over fifty people counting mistresses and maids. Where possible she caters to individual needs, such as Skybright's 晴雯 vegetarianism or sudden ailments that require the creation of invalid menus. But her patience is tested as the economy of the mansion tightens and shortages of key ingredients, such as eggs, make it difficult for her to make ends meet for even the two core meals per day. Food shortages such as those identified by Cook Liu's grumblings signal the slow decline of the Jia household's finances and, as we will see in the next section, the movement of food and drink into the garden signals the inevitable decay of its moral division between purity and pollution as well.[10]

Within Baoyu's garden residence there are clear divisions about the serving of food and drink based on his unique hierarchy of purity—the older women are expressly prohibited from handling his food. In Chapter 24, Baoyu calls for a cup of tea; two old ladies 老婆子 come to help and he dismisses them perfunctorily 罷罷，不用了 leaving them perplexed as they depart—why would he not accept their help when he clearly called for tea? Rather than be served by two old women, Baoyu gets up to pour himself a cup. Just at that moment a young maid from his outer chambers, Crimson 小紅, enters to assist lest he scald himself. Baoyu accepts the service of a young girl, but not of the older women, even though all the servants are transgressing their space-defined status boundaries. Crimson should not have been allowed to enter Baoyu's personal rooms because of her lowly rank within the hierarchy of young maids. The point is reiterated when

Baoyu's 'inner maids' return and berate Crimson for being in a space beyond her status. Baoyu's demand for tea in the absence of the normal hierarchy of inner and outer maids and young and old servants provides a prompt for readers to learn about the peculiarities of space and hierarchy that permeate the garden world, but it also shows us that while Baoyu would not countenance drinking tea poured by an old (and therefore polluted) woman servant, he has no qualms about the young (pure) girl servant even if she is out of her designated space.[11]

In Chapter 58 we read of another incident that demonstrates the way food marks the garden's unique hierarchy and spatial boundaries. In this scene, Baoyu is being served some gruel to assist in his recovery from a debilitating illness. The food is delivered to his rooms and one of the young actresses, Parfumée 芳官, is instructed to cool the broth by blowing across the surface of the bowl. Her instructions are strict. She must blow gently to avoid spitting on the soup.

你也學些服侍，別一味傻頑傻睡。口兒輕著些，別吹上唾沫星兒 (2.58.1432–3)

Her foster-mother, who is at that time waiting outside the room, rushes in to take charge lest the young actress spill the bowl. Baoyu's maid, Skybright 晴雯, yells sharply at the foster-mother, 'Get out of here!' and instructs her that the task of cooling Baoyu's soup would under no circumstances *ever* pass to her.

快出去！你讓她砸了碗，也輪不到你吹！你什麼空兒跑到裏欄兒來了！(2.58.1433)

Not only has the foster mother entered forbidden space, but she has dared to suggest she handle Baoyu's food. Further humiliating the older women, and reminding the readers of the age and space markers of purity, Parfumée is then told to *taste* the soup to make sure it is cool enough. Skybright proceeds to taste the soup herself by way of reassuring the puzzled Parfumée that it is also fine for *her* to do so. The freedom of food exchange between the young members of the garden's household across the boundaries of servants and master, and the exclusion of the older women, is reiterated when Baoyu hands his half-finished bowl of gruel back to Parfumée for her to enjoy. The sharing of food, albeit still within the hierarchy that places Baoyu at the pinnacle, is possible among young people but not between the old, married (impure) and the young, virginal (pure).

A similar soup-sharing episode occurs in Chapter 35 prior to the establishment of the special garden kitchen, when Baoyu is trying to win the good favour of Silver 玉釧, his mother's maid. Silver's sister, Golden 金釧, has just committed suicide after being sacked by Baoyu's mother, Lady Wang 王夫人, for 'seducing Baoyu'. In fact, Baoyu had been flirting outrageously with Golden leading to her demise. Silver is sent to deliver an intricately made soup to Baoyu. Silver's

delivery of the soup to Baoyu provides him with the chance to seek her forgive-
ness for his role in provoking Golden's death so he tricks her into tasting the
soup by declaring it to be tasteless. Through this ruse she is goaded into tasting
the soup and only afterwards realizes that he was tricking her into the intimacy
of sharing the soup when he declares 'Ah, now it'll taste all right!' (2.35.186) 這
可好喫了! (1.35.845). She refuses to return the bowl to him by way of resisting
his flirtation. The standoff is interrupted by the arrival of two old ladies. In a
moment of distraction prompted by their visit, the bowl accidently spills onto
Baoyu's hand, scalding him. The contrast between young and old women is
clear—the young maid, Silver, has the power to give flavour to the soup whereas
the presence of the old women causes Baoyu direct physical injury.

Outside Prospect Garden, in the rest of the Rong mansion, food provision
marks status, but there is no anxiety about the source of the food or the age of
those serving it. For example, Grandmother Jia 賈母, the matriarch of the clan,
has a distinct menu from the rest of the household, yet she is happy to receive the
farm produce brought in by the rustic, and highly polluting, Granny Liu 劉姥姥,
who visits the mansions. Wang Xifeng 王熙鳳, the daughter-in-law responsible
for household management, shares her food with Liu in her private chambers—
and even provides the most tender meat for the elderly woman on the basis that
it is easier for older folk to chew.

A significant aspect of the food sharing hierarchies is the response to the
foodstuffs produced for or inspired by the imperial household. While Baoyu is
often reluctant to join men in sharing their food he is an enthusiastic consumer of
comestibles with a royal connection. The soup Silver delivered to Baoyu required
the use of special moulds for flour dumplings in the shapes of caltrops, lotus
leaves and pods, chrysanthemums and plum flowers and was only once previously eaten in the Jia household—during the Imperial Concubine's visitation.
Baoyu had especially requested the soup as his first meal after suffering a life-
threatening beating by his father—seeking comfort from food that invoked his
proxy mother, his beloved elder sister. As they are items of rare use, the moulds
are found by Xifeng using the elaborate inventory system for household goods
and she decides that rather than simply making one bowl for the ailing Baoyu,
all the women of the household should share the experience. During this period
of Baoyu's recovery another item from the Imperial Household is delivered to
his rooms—two small glass bottles with silver screw-on lids filled with drink
flavourings. Made especially for the imperial household, one bottle contains
'Essence of Cassia Flowers' 木樨清露 and the other 'Essence of Roses' 玫瑰清露.
The grace of Her Eminence, Baoyu's elder sister, signals the healing power of the

most prominent of women, the Imperial Concubine, over the destructive power of the male world that reduces his body to a bloody pulp through beating.

Food as a Conduit for Impurities Entering the Garden

While food can have protective powers, it can also have a destructive and dangerous aspect. Two key episodes show the danger the garden dwellers face from non-imperial food that is brought in from outside. In Chapter 39, on the formation of the Crab Flower Poetry Club 海棠社, Baochai 寶釵 arranges to have some crabs brought in from her brother, Xue Pan, for an autumn feast that will conclude with a poetry writing competition. The celebration includes all the garden residents as well as some of the older, married women of the household, such as Wang Xifeng, Grandmother Jia and Baoyu's mother, Lady Wang. The excess supply of such a luxury food item marks the extravagance typical of the Jia household. According to Granny Liu, the quantity of crabs purchased for this one party is 'enough to keep a farmer and his family for a year (2.39.265).' 這一頓的錢夠我們莊家人過一年的了 (2.39.945) Moreover, readers have earlier learned, through the carelessness of its consumption, that this expensive foodstuff was not particularly valued once in the household. For example, Patience smears crab roe on Xifeng's face in a play fight—her original target was Amber. Events that occur in the novel before and after this frivolity also suggest one of the novel's key overarching themes: 'the good times must end'. The feast is presaged by Grandmother Jia's grim tale of her near-death-by-drowning experience as a child in a pavilion similar to that in which they are about to feast on the crab, and the night concludes with an unexplained fire in the Jia stables. These disasters are still outside of the Garden walls, and the residents can continue their idyllic, privileged lives in its safe confines, but both create a sense of impending doom—the chaos from outside will soon penetrate into the garden. As they eat the crabs, the party-goers comment that crab is a 'cold' food and in order to balance the temperatures one should drink wine, but ultimately, the huge stable fire overcomes their 'cold' with a massive outburst of heat.[12]

Another case where celebrations with special foodstuffs presage danger and demise comes in Chapter 49. On this occasion venison is brought into the garden in its raw state for Baoyu and the girls to barbeque on skewers over an open fire. Initially Li Wan 李紈 thinks that they are planning on eating the meat raw and hurries out to stop them lest they make themselves sick. But she acquiesces on hearing of their planned 'cook-out'. Baoyu and Shi Xiangyun 史湘雲, the organizers of the banquet carve up the raw meat and cook and eat with gusto. Xifeng joins in too, but Daiyu and Baochai demur, and Baoqin 寶琴 has to be

persuaded to try some although her initial reaction is that it was 'Too dirty!' 怪
醃臢的 (2.49.1190). Jokes about the polluting nature of the butchering of the deer
in the garden pavilion abound. Daiyu mockingly laments that Yun threatens to
sully Baoqin's purity across multiple potential Buddhist reincarnations.

> 罷了，罷了，今日蘆雪廣遭劫，生生被雲丫頭作踐了！我們蘆雪廣一大
> 哭！(2.49.1191)

Xiangyun parries by accusing Baoqin of 'false purity' and asserts the cleansing
power of verse saying that once their feast is done, she and her fellow venison-
eaters will soar as literary talents.

> 你知道甚麼！「是真名士自風流」，你們都是假清高，最可厭的。我們這會子腥的
> 膻的大喫大嚼，回來卻是錦心繡口。(2.49.1191)

Amidst the jocular festivities, this polluting event provides the opportunity for
one of Baoyu's maids, Trinket, to steal Patience's gold 'shrimp whisker' bracelet
(2.52.535). The discovery of the theft worsens the vegetarian Skybright's illness—
an illness that will eventually lead to her death. The rot and decay from the real
world has penetrated deep into Baoyu's apartment at the heart of the garden
with excessive luxurious food consumed in a primal, carnivorous celebration as
its conduit.

Throughout the middle of the novel, the increasing incidents of theft and
smuggling in and out of the garden enhance the narrative tension—the protective barrier to the sanctity of the garden is crumbling. In Chapter 60, Cook Liu
herself unwittingly becomes a transmission zone rather than a cleansing zone.[13]
Her relatively elevated power within the mansions as the provider of food to
the garden has already prompted jealousy among the other older women and
they pounce when Liu errs—Cook Liu and her daughter Fivey 五兒 are accused
of theft and the kitchen is ransacked in the search for more stolen property. The
crisis is sparked by Baoyu's maid, Parfumée, who gives Cook Liu some Rose
Essence 玫瑰露 for her ailing daughter, Fivey. Cook Liu asks if it is possible to
get more and Parfumée obliges by asking Baoyu if he can spare some more. He
gives her a half-full bottle saying, 'I don't drink it very often myself.' In this
transfer, by gifting the essence to Cook Liu, control of the 'pure' garden essence
is then lost to the outside world. In a show of generosity, Cook Liu takes a cup of
the 'pure' and 'precious' essence out of the garden to her relatives to help their
ailing son recover. Fivey warns her that this action could invite trouble if anyone
asks about the origins of the essence. 依我說，竟不給他也罷了。倘或有人盤問
起來，倒又是一場是非 (2.60.1474). Her mother dismisses this cautionary voice
and takes the garden essence out into the impure world. Further compounding

this error, she is then responsible for bringing another, equally precious, but unauthorized medicinal herb into the garden. Her relatives had secured a small packet of Fu Ling Snow 茯苓霜 as part of Liu's husband's work at the front gates of the Mansion.[14] Another tonic designed to boost her daughter's constitution, these two products as they surreptitiously move in and out of the garden ultimately lead to her daughter's downfall.

Fivey, despite her own warning to her mother about transporting food products in and out of the garden, decides to take a small amount of the Fu Ling Snow to Parfumée and sneaks into the garden at nightfall. She is not an authorized garden resident, being the daughter of a cook, and so when the older garden women discover her on one of their nightly patrols just as she is about to make good her departure, Fivey feels the full weight of their jealousy, resentment and enthusiasm to wield power. During her interrogation, it becomes apparent that a bottle of Rose Essence is missing from Lady Wang's supply; and that the Fu Ling Snow is a 'sweetener' taken by the doormen and therefore is also ill-gotten gain. Suspected of theft, Fivey spends the night locked in with the gatekeepers awaiting her punishment. As household manager, Wang Xifeng passes hasty judgment on the mother and daughter declaring that Cook Liu must be expelled from the garden and never allowed to work inside again. Fivey is to be sold or married off and expelled from the Jia mansions altogether. Both will receive a beating of forty strokes as well. To reverse this ruling, Baoyu takes the blame for the incident so that both mother and daughter gain a reprieve and resume their normal lives. But suspicion remains about the lax security of the garden and, despite Patience's optimism that 'It's the sign of a really thriving household that their big troubles turn into little one and their little ones into nothing at all' (3.62.164) 大事化為小事，小事化為沒事，方是興旺之家 (2.62.1503), readers know that this incident is another crack in the sanctity of the Garden as the impurities from outside enter.

Equally, the magical garden resists polluting influences from outside through the power of food. For example, in Chapter 41, the rustic Granny Liu visits the garden and joins in a special banquet to return the favour of the crab party that Shi Xiangyun organized. The women and girls of the household give a lunch party in the garden and Granny Liu is included for the entertainment that her rough, uncultured ways provide to the refined Jia ladies. She is given a pair of heavy silver chopsticks so that her inevitable clumsiness will provide the women with humorous diversion. Xifeng explains that the silver is useful for detecting if the food is poisoned because the utensils will change colour in the presence of poison. To which Granny Liu replies: 'If this food is poisoned ... then what

we eat at home must be pure arsenic' (2.40.290) 這個菜裡有毒，我們那些都成
了砒霜了 (1.40.970). Among the many dishes she eats are the most famous of all
the foods described in the novel—the dried aubergine. This dish requires ten
chickens in its preparation through steaming and drying aubergine over chicken
stock multiple times (2.41.306). Some delicate snacks follow the aubergine
including goose-fat rolls and pastries shaped in intricate flower patterns. She
proceeds to eat all these delicacies with gusto only to discover that the food is
indeed unsuited to *her* stomach. She spends a long time in the toilet as she expels
the rich food and drink she has just consumed. While suited for the aristocratic
garden dwellers and elite Jia women, these refined foods are indigestible for the
old, poor, rural Granny.

Bearers of Breast Milk as Sources of Pollution

Elsewhere I have demonstrated that the novel confirms long-standing beliefs
that the most polluting women are married women because they exude polluting substances like menstrual and post-partum blood and breast milk (2000,
419). These two body fluids carry moral significance and not merely biological
significance. Limin Bai notes that from the Han through the Qing 'writers about
infant care repeatedly urged parents to examine the physical and moral quality
of wet-nurses carefully' because 'the milk became a crucial channel to transmit
not only physical attributes or diseases but also moral character from the mother
or wet-nurse to the child'.[15] Similarly, Charlotte Furth has shown that breast milk
has the potential to pollute babies through foetal poisoning since it was thought
to be a postpartum transformation of the mother's highly polluting yin blood.[16]
Hiring wet nurses was one method mothers avoided blame for foetal poisoning—the burden for any infant illness passed instead to the wet nurse (Furth,
23). She notes that in elite families the wet nurses usually assumed positions of
relatively high status domestics and lived with the families of their nurslings.
This phenomenon is evident in *Honglou meng* through the appearance of myriad
wet nurses. For example, Lin Daiyu arrives at the Jia household accompanied
by one maid and her wet nurse 王嬤嬤. Jia Lian's wet nurse Nannie Zhao 趙嬤
嬤 appears in Chapter 16 and Jia Baoyu's wet nurse Nannie Li 李嬤嬤 appears
multiple times. They are all integral members of the Jia household even though
their breast-feeding duties have long ceased. Breast milk features frequently in
the foodscape of the novel prior to the entrance of the young people into the
garden. The garden walls act as a protective barrier against the threat of pollution from breast milk and its bearers, the wet nurses. The wet nurses of the novel
develop a sense of entitlement to special favours from their former nurslings

as a result of their intimate, nurturing role. But, readers become aware that the poison they potentially carry continues well after their breast-feeding duties are over.

The first example we have of this motif comes in Chapter 8 when Baoyu is still living in his Grandmother's quarters. He returns from drinking with Baochai, Daiyu and Aunt Xue 薛姨媽 slightly inebriated to find that the Beancurd Dumplings he had sent to Skybright had been taken by Nannie Li for her grandchildren and that she had also drunk the special tea he had been saving for 'later', a certain Fung Loo tea. On hearing about her actions he rages angrily, 'Merely because I drank her milk for a few days when I was a baby she is as spoiled and pampered as if she were some sort of divinity. Let's get rid of the old woman now and have done with it!' (1.8.198). David Hawkes uses the phrase 'have done with it' but it is important to notice that the Chinese text uses the word 'clean' 乾淨 in keeping with Baoyu's notion that older women are impure.

> 不過是我小時候喫過他幾日奶罷了，如今怪的比祖宗還大！攆了出去，大家乾淨！(1.8.206)

Nannie Li provided nourishment for the infant Baoyu and years later still demands repayment in kind by taking food at will from her former charge, or more specifically from his current servants—the young women that have replaced her in caring for Baoyu.

A second example of this feature comes in Chapter 19, when Nannie Li visits Baoyu's chambers and finds a bowl of rare mare's milk (*sulao* 酥酪), or koumiss, that he had put aside for Aroma 襲人. The koumiss was a gift to Baoyu from his elder sister, the Imperial Concubine, Yuanchun. However, Nannie Li mistakes the substance for ordinary junket and guzzles the precious bowl of koumiss despite protests from those all around. She declares:

> I won't believe he would be so wicked as to grudge his old Nannie a bowl of milk. Why, he *owes* it to me ... He ought to stop and ask himself how he grew up to be the big boy he is today. It's my milk he sucked, that came from my own heart's blood:[17] that's what he grew up on. And you mean to tell me that now, if I drink one little bowlful of *his* milk—*cow's* milk—he's going to be angry with me? (1.19.384)
>
> 我不信他這樣壞了腸子！別說我喫了一碗牛奶，就是在比這個值錢的，也是應該的。…… 難道他不想想怎麼長大了？我的血變的奶喫的長這麼大；如今我喫他一碗牛奶，他就生氣了？我偏喫了，看他怎樣！(1.19.423)

Nannie Li's assertion of right to special privilege above the young maidservant Aroma results in her jealous rage at Baoyu in Chapter 20 with accusations that he has no gratitude for the life she gave him. 'Let them [Her old Ladyship and

Her Ladyship] hear how you have cast me off—me that reared you at my own breast—now that you don't need my milk any more.' (1.20.401)[18] 我只和你在老太太，太太跟前去講。把你奶了這麼大，到如今喫不著奶了，把我丟在一旁 (1.20.447). The power of the wet nurses decreases as the youngsters move into the Garden and become rulers of their own kingdoms, but the threat from the corrupting power of the once-nurturing breast milk continues. Wet nurses and breast milk are symbols of the potential leakage of pollution into the garden and the forbidden transport of garden objects out. In one case a young girl, rather than a wet nurse, becomes an unwitting trafficker of breast milk-related contraband. Readers learn that the Fu Ling Snow secreted into the garden by Fivey, and the cause of much grief to her and her mother, Cook Liu, is most efficacious when mixed with breast milk.

In Chapter 73, readers learn that wet nurses are particularly problematic domestics. In this incident, Parfumée sees a man jumping into the garden from over the wall and the once-quiet kingdom of girls is plunged into panic and chaos. The ensuing search and investigation of the garden's security processes finds that the supervisors had become lax in their duties as a result of a distracting gambling network that had formed among the women. One of the ringleaders is Jia Yingchun's wet nurse. Grandmother Jia points out:

> These old nannies are all the same. They think that because they suckled you when you were babies it entitles them to special treatment now. They're worse trouble than all the other servants put together, because whenever they have done wrong they think they can always get you to cover up for them. I know, I have had a lot of experience of these people. (3.73.442)
>
> 大約這些奶子們，一個個仗著奶過哥兒姐兒，原比別人有些體面，他們就生事比別人更可惡，專管調唆主子，護短偏向。我都是經過的。況且要拿一個作法，恰好果然就遇見了一個。你們別管，我自有道理 (2.73.1785–86).

Indeed, Yingchun's nannie finds herself in financial strife as a result of her gambling activities and begins stealing from Yingchun—pawning her jewellery for cash. When the gambling network is exposed, the nannie's daughter-in-law pleads with Yingchun: 'I've come to ask the mistress for the sake of the milk she sucked from her as a baby, to go to her Old Ladyship and plead with her for our old missus' (3.73.447). 如今還要求姑娘看著從小兒吃奶的清常，往老太太那邊去討一個情，救出他來纔好 (2.73.1789–90). With the 'bank' money confiscated, there is no way to redeem the latest pilfered piece, a pearl and gold phoenix. The nannie's daughter-in-law tries to hide the crime by threatening Yingchun with accusations that *she* has been overspending and actually owes nannie the money.

Illegal and Excessive Alcohol Weakens the Boundaries

Alcohol is consumed in copious amounts throughout the novel by all classes of characters. Young children are given wine to accompany their meals and the family shares wine in rituals, celebrations and at impromptu gatherings. Dissolute men known for hard drinking are marked as causing misery to their families and a young man's drunken cavorting with prostitutes stands as a marker of the impending decline of a family. For example, Xue Pan, scion of the Xue clan is a renowned wastrel and a buffoon of the first order; Jia Zhen and son, Jia Rong, senior males of the Ning mansions, spend large amounts of their extensive recreational time drinking and gambling with like-minded cronies, and Xing Xiuyan's father neglects his family as a result of his drunkenness. Other times, alcohol is used as a device to allow for the revelation of 'truth'—the most famous incident being Big Jiao's drunken abuse of the declining morals of the Ning mansion and his hint that Jia Zhen was involved in an illicit relationship with his daughter-in-law, Qin Keqing 秦可卿.

Yet, wine does not always carry a completely negative association, and neither does drinking to excess. Chapter 5 of the novel describes Baoyu's dream visit to the Land of Illusion where he joins a fairy party in which fairy wine is served called Lachrymae Rerum and the Fairy Disenchantment explains its delectable flavour as:

> This wine … is made from the petals of hundreds of different kinds of flowers and extracts from thousands of different sorts of trees. These are blended and fermented with kylin's marrow and phoenix milk (1.5.139).
>
> 此酒乃以百花之蕊，萬木之汁，加以麟髓之醅，鳳乳之麴釀成，因名為「萬艷同杯」。(1.5.124)

Baoyu proceeds to drink the magical wine while reading the libretto for the 'Dream of Golden Days' suite in which the fate of the twelve beauties of the Jia household are outlined in a premonitory musical performance designed to reveal to Baoyu the folly of love. However, the wine makes Baoyu dizzy and he fails to understand the significance of the songs—instead he requests to lie down. At this, Fairy Disenchantment reveals that her motive for making him drunk with fairy wine is to teach him about the illusion of love in order that he free himself and concentrate on 'devoting your mind seriously to the teachings of Confucius and Mencius and your person wholeheartedly to the betterment of society' (1.5.146) 而今後萬萬解釋，改悟前情，留意於孔孟之間，委身於經濟之道 (1.5.130). In the mystical Land of Illusion, alcohol is designed as a trigger for enlightenment and a spur to self-realization.

In the Land of Illusion's mirror world on earth, wine accompanies all the activities of the garden dwellers celebrations with drinking games and poetry forfeits. Drunkenness takes on a recreational aspect with positive connotations when it occurs in the garden. For example, in several meetings of the Crab Flower Poetry Club wine is regarded as being a spur to improved creativity: 'I need wine to inspire my verse' says Xiangyun (2.49.485) 喫了酒纔有詩 (2.49.1190). It also appears frequently in a medicinal role—balancing the humours with the 'hot' nature of wine. Baochai and Daiyu request wine for its warming qualities to balance the cool properties of the crab they have just consumed (see Chapter 38).

The episode in which the greatest quantity of drinking takes place in the garden is during the four-way birthday celebrations for Baoyu, Baoqin, Xingyan and Patience held in the evening after the formal birthday rituals have been completed. Mistresses and maids alike reach a happy level of inebriation through their drinking games. Midway through the party some older serving women enter to check on them and offer some snacks to dull the impact of the alcohol. Tanchun reassures everyone that 'As long as we don't do any serious drinking, it's perfectly all right' (3.62.204) 橫豎咱們不認真喝酒就罷了 (2.62.1520–21). Just at this moment a young maid enters with news that Xiangyun has fallen into a drunken stupor on a granite bench nearby in the garden. She was unconscious to the world and covered in peony petals that had dropped from the bushes around and her 'flowery heap' had attracted butterflies and bees (3.62.204). After sucking a couple of 'hangover rocks' 醒酒石 and taking some cups of strong tea she is almost back to normal again. This scene of Xiangyun drunk asleep among the peony petals becomes her totemic image. Alcohol consumption by the young women when inside the garden leads to no ill effect and, in fact, is likened to the magical fairy party of beautiful women that Baoyu visits in his premonitory dream in Chapter 5. This carefree pleasure of inebriation is not possible in the novel's moral order for the older or married women.

The excessive drinking at Wang Xifeng's birthday party results in calamity for her household. Grandmother Jia encourages Xifeng to drink toast after toast to the point where the normally sober and controlled Xifeng is quite dizzy. She escapes from the party early, planning on briefly resting in her quarters, and surprises her husband, Jia Lian in bed with a servant woman, Bao Er's wife. The excessive consumption of alcohol fuels her jealous rage and in the ensuing fight between husband and wife and its aftermath their loyal senior maid, Patience, unjustly receives a slap and a hail of abuse from her mistress and Bao Er's wife commits suicide.[19] Both master and mistress make public apologies to Patience, and Bao Er is paid off in cash.

Alcohol consumption plays a crucial role in signalling the impending decline of the garden's utopian world. When their rural relative, Granny Liu, visits the mansions in Chapters 40–41 she is treated to a banquet in the garden where she is tricked into drinking beyond her capacity. In her drunken state she wanders through the garden and accidentally stumbles into Baoyu's bedchamber. She promptly falls into a drunken stupor on his bed where Aroma discovers her polluting the room with the stench of farts and belches. Aroma whisks her hastily from the room and then adds handfuls of aromatics to the incense burner to mask the old woman's smell. The fumes of age, poverty and uncouthness have literally polluted the purity of the garden paradise.

The older women charged with maintaining security at the garden gates use the relative freedom of their positions to drink and gamble. Taking turns to keep watch for any of the masters or mistresses that might discover their antics, the old women play cards and drink, setting up an elaborate system that involves a 'bank' that loans to women wishing to incur debts to continue their gambling. Eventually this social scourge and threat to the safety of the garden becomes common knowledge. Lady Wang comments: 'They drink and play cards whenever they have a moment to spare. They sleep in the daytime and play cards at night.' (3.55.46) 老婆子們不中用，得空兒喫酒鬪牌，白日裡睡覺，夜裡鬪牌 (2.55.1328). When Xifeng is unable to continue to monitor every aspect of the household's management as a result of her miscarriage, three of Prospect Garden's residents take over management of their world—Jia Tanchun, Li Wan and Xue Baochai. Aware of the ongoing problem of gambling and drinking they clamp down on the activities in the gatehouses. Their impact is clear when the old women complain: 'No sooner is the Terror of the Seas put out of action than along come these three Scourges of the Mountains to take her place. Nowadays you can't even take time off for a quiet drink of a night or a little game of cards!' (3.55.48) 剛剛的倒了一個「巡海夜叉」，又添了三個「鎮山太歲」，越發連夜裡偷著喫酒頑的工夫都沒了 (2.55.1330).

Tea as Social Hierarchy

Tea is more commonly consumed than alcohol in the novel and not surprisingly also contributes to the core principles underlying the novel's detail. A wide range of top-range teas are mentioned in the text and tea connoisseurship is a key aspect of civility and graceful living described therein. Tea consumption serves to mark social hierarchy and high levels of cultural refinement but it also operates to extend the novel's discussion of purity and pollution.

For example, in Chapter 41, we read of a tea-drinking episode that illustrates perfectly the division between the pure and the profane. During Granny Liu's visit to the Jia mansions Grandmother Jia shows remarkable solicitude to her food needs. But when the two older women visit Prospect Garden's young Buddhist nun, Adamantina 妙玉, the division between the two moral positions is laid out for all to see. Adamantina's desire to maintain her distance from the pollution of poverty, age and uncultured rustic ways is manifest through an incident involving tea. She aspires to the highest levels of purity having sought protection from worldly pollution by living in a nunnery that is itself within Prospect Garden. This double-layered protective wall is penetrated by age, illness, poverty and the taint of ignorance when she receives a visit from the two elderly women, Grandmother Jia and Granny Liu. Her superior knowledge of tea and her refined manner of serving the tea are all demonstrated within a few short lines.

Adamantina provides the women with Old Man's Eyebrows 老君眉 tea served from an elaborately decorated lacquer tray. Grandmother Jia assumes the tea to be Liu'an 六安茶, but Adamantina demonstrates her prescience by correcting the elder woman and assuring her that she would not serve Liu'an because she is aware that the Grandmother Jia does not drink this form of tea.[20] Instead she is serving Old Man's Eyebrows. Thus reassured, Grandmother Jia then asks about the water used to brew the tea and is told that it is 'last year's rain-water'. Liu'an tea is one of the ten superior green teas of the entire country and is produced in Anhui, one of the best tea growing regions. Liu'an tea is renowned for its natural colour and slightly bitter flavour.[21] Grandmother Jia's rejection of this luxury item underscores yet again the luxury to which the family is accustomed. The Old Man's Eyebrows tea remains a point of conjecture since this name is not recorded in the traditional lists of tea 茶譜. The eminent scholar Deng Yunxiang argues that it is another name for Shoumei 壽眉 tea and argues that Grandmother Jia was actually asking for 'red tea' rather than a 'green tea' because the popularity of Liu'an tea among the elites in the Qing had meant that the name often stood in for 'green tea'.[22] But Deng's neutralization of Grandmother Jia's choice as a mere act of taste preference minimizes the significance of this choice in a novel where every small detail carries broader meaning.

Further compounding the atmosphere of refinement and exclusivity, the cup that she proffers to Grandmother Jia is a brightly glazed Chenghua porcelain 成窯五彩小蓋鐘. Grandmother Jia sips the tea and then hands the very same cup to Granny Liu. Granny gulps instead of sipping and further exposing her lack of refinement declares that it is a bit weak and would have been improved by longer brewing. While Grandmother Jia finds this amusing it is evident later that Adamantina is far from amused. Instead she feels Granny Liu has contaminated her space and that the once-precious cup the old women drank from is also polluted. At the end of the visit, she discards the cup that Granny Liu drank from refusing even to have it brought into the nunnery from the foyer. Baoyu immediately understands Adamantina's revulsion at the now-contaminated object since this regimen is something he maintains within his own residence in the garden. He relieves Adamantina of the cup and while she reminds him that if she had ever used it, then the cup would be smashed to pieces. Baoyu eventually makes a present of the cup to Granny Liu when she is about to return home.

In contrast to her cold response to the elderly women visitors, Adamantina's interactions with Baochai and Daiyu, whom she personally invites into her room, show no concern for potential pollutants. On their arrival at the priory Grandmother Jia says that the party should remain outside because they had just eaten meat and taken wine so that that their presence inside would be 'sacrilege' 沖了罪過. But these rules clearly do not apply to the young and refined because Adamantina targets them for a special invitation even though she has never met them before. Baoyu enters her room uninvited and joins this refined and pure coterie. Adamantina explains to Baoyu, Baochai and Daiyu that the water she is brewing their particular tea with is of a level of superiority that leaves 'last year's rain water' far behind. She had indeed given the elderly women a superior form of water but one that is not as refined as the one she shares with her younger visitors. The youngsters are given water derived from the melted snow collected from the branches of winter-flowering plum trees five years earlier. Adamantina had only just opened the jar and it was the second time that she herself had drunk the pure liquid. She instructs them on its qualities of superior clarity and lightness in their short time with her. But, in their brief encounter we also become aware of her excessive search for purity—a quality that will inevitably lead to her fall into impurity. Daiyu asks about the water and is dismissed perfunctorily with the comment: 'I am most surprised that you cannot tell the difference (2.41.315).' She goes on to explain that stored rainwater could never have such 'purity and simplicity' 清淳.[23] '你怎麼嚐不出來？隔年蠲的雨水那有這樣清淳，如何喫得' (2.41.1999). Adamantina, it seems, is more pure than the pure, more refined than the refined and more cultured than the cultured.

Tea also plays a role in establishing the boundaries of Baoyu's girls' world in Chapter 63 during the lively birthday celebrations his maids hold for him. Although the entire day has been occupied with celebrating Baoyu's birthday with Grandmother Jia and the other older women, that evening Baoyu's maids have prepared a private party for him. Cook Liu, despite her recent travails in fending off the allegations of theft outlined in Chapter 60, prepares a special meal for Baoyu's secret party, which has been paid for by donations from each of his maids. The food is designed to aid digestion, since the entire day has been spent eating. However, organizing a party of this kind is not a simple matter for the young people. The usual evening patrols to secure each household's gates have to be endured before their party can commence. Lin Zhixiao's 林之孝 wife comes to check on Baoyu's household and advises his senior maids to give him some Puer tea to settle him down after a day of heavy indulgence.[24] Aroma and Skybright reply that they have indeed already just done that by brewing a pot of 'girls' tea' 女兒茶 and in order to keep the old woman on side, they offer her a cup as well. 'Girls' tea' is a form of Puer tea which grows in Yunnan province and is harvested just around the sixth solar term 穀雨. According to Zhang Hong's 張泓 Qianlong era text *New Words from Southern Yunnan* (*Diannan xin yu* 滇南新語), its name derives from the fact that it is picked, cured and processed by girls who use the money earned for their bridal trousseau (cited in Deng, 257). Cao Xueqin's identification of a particular type of Puer tea that so clearly invokes the singular work of virginal young girls in its production is designed to alert readers to the formation of a new space—a pure and clean girls' world in the form of the birthday party that is about to take place. The older woman, Lin Zhixiao's wife, is given a cup of this tea to seduce her into a more compliant position and enable Baoyu's party with his beauties to begin. The event mirrors the party Baoyu enjoyed in his dream sequence in the Land of Illusion in Chapter 5 since he is the only man within a world of beautiful, talented and desirable girls. The consumption of Girls' Tea presaged this shift in spatial and moral orders by serving as the potion by which this world is created.

***

The manner in which Cao Xueqin has drawn food and drink into his novel's deeper philosophical commentary on the impossibility of separating purity and impurity attests to his mastery as a writer. Food and drink are deployed not merely to reveal the refinement of the Jia clan and their extreme privilege, nor are they decorations dotted through the books to display Cao Xueqin's own superior level of cultivation. Rather, they are intimately entwined with the core of the novel's engagement with the tragedy of impermanence. The consumption, preparation, transmission and trade of food and drinks are integral to the novel's explication of the permeability of the boundaries between the pure and the profane. The extensive and exotic feasting sustained throughout the novel creates not only a sense of luxury and privilege but also builds narrative tension as the Jia family's excessive, albeit exquisite, lifestyle is made manifestly unstable.

As with masterpieces the world over, *Honglou meng*'s influence reaches well beyond the literary scene and into the realm of mass commercial culture. Prospect Garden has been reconstructed in multiple locations around China for tourists to walk amidst the pavilions and loggias and experience the luxury of aristocratic garden landscaping. And restaurants offer 'Red Chamber Cuisine' to meet increasing epicurean desires to taste the exquisite foods so eloquently described in the novel.[25] The intermingling of elite and mass cultures occurs today as inevitably as the mixing of the pure and the profane or the real and the unreal.

Notes

Chapter 1

1. Sidney W. Mintz, 'Foreword: Food for Thought', in *The Globalization of Chinese Food*, eds. David Y. H. Wu and Sidney C. H. Cheung (Surrey: Curzon Press, 2002), xii.
2. Chang Kwang-chih, ed., *Food in Chinese Culture: Anthropological and Historical Perspectives* (New Haven: Yale University Press, 1977), 11.
3. Roel Sterckx, 'Introduction', in *Of Tripods and Palate* (London: Palgrave, 2005), 6.
4. A collection of essays dealing with such questions can be found at Roderick Whitfield, ed., *The Problem of Meaning in Early Chinese Ritual Bronzes* (London: Percival David Foundation of Chinese Art, School of Oriental and African Studies, University of London, 1993).
5. Some scholars, however, remain unconvinced by the equivalence of *taotie* and the beast-like motif on the bronzes. Wang Tao, for example, points out that while the beast-like motif was already common in Shang bronzes, *taotie* as a literary term appeared relatively late in Zhou. He suggests that since the meaning of the term *taotie* was not necessarily the original meaning for the Shang people, it is better to use the term 'two-eyed motif' instead of the *taotie* when referring to the motif on the bronzes. For more information, see Wang Tao, 'A Textual Investigation of the *Taotie*', in *Ritual Bronzes*, 102–18.
6. Chen Qiyou 陳奇猷, ed., 'Prophecies 先識 16.1', in *Lüshi chunqiu* 呂氏春秋 (Shanghai: Xuelin chubanshe, 1995), 947.
7. Yang Bojun 楊伯峻, ed., 'Wengong 文公 18.7', in *Chunqiu Zuo zhuan zhu* 春秋左傳注 (Beijing: Zhonghua shuju, 1981), 633–42. See also James Legge, *The Chinese Classics: The Ch'un Ts'ew with The Tso Chuen* (Hong Kong: Hong Kong University Press, 1960), 279–83.
8. Because the *taotie* is commonly featured as a decorative pattern of the tripods (*ding* 鼎) since the Shang era, Sarah Allan theorizes that a connection is eventually forged between its insatiable greed and the motif of eating for which the tripod is designed. For more information, see Sarah Allan, *The Shape of the Turtle: Myth, Art, and Cosmos in Early China* (New York: SUNY Press, 1991), 145–48.
9. Du Fu's critique is clearly indicated by the last line of the poem, which compares a thief who tries to pretend to be otherwise to the appetite of the *taotie*: 'A thief in spite of fancy attires, like a feasting *taotie*' 衣冠兼盜賊，饕餮用斯須.
10. James Legge, trans., *The Chinese Classics* (Hong Kong: Hong Kong University Press, 1960), Ode 230.

11. D. C. Lau, ed., *A Concordance to the Xunzi* 荀子逐字索引 (Hong Kong: The Commercial Press, 1996) 32.130.24–131.1; also John Knoblock, *Xunzi: A Translation and Study of the Complete Works*, 3 vols. (Stanford: Stanford University Press, 1988–94), 27.52.

12. D. C. Lau, trans, *Mencius* (Hong Kong: Chinese University Press, 2003), 1.A3 & 1.A7.

13. *Mencius*, 6.A17.

14. Legge, *The Chinese Classics*, Ode 247.

15. James Legge, *The Sacred Books of China: The Text of Confucianism* (Oxford: Clarendon Press, 1879–1885), 3.406.

16. Lau, *Concordance*, 19.90.1–8; Knoblock, *Xunzi: A Translation*, 19.1a.

17. Legge, *Sacred Books*, 4.318.

18. Lau, *Concordance*, 19.95.1–4; Knoblock, *Xunzi: A Translation*, 19.6.

19. D. C. Lau, trans, *The Analects* (Hong Kong: Chinese University Press, 1992), 6.18.

20. Patricia Buckley Ebrey, *Confucianism and Family Rituals in Imperial China* (Princeton, NJ: Princeton University Press, 1991), 3.

21. Lau, *Concordance*, 19.91.7–9; Knoblock, *Xunzi: A Translation*, 19.2b.

22. Legge, *Sacred Books*, 3.444.

23. E. N. Anderson, *The Food of China* (New Haven and London: Yale University Press, 1988), 201.

24. Luo Guanzhong, *Three Kingdoms: A Historical Novel*, trans. Moss Roberts (Berkeley: University of California Press, 1994), 1083.

25. Ibid., 1084.

26. Several decades before the time of Zhuge, a type of food called the 'steamed cake' (*zhengbing* 蒸餅), which bears very close resemblance to the dough-head, has already been documented by Liu Xi 劉熙. Zhuge, therefore, is unlikely to have been the first person to come up with this idea. See Liu Xi 劉熙, *Shiming* 釋名, in *Zhongguo gudai gongjushu congbian* 中國古代工具書叢編 (Tianjin: Tianjin guji chubanshe, 1999), 20.

27. Dongfang Shuo and Lin Hongcheng, 'Separation of Politics and Morality: A Commentary on *Analects of Confucius*', trans. Huang Deyuan, *Frontiers of Philosophy in China*, 3 (2006), 402.

28. For a detailed study of these three poems, see Gong Pengcheng 龔鵬程, 'Jiani, daiyan, xixue shiti yu shuqing chuantong jian di jiuge' 假擬、代言、戲謔詩體與抒情傳統間的糾葛, *Tangdai sichao* 唐代思潮 (Yilan: Foguang renwen shehui xueyuan, 2001), 715–39.

29. See Zhao Xiaolan 趙小蘭, 'Shouma, bingju, kuzong: luelun Dushi biaoxian shangshi youshi zhuti de yizu geren yixiang' 瘦馬、病橘、枯棕：略論杜詩表現傷時憂世主題的一組個人意象, *Du Fu yanjiu xuekan* 杜甫研究學刊, (1) 2002, 51–56.

30. Su Shi 蘇軾, *Chouchi biji* 仇池筆記 (Shanghai: Huadong shifan daxue chubanshe, 1983), 257.

31. Ye Jiaying 葉嘉瑩, *Ye Jiaying shuo Tao Yuanming yinjiu ji nigushi* 葉嘉瑩說陶淵明飲酒及擬古詩 (Beijing: Zhonghua shuju, 2007), 79.

32. Michel Jeanneret, *A Feast of Words; Banquets and Table Talk in the Renaissance* (Chicago: University of Chicago Press, 1991), 1.

33. Its ubiquitous omission in *The Travels of Marco Polo*, for example, is one of the most often cited reasons for critics to doubt the authenticity of the work.

34. C. T. Hsia, *The Classic Chinese Novel: A Critical Introduction* (New York: Columbia University Press, 1968), 181.

35. Martin W. Huang, *Desire and Fictional Narrative in Late Imperial China* (Cambridge, MA: Harvard University Asia Center), 93.

36. David R. Knechtges, 'A Literary Feast: Food in Early Chinese Literature', *Journal of the American Oriental Society*, 106 (1986), 63.

Chapter 2

1. Liu Xiang 劉向, *Zhanguo ce* 戰國策 (Shanghai: Shanghai guji chubanshe, 1985), 'Wei ce 2' 魏策二, 846–7. This story of Yu 禹 is cited by the ruler of Lu 魯 to exhort King Hui of Wei 魏惠王 during a banquet with other feudal lords at Fantai 范臺.

2. Liu Xiang 劉向, *Xinxu [yizhu]* 新序譯注, annot. Zhao Zhongyi 趙仲邑 (Beijing: Zhonghua shuju, 1997), Ch. 6, 'Cì she' 刺奢, 180.

3. Qu Wanli 屈萬里, *Shangshu shiyi* 尚書釋義 (Taipei: Zhonghua wenhua chubanshe, 1963), 86.

4. Zhu Xi 朱熹, *Sishu jizhu* 四書集注 (Taipei: Shijie shuju, 1977), 65; quotation from the 'Xiangdang' 鄉黨 chapter in *The Analects* 論語.

5. Ibid., 59; quotation from the 'Zihan' 子罕 chapter in *The Analects*.

6. See Guo Qingfan 郭慶藩, ed., *Zhuangzi jishi* 莊子集釋 (Beijing: Zhonghua shuju, 1961), 3.636.

7. Ibid., 3.685.

8. Ibid., 4.947. See also Wei Chongzhou 魏崇周, 'Dui zhi de qijie yiji dui zhiyan de wudu' 對卮的歧解以及對卮言的誤讀, *Henan Social Sciences* 河南社會科學, 16 (2008), 129–31.

9. See Burton Watson, trans., *The Complete Works of Chuang Tzu* (New York: Columbia University Press, 1968), 303.

10. Yang Bojun 楊伯峻, *Liezi jishi* 列子集釋 (Hong Kong: Taiping shuju, 1965), 142.

11. Wang Xianqian 王先謙, *Xunzi jijie* 荀子集解 (Beijing: Zhonghua shuju, 1988), 104.

12. See John Knoblock, *Xunzi: A Translation and Study of the Complete Works* (Stanford: Stanford University Press, 1988–94), 1.229. See also Confucius, *The Analects*, trans. Arthur Waley (New York: Alfred A. Knopf, 2000), 134.

13. Sima Qian 司馬遷, *Shiji* 史記 (Beijing: Zhonghua shuju, 1959), 8.2528.

14. Ibid., 9.2847.

15. Sima Qian, 'Bao Ren An shu' 報任安書, in *Zhongguo lidai sanwen xuan* 中國歷代散文選, eds. Liu Pansui 劉盼遂 and Guo Yuheng 郭預衡 (Beijing: Beijing chubanshe, 2003), 1.331.

16. Lu Xun 魯迅, 'Wei Jin fengdu ji wenzhang yu yao ji jiu zhi guanxi' 魏晉風度及文章與藥及酒之關係, in *Lu Xun xuanji* 魯迅選集, ed. Zeng Yanxiu 曾彥修 (Chengdu: Sichuan renmin chubanshe, 1983), 276.

17. Liu Yiqing 劉義慶, *Shishuo xinyu [yizhu]* 世說新語譯注, trans. Zhang Huizhi 張撝之 (Shanghai: Shanghai guji chubanshe, 1996), 625.

18. For instance, Zou Yang's 'Wine *fu*' briefly states the various purposes of drinking according to the drinkers' social status: 'The populace drink for merriment; gentlemen drink for rites' 庶民以為歡，君子以為禮. See Zou Yang 鄒陽, 'Jiu fu' 酒賦, in

Quan Hanfu jiaozhu 全漢賦校注, ed. Fei Zhen'gang 費振剛 (Guangzhou: Guangdong jiaoyu chubanshe, 2005), 54.

19. Cao Zhi's 'Wine *fu*' describes officials and common folk sharing merriment in drinking irrespective of social status: at such moments 'inferior people forget their humbleness, destitute ones forget their poverty' 卑者忘賤，寠者忘貧. See Zhao Youwen 趙幼文, *Cao Zhi ji jiaozhu* 曹植集校注 (Beijing: Renmin wenxue chubanshe, 1984), 125.

20. Partly as a result of frequent drinking, Cao Zhi finally lost his father's trust, and the right to succession was conferred on his elder brother Cao Pi 曹丕. Cao Zhi paid a heavy political price partly for the love of wine.

21. '*Duanjiu jie*' 斷酒戒 can be found in *juan* 72, 'Shiwu bu' 食物部, in *Yiwen leiju* 藝文類聚, ed. Ouyang Xun 歐陽詢 (Hong Kong: Zhonghua, 1973), 1250–1. Allusions are cited to support the sacredness of wine. 'Springs of sweet water gushed in primeval times' 醴泉涌於上世 suggests that Nature provides ample resources for man to make wine, while 'the Plough shines brighter than all other stars' 懸象煥乎列星 implies that the asterism is named to exalt drinking (a plough for dipping wine). 'He who killed the serpent [after getting drunk] rose to power' 斷蛇者以興霸 refers to Liu Bang 劉邦 slaying a white serpent and starting an uprising after he got drunk. The source for 'he who settled disputes [while intoxicated] left his good name to posterity' 折獄者以流聲 is uncertain, but possibly refers to the early Han statesman Cao Shen 曹參 (?–190 BCE), who loved drinking and ruled the country in a simple way, thus earning himself a good name.

22. Liu Ling, 'Jiude song' 酒德頌, in *Wen xuan* 文選, ed. Xiao Tong 蕭統 (Shanghai: Shanghai guji chubanshe, 1986), 5.2098–100.

23. Fang Xuanling 房玄齡 et al., *History of the Jin Dynasty* 晉書 (Beijing: Zhonghua shuju, 1974), 5.1375–6.

24. Chen Bojun 陳伯君, *Ruan Ji ji jiaozhu* 阮籍集校注 (Beijing: Zhonghua shuju, 1987), 161.

25. Ji Kang, 'Yu Shan Juyuan juejiao shu' 與山巨源絕交書, in *Zhongguo lidai sanwen xuan*, 1.447.

26. Wang Xizhi, 'Lanting ji xu' 蘭亭集序, in *Zhongguo lidai sanwen xuan*, 1.506.

27. 'Drinking Wine' 飲酒 (Poem No. 14), in *Tao Yuanming ji* 陶淵明集, annot. Lu Qinli 逯欽立 (Beijing: Zhonghua shuju, 1973), 95.

28. For example, the early Tang writer Wang Ji 王績 wrote a 'Biography of Mr. Five Decalitres' (Wudou xiansheng zhuan 五斗先生傳) modelled on Tao Yuanming's prototype, and a piece entitled 'Drunkenland' 醉鄉記. In 'Drunkenland', he mentions an imaginary place without seasonal changes or land elevations; different from the hardworking peasants in Peach Blossom Spring, its inhabitants are more like a group of drunkards who indulge in drinking all day without worldly concerns, living freely and easily. See Wang Ji, *Wang Wugong wenji* 王無功文集 (Shanghai: Shanghai guji chubanshe, 1987), 181–2.

Chapter 3

1. William James, *The Varieties of Religious Experience* (New York: New American Library, 1958), 297.

2.   I will generally translate *jiu* 酒 as 'wine' in this chapter in the interest of euphony, even though 'ale' would be a more accurate description of what Chinese people were actually drinking in this period. On the other hand, note that 'wine' in common English can be used to refer to a generic term for alcoholic drinks, not merely grape wine, e.g. 'rice wine' or 'plum wine'. Moreover, grape wine was one of the beverages consumed by the Chinese even as early as the third century; see David R. Knechtges, 'Gradually Entering the Realm of Delight: Food and Drink in Early Medieval China', *Journal of the American Oriental Society*, 117 (1997), 237.

3.   Xu Shen 許慎, *Shuowen jiezi zhu* 說文解字注 (Nanjing: Fenghuang chubanshe, 2007), 14B.1296a. According to Duan Yucai's commentary, Xu Shen has drawn his retelling of the origins of wine from the Warring States text *Shiben* 世本.

4.   *Mao shi*, Ode 154. For a number of anecdotes on alcohol throughout Chinese history, see Hu Shanyuan 湖山源, *Gujin jiushi* 古今酒事 (Shanghai: Shanghai shudian, 1987); another useful survey is Mu-chou Poo, 'The Use and Abuse of Wine in Ancient China', *Journal of the Economic and Social History of the Orient*, 42 (1999), 123–51.

5.   Ouyang Xun 歐陽詢, ed., *Yiwen leiju* 藝文類聚 (Shanghai: Shanghai guji chubanshe, 1982), 72.1247. The *Shenyi jing* was originally attributed to Dongfang Shuo東方朔 (154–93 BCE) but probably dates in fact to the Six Dynasties.

6.   Li Bai 李白, 'Sharing a Drink Beneath the Moon' 月下獨酌, in *Li Bai ji jiaozhu* 李白集校注, ed. Qu Tuiyuan 瞿蛻園 (Shanghai: Shanghai guji chubanshe, 1980), 23.1332.

7.   Yu Xin 庾信, 'Ni "Yong huai"' 擬詠懷, in *Yu Zishan jizhu* 庾子山集注 (Beijing: Zhonghua shuju, 1980), 3.236.

8.   Zhuangzi 莊子, *Zhuangzi jishi* 莊子集釋 (Beijing: Zhonghua shuju, 2004), 7A.636. The identical passage occurs in *Liezi* as well, and I adopt the elegant translation of A. C. Graham, *The Book of Lieh-tzŭ* (London: John Murray, 1960), 38.

9.   'Yue ji' 樂記, *Li ji zhengyi* 禮記正義, 38.306c, in *Shisanjing zhushu* 十三經注疏 (Beijing: Zhonghua shuju, 1980, 1982).

10. Perhaps the outstanding study of the role of alcohol in this period is Wang Yao 王瑤, 'Wenren yu jiu' 文人與酒, in *Zhonggu wenxue shi lun ji* 中古文學史論集 (Shanghai: Shanghai guji chubanshe, 1982), 28–48.

11. For a text with an insightful introduction, see E. R. Dodds, ed. and comm., *Bacchae* (Oxford: Clarendon Press; New York: Oxford University Press, 1986).

12. Gu Yanwu 顧炎武 has an interesting discussion of prohibitions of drinking in Chinese history: 'Jiu jin' 酒禁, in *Ri zhi lu* [*ji shi*] 日知錄集釋 (Shanghai: Shanghai guji chubanshe, 1985), 28.15a–17b. Like American Prohibition, these Chinese efforts were never entirely successful.

13. See Yan Kejun 嚴可均, 'Quan Hou Han wen' 全後漢文, 83.8–9, in *Quan shanggu sandai Qin Han Sanguo Liuchao wen* 全上古三代秦漢三國六朝文 (Beijing: Zhonghua shuju, 1958). Note that Yan's text is a reconstruction from *Yiwen leiju* 72.1251 and Fan Ye范曄, *Hou Han shu* 後漢書 (Beijing: Zhonghua shuju, 1997), 70.2273, n. 1. Chen Shou 陳壽, *Sanguo zhi* 三國志 (Beijing: Zhonghua shuju, 1997), 12.372, n. 1, also quotes a speech by Kong Rong that overlaps with part of the letter.

14. Recalling *Mao shi*, Ode 14: 'Once I have seen him, / Once I have met him, / My heart will then be calm' 亦既見止、亦既覯止、我心則降.

15. This section is preserved only in the *Yiwen leiju*. The transition from this section to the next seems awkward and suggests textual instability.

16. An abbreviated quotation from the *Shang shu* 尚書: 'make offerings to the Supreme Lord and sacrifices to the ancestors' 肆類於上帝，禋於六宗. See Kong Yingda 孔穎達, *Shangshu zhengyi* 尚書正義, 3.14b, in *Shisanjing zhushu*.

17. This section is preserved in the *Hou Han shu* but not in the *Yiwen leiju* text.

18. The Wine Stars form a three-star constellation in Leo (consisting of the stars ξ, φ, and ω). It is also known as the Wine Banner (*jiu qi* 酒旗) and that is in fact the *Yiwen leiju* variant. We have already discussed the Wine Spring above.

19. This seems to have been a common proverb derived loosely from the *Analects*, which state that Confucius had a high tolerance for alcohol and was never drunk (e.g. 9/16). Cf. *Kong congzi* 孔叢子 (*Congshu jicheng*, v. 517), B.87: 'The thousand cups of Yao and Shun, the hundred goblets of Confucius' 堯舜千鐘，孔子百觚, identifying the phrases as an 'old proverb' 遺諺. This text was traditionally attributed to Kong Fu孔鮒 (c. 264–208 BCE), but was probably compiled later.

20. Referring to the famous incident when Fan Kuai saved Liu Bang 劉邦 (247–195 BCE) at the Hongmen feast. See Sima Qian 司馬遷, *Shi ji* 史記 (Beijing: Zhonghua shuju, 2003), 7.312–4.

21. A servant rescued the King of Zhao from captivity in Yan by a clever intrigue. See Sima, *Shi ji*, 89.2576–2577 and Ban Gu 班固, *Han shu* 漢書 (Beijing: Zhonghua shuju, 2002), 32.1833–1834. Like the previous example, it was a case of boldness instilled by drinking. In fact alcohol does not appear in the *Shi ji* or *Han shu* records of the incident.

22. Liu Bang once killed a great serpent while drunk. See Sima, *Shi ji*, 8.347.

23. A.k.a. Yuan Ang 爰盎 (?–148 BCE). An officer who owed Yuan a favour saved him from the insurgent Prince of Wu's army by offering the soldiers two *shi* 石 of strong wine, and thereby incapacitating them. See Sima, *Shi ji*, 101.2743

24. Yu Dingguo 于定國 (?–40 BCE) was renowned for his fair judgments as a chamberlain for law enforcement, and was especially judicious after drinking to excess.

25. Liu Bang refused to see Li Shiji 酈食其 (?–203 BCE), thinking he was a Confucian scholar, until Li declared himself a 'drinker of Gaoyang' and was received as a follower of Liu Bang, whom he then helped to conquer China. See Sima, *Shi ji*, 97.2704.

26. This line alludes to the famous speech of the fisherman criticizing Qu Yuan 屈原, 'Yufu' 漁父, in *Chuci buzhu* 楚辭補注 (Beijing: Zhonghua shuju, 1983), 7.179–180: 'The sage does not let himself get stuck in things, but can move along with the world. All the people in the world are dirty, so why not stir up their muck, and raise some waves? The masses are all drunk, so why not feed off the dregs, and drink up the light wine?' 聖人不凝滯於物，而能與世推移。世人皆濁，而揚其波？紅人皆醉，何不餔其糟而歠其醨.

27. This section is preserved in both the *Hou Han shu* and *Yiwen leiju* texts with some variants.

28. See Wu Yun 吳雲, ed., *Jian'an qizi ji jiaozhu* 建安七子集校注 (Tianjin: Tianjin guji chubanshe, 2005), 93, n. 23.

29. See Liu Yiqing 劉義慶, *Shishuo xinyu* 世說新語 (Beijing: Zhonghua shuju, 1991), 4.91; Richard Mather, 'The Controversy Over Conformity and Naturalness in the Six Dynasties', *History of Religions*, 9 (1969–1970), 174–5.

30. See Ban, *Han shu*, 92.3712–3, and translation in David R. Knechtges, 'Wit, Humor, and Satire in Early Chinese Literature', *Monumenta Serica*, 29 (1970–1971), 93.

31. Fan, *Hou Han shu*, 70.2273; Wu, *Jian'an qizi ji jiaozhu*, 90.

32. See Yan Kejun, 'Quan Jin wen', 85.2b–3a. For more on Ling ale, see Knechtges, 'Gradually Entering the Realm of Delight', 238.

33. For general discussions of the Seven Worthies, see Donald Holzman, 'Les Septs Sages de la Forêt des Bambous et la societé de leur temps', *T'oung Pao*, 44 (1956), 317–46; and He Qimin 何啟民, *Zhulin qixian yanjiu* 竹林七賢研究 (Taipei: Shangwu yinshuguan, 1966).

34. On nonconformity, see Mather, 'The Controversy Over Conformity and Naturalness in the Six Dynasties'.

35. Michael Nylan, 'Confucian Piety and Individualism in Han China', *Journal of the American Oriental Society*, 116 (1996), 1–27.

36. Henry Reeve, trans., *Democracy in America* (New York: Langley, 1840), 2.98. Cf. Nylan (25): 'a term coined by the political commentator Alexis de Tocqueville that denotes the freedom of the individual to operate in a self-directed, self-contained, and comparatively unrestrained fashion, without undue government interference or institutional control (including control by the family).'

37. Liu, *Shishuo xinyu*, 23.6.

38. Kong, *Shangshu zhengyi*, 16.110b, in *Shisanjing zhushu*.

39. The adoptive relationship of these insects first appears in *Mao shi*, Ode 196, but there is an elaboration in Yang Xiong's *Fayan*: 'The moth larvae were hiding, when they met the wasp, who encouraged them saying: 'Be like me! Be like me!' So after a time they begin to resemble the wasp in fact. So swiftly did the seventy disciples come to resemble Confucius' 螟蛉之子殪而逢蜾蠃，祝之曰：類我，類我。久則肖之矣。速哉，七十子之肖仲尼也. See *Fayan yishu* 法言義疏 (Beijing: Zhonghua shuju, 1987), 1.9.

40. Xiao Tong 蕭統, ed., *Wen xuan* 文選 (Beijing: Zhonghua shuju, 1974), 47.2098–9; Yan Kejun, 'Quan Jin wen', 66.1; *Shishuo xinyu*, 4.69, note; previous translation in Richard Mather, *A New Account of Tales of the World* (Ann Arbor: Center for Chinese Studies, University of Michigan, 2002), 137–8.

41. Modern entomologists know that the wasp actually uses them as food, casting a new satirical hue on the traditional allegory.

42. Liu, *Shishuo xinyu*, 23.51.

43. Sima Zhao 司馬昭 (211–265), who did not actually assume the title of emperor during his lifetime, but posthumously after his son Sima Yan 司馬炎 (236–90) established the Jin as Emperor Wu.

44. Over 16 gallons.

45. Fang Xuanling 房玄齡 et al., *Jin shu* 晉書 (Beijing: Zhonghua shuju, 1974), 49.1360–61. Donald Holzman discusses these in *Poetry and Politics*, 48–9, but downplays the significance of alcohol in the anecdotes.

46. Liu, *Shishuo xinyu*, 23.8.

47. See, e.g. James Hightower's discussion of the Han precedents for Tao Qian's own *fu* on 'Stilling the Passions' in 'The *Fu* of T'ao Ch'ien', *Harvard Journal of Asiatic Studies*, 17 (1954), 169–230.

48. Liu, *Shishuo xinyu*, 23.9.

49. Ibid., 23/7.

50. See *Ruan Ji ji jiaozhu* 阮籍集校注 (Beijing: Zhonghua shuju, 1987), 161–92.

51. Paul Kroll, 'Between Something and Nothing', *Journal of the American Oriental Society*, 127 (2007), 403–13.

52. On the particular place of Ruan Ji and Xi Kang relative to *xuanxue*, see Yu Dunkang 余敦康, *Wei Jin xuanxue shi* 魏晉玄學史 (Beijing: Beijing daxue chubanshe, 2004), 299–324.

53. Xiao Gongquan [Hsiao Kung-Ch'üan] 蕭公權, *Zhongguo zhengzhi sixiang shi* 中國政治思想史 (Taipei: Huagang, 1963, 1976), 365–70.

54. Ibid., 370–4. Bao Jingyan's doctrines are known only from chapter 49 of the *Baopuzi* 抱朴子, which critiques them.

55. Originally published in 1927; collected in *Lu Xun quanji* 魯迅全集 (Beijing: Renmin wenxue chubanshe, 2005), 3.532–3.

56. An intriguing variant has *da* 達 for *yi* 遺. There are all kinds of possible interpretations of this line, including Hightower's 'To strengthen my resolve to leave this world' ('T'ao Ch'ien's "Drinking Wine" Poems', in *Wen-lin* [Madison: University of Wisconsin Press, 1968], 14), but I prefer this reading simply because it is challenging, one of those surprising twists that occur frequently in Tao's poetry.

57. No. 7 in the series. See Lu Qinli 逯欽立, *Tao Yuanming ji* 陶淵明集 (Hong Kong: Zhonghua shuju, 1987), 90.

58. As Wang Yao points out, it was Tao Qian's special contribution to write drinking into his poetry, unlike the earlier poets who had kept it mostly separate. See 'Wenren yu jiu', 45.

59. Cf. Ding Xiang Warner, 'Mr. Five Dippers of Drunkenville: The Representation of Enlightenment in Wang Ji's Drinking Poems', *Journal of the American Oriental Society*, 118 (1998), 347–55.

Chapter 4

1. The Chinese term *jiu* 酒, translated as 'wine' for convenience, is usually not grape wine but an alcoholic drink made from one of a number of fruits or grains; see references to it in Kwang-chih Chang, ed., *Food in Chinese Culture* (New Haven: Yale University Press, 1977).

2. For instance, in Poem 3 wine serves as an anaesthetic 'to still the heart's pain' of homesickness and longing; in Poem 191 the sad feelings themselves are figuratively likened to the physiological effects of drunkenness: 'The [people's] hearts are worried like a bad hangover'. See also Poems 65 and 132.

3. By Liu Yangzhong's 劉揚忠 count, 48 of the 305 poems in *Shi jing* (16%) are related to wine: 9 of 160 (5%) in 'Airs of the States', 22 of 74 (30%) in the 'Minor Odes', 10 of 31 (32%) in the 'Major Odes', and 7 of 40 (18%) in the 'Hymns'. See his *Shi yu jiu* 詩與酒 (Taipei: Wenjin chubanshe, 1994), 33.

4. Joseph Allen notes that 'wine is mentioned four times more often in "The Minor Odes" than in the rest of the collection. And rather than the sombre libations of the ancestral rituals [seen in the "Hymns"], it is boisterous drinking that celebrates the here and now: "Set out your dishes and meat-stands, / Drink wine to your fill; / All you brothers are here together, / Peaceful, happy, and mild." (164)' See Arthur Waley, trans., *The Book of Songs*, ed. Joseph R. Allen (New York: Grove Press, 1996), 131. Note that Liu's figures and Allen's general statement do not exactly match each other.

5. A similar use of wine can be found in the 'Major Odes', e.g. Poem 239.

6. See also Poems 161 and 164.

7. For instance, he makes a formal 'Announcement against Drinking' 酒誥 to Yin subjects in the former Shang capital area, and a similar exhortation to King Cheng 成王 in 'No Idle Comfort' 無逸. Indeed, even the deposed King Zhou's 紂王 elder brother and senior adviser purportedly admit to the alcoholic overindulgence and dissolution of the Yin kings in 'Viscount of Wei' 微子.

8. Suffice it to quote a saying from *Proverbs* 20.1 in *The Old Testament*: 'Wine is a mocker, strong drink a brawler; and whoever is led astray by it is not wise.' Note that this does not entail teetotalism; Jesus himself drank wine, which is also part of the sacrament.

9. See for instance, D. C. Lau, trans., *The Analects* (Hong Kong: Chinese University Press, 1992), 3.7, 10.8, 9.16.

10. See also D. C. Lau, trans., *Mencius* (Hong Kong: Chinese University Press, 2003), 4B.20, 7B.34.

11. See also Chapters 53 and 63.

12. See Chapters 19 'Mastering Life' 達生, 32 'Lie Yukou' 列禦寇 and 20 'Mountain Tree' 山木.

13. The use of wine to lure back dead spirits in 'Zhao hun' 招魂 and 'Da zhao' 大招 is derived from its sacrificial use; see 'Donghuang Taiyi' 東皇太一 and 'Dong jun' 東君 in the *Nine Songs* 九歌, in Jin Kaicheng, Dong Hongli and Gao Luming 金開誠、董洪利、高路明, *Qu Yuan ji jiaozhu* 屈原集校注 (Beijing: Zhonghua shuju, 1996), 1.187–95, 255–65.

14. The authorship of 'Yu fu' is a matter of dispute, but the force of the poet's voice remains unaffected. Qu Yuan does seem to stay sober, for instead of mentioning wine in 'Li Sao' 離騷, he prefers to be loaded with fragrant plants.

15. See, for instance, the late Han 'Three Poems to Su Wu' 與蘇武三首 attributed to Li Ling 李陵 (?–74 BCE): 'I only have this full jar of wine, / To seal a close bond with you.' 獨有盈觴酒，與子結綢繆.

16. For a discussion of the *carpe diem* theme in the Han *yuefu* poems, see Anne Birrell, *Popular Songs and Ballads of Han China* (Honolulu: University of Hawaii Press, 1993), 78–93. The *carpe diem* theme has been expressed before in the *Shi jing*, in Ode 115 'On the Mountain is Thorn-Elm' 山有樞; see also Ode 217 'Pointed is the Cap' 頍弁.

17. For some other examples, see 'Xianghe geci, shanzai xing (guci)' 相和歌辭・善哉行 (古辭), in *Yuefu shiji* 樂府詩集, ed. Guo Maoqian 郭茂倩 (Beijing: Zhonghua shuju, 1979), 2.535–6; 'Gushi shijiu shou', No. 3 古詩十九首其三; Ruan Yu's 阮瑀 'Qi ai shi' 七哀詩, *Jian'an qizi ji* 建安七子集, ed. Yu Shaochu 俞紹初 (Beijing: Zhonghua shuju, 2005), 160.

18. See Sima Qian 司馬遷, *Shi ji* 史記 (Beijing: Zhonghua shuju, 1982), 2.389 ('Annals of Gaozu' 高祖本紀). Similar effects of wine can be seen in his portrait of the assassin Jing Ke 荊軻; ibid., 8.2526–38, esp. 2528 ('Biographies of Assassins' 刺客列傳).

19. Ban Gu, *Han shu* 漢書 (Beijing: Zhonghua shuju, 1962), 4.1182 ('Treatise on Food and Commodities' 食貨志).

20. 'Congjun shi wu shou', No. 1 從軍詩五首其一, in *Jian'an qizi ji*, 90.

21. For instance, Ruan Ji regularly stays drunk to protect himself and to avoid expressing political opinions; see his biography in Fang Xuanling 房玄齡 et al., *Jin shu* 晉書 (Beijing: Zhonghua shuju, 1974), 5.1360.

22. See Cao Zhi's 曹植 'Jiu fu' 酒賦, in *Cao Zhi ji jiaozhu* 曹植集校注, ed. Zhao Youwen 趙幼文 (Beijing: Renmin wenxue chubanshe, 1998), 125. Note that Cao Zhi still warns against over-indulgence in drinking, as does Wang Can in a *fu* piece of the same title; in *Jian'an qizi ji*, 107.

23. See Xiao Tong 蕭統, ed., *Wen xuan* 文選 (Shanghai: Shanghai guji chubanshe, 1986), 5.2098–100.

24. See biography in *Jin shu*, 8.2384. Another Jin writer Bi Zhuo 畢卓, who often neglected his official duties because of drinking, says that 'holding a wine cup in my right hand and a crab's pincer in my left will suffice for spending the rest of my life'; in *Jin shu*, 5.1381.

25. One critic has suggested that over forty per cent of Tao's poems are related to wine; see Lu Kebing 魯克兵, *Zhizhuo yu xiaoyao—Tao Yuanming yinjiu shiwen de shenmei guanzhao* 執著與逍遙——陶淵明飲酒詩文的審美觀照 (Hefei: Anhui daxue chubanshe, 2009), 82. However, the first editor of Tao's works, Xiao Tong, states in his 'Preface to Tao Yuanming's Collected Works' 陶淵明集序 that ultimately, the poet's 'spirit lies not in wine'.

26. See Tao's biographical composition on Meng Jia: 'Jin gu zhengxi dajiangjun zhangshi Meng Fujun zhuan' 晉故征西大將軍長史孟府君傳, in *Tao Yuanming ji jiaojian* 陶淵明集校箋, ed. Gong Bin 龔斌 (Shanghai: Shanghai guji chubanshe, 1996), 412.

27. Routinely translated as 'drunk' in English due to the lack of a semantic equivalent, the word 醉 can range from a mildly tipsy state to a total loss of consciousness.

28. Legendary ancient sage-rulers.

29. 'Zashi shier shou', No. 5 雜詩十二首其五 and 'Gan shi buyu fu' 感士不遇賦; in Gong (1996), 296, 365.

30. William Cowper, 'The Task', Book IV 'The Winter Evening', ll. 282, 291, 297.

31. William Wordsworth, 'Lines Composed a Few Miles above Tintern Abbey', ll. 47–9.

32. For instance, Bao Zhao writes of wine as a 'sealant' of friendship in 'Dai zhi chao fei' 代雉朝飛, and wine also features in occasional and trivial contexts in the palace-style poetry of the Southern Dynasties.

33. See Zuo's 'Yongshi ba shou', No. 6 詠史八首其六, in *Xian-Qin Han Wei Jin Nanbeichao shi* 先秦漢魏晉南北朝詩, ed. Lu Qinli 逯欽立 (Beijing: Zhonghua shuju, 1998), 1.733, and Tao's 'Yong Jing Ke' 詠荊軻, in *Tao Yuanming ji jiaojian*, 330–1.

34. See, for instance, her 'Pusa man' (feng rou ri bo chun you zao) 菩薩蠻 · 風柔日薄春猶早, in *Quan Song ci* 全宋詞 (Beijing: Zhonghua shuju, 1995), 2.927 and 'Su zhongqing' (ye lai chen zui xie zhuang chi) 訴衷情 · 夜來沈醉卸妝遲, in *Quan Song ci*, 2.930.

35. See Li Bai's 'Jinling yu zhuxian song Quan Shiyi Zhaoyi xu' 金陵與諸賢送權十一昭夷序, in *Quan Tang wen* 全唐文, ed. Dong Gao 董誥 et al. (Shanghai: Shanghai guji chubanshe, 1990), 2.1566, where he calls himself an 'elderly banished immortal'.

36. Of course, as seen in Wang Changling's 王昌齡 'frontier poems' (e.g. 'Congjun xing qi shou' 從軍行七首, in *Quan Tang shi* 全唐詩 [Beijing: Zhonghua shuju, 1960], 4.1443) show, wine is not a necessary ingredient in heroic poetry.

37. See also Wang Wei's 'Wangchuan xianju zeng Pei xiucai di' 輞川閒居贈裴秀才迪, in *Quan Tang shi* , 4.1266.

38. See respectively 'Qiupu Songs', No. 15 秋浦歌其十五 and 'Mengyou Tianmu yin liubie' 夢遊天姥吟留別; in *Quan Tang shi*, 5.1723 and 5.1779.

39. For another classic example, see 'Duzuo Jingtingshan' 獨坐敬亭山, in *Quan Tang shi*, 6.1858.

40. Examples abound, e.g. 'Zi qian' 自遣, 'Kezhong xing' 客中行 and 'Xinglu nan' 行路難; in *Quan Tang shi*, 6.1858, 6.1842, and 6.1684.

41. Examples are too numerous to reckon in detail, but see for instance Du Fu's 'Deng gao' 登高, in *Quan Tang shi*, 7.2467; Li Shangyin's 李商隱 'Fengyu' 風雨, in *Quan Tang shi*, 16.6155; Du Fu's 'Ke zhi' 客至, in *Quan Tang shi*, 7.2438; Bai Juyi's 白居易 'Wen Liu Shijiu' 問劉十九, in *Quan Tang shi*, 13.4900; Sikong Shu's 司空曙 'Yunyangguan yu Han Shen subie' 雲陽館與韓紳宿別, in *Quan Tang shi*, 9.3317; Li Bai's 'Kezhong xing'; Dai Shulun's 戴叔倫 'Jiangxiang guren ouji keshe' 江鄉故人偶集客舍, in *Quan Tang shi* , 9.3073; Li Bai's 'Zeng Meng Haoran'孟浩然, in *Quan Tang shi*, 5.1731; Li Bai's 'Zi qian' respectively. Some poets also mention wine in the context of pleasure in entertainment quarters, e.g. Li Bai's 'Shaonian xing' 少年行, in *Quan Tang shi*, 5.1708; and Du Mu's 杜牧 'Qian huai' 遣懷, in *Quan Tang shi*, 16.5998.

42. See Du Fu's 'Zi Jing fu Fengxianxian yonghuai wubai zi' 自京赴奉先縣詠懷五百字, in *Quan Tang shi*, 7.2265–6; and Du Mu's 'Zengbie er shou', No. 2 贈別二首（其二）, in *Quan Tang shi*, 16.5998.

43. Respectively Ouyang Xiu's 'Ti Chuzhou Zuiwengting' 題滁州醉翁亭, in *Ouyang Xiu shiwen ji jiaojian, waiji* 歐陽修詩文集校箋・外集, ed. Hong Benjian 洪本建 (Shanghai: Shanghai guji chubanshe, 2009), 3.1350; Su Shi's 'Shieryue ershibari, meng'en zeshou jianxiao shuibu yuanwailang Huangzhou tuanlian fushi, fuyong qianyun er shou', No. 1 十二月二十八日，蒙恩責授檢校水部員外郎黃州團練副使，復用前韻二首（其一）, in *Su Shi shiji* 蘇軾詩集, ed. Wang Wen'gao 王文誥 (Beijing: Zhonghua shuju, 1982), 3.1005; Lu You's 'Zuihou caoshu geshi xizuo' 醉後草書歌詩戲作, in *Lu You ji: Jiannan shigao* 陸游集・劍南詩稿 (Beijing: Zhonghua shuju, 1976), 1.120; and He Jingming's 'Wu Wei Jiangshantu ge' 吳偉江山圖歌, in *Ming shi zong* 明詩綜, ed. Zhu Yizun 朱彝尊 (Beijing: Zhonghua shuju, 2007), 3.1528.

44. The three excerpts are taken from poems entitled 'Bie sui' 別歲, 'Zhengyue ershiri yu Pan, Guo ersheng chujiao xunchun, huji qunian shiri tongzhi Nüwangcheng zuoshi, nai he qianyun' 正月二十日與潘、郭二生出郊尋春，忽記去年是日同至女王城作詩，乃和前韻, and 'Xi xin qiao' 西新橋; in *Su Shi shiji*, 1.160, 4.1105 and 7.2199 respectively. For some other examples by Song poets, see also Zhang Lei's 張耒 'Tianjia san shou' 田家三首, in *Quan Song shi* 全宋詩 (Beijing: Peking University Press, 1991–1998),

20.13124; Huihong's 惠洪 'Chuxia si shou', No. 2 初夏四首（其二）, in *Quan Song shi*, 23.15306; and Lu You's 'You Shanxi cun' 遊山西村, in *Lu You ji*, 1.29, etc.

45. For some poetic examples of social criticism through wine imagery, see, for instance, Mei Yaochen's 梅堯臣 'Cunhao' 村豪, in *Mei Yaochen shixuan* 梅堯臣詩選, ed. Zhu Dongrun 朱東潤 (Beijing: Renmin wenxue chubanshe, 1980), 122; Zhang Shunmin's 張舜民 'Da mai' 打麥, in *Quan Song shi*, 14.9670–1; and Liu Kezhuang's 劉克莊 'Kuhan xing' 苦寒行, in *Quan Song shi*, 58.36256–7.

46. Some traditional critics have considered 'farmers' language' 田家語 unworthy of poetic writing, an attitude that stubbornly lingered as late as the Qing, as criticism of Tao Qian's 'vulgarisms' attest. See Mao Xianshu's and Wang Fuzhi's remarks collected in *Tao Yuanming yanjiu ziliao huibian* 陶淵明研究資料彙編, eds. Department of Chinese, Peking University and Beijing Normal University (Beijing: Zhonghua shuju, 1962), 1.178–9, 1.184. Since Song times, however, more and more poets have written on farming subjects, often with poem titles including the term 田家.

47. See, for instance, Li Yu's 李煜 'Wu ye ti: linhua xieliao chunhong' 烏夜啼 · 林花謝了春紅, in *Quan Tang Wudai ci* 全唐五代詞 (Beijing: Zhonghua shuju, 1999), 1.750; Feng Yansi's 馮延巳 'Que ta zhi: shuidao xianqing paozhi jiu' 鵲踏枝 · 誰道閑情拋擲久, in *Quan Tang Wudai ci* , 1.650; Yan Jidao's 晏幾道 'Lin jiang xian: menghou loutai gaosuo' 臨江仙 · 夢後樓臺高鎖, in *Quan Song ci*, 1.221; and Li Qingzhao's 李清照 'Shengsheng man' (xunxun mimi) 聲聲慢 · 尋尋覓覓, in *Quan Song ci*, 2.932.

48. See her poems 'Dui jiu' 對酒 and 'Huanghai zhouzhong Riren suoju bingjian Ri'E zhanzheng ditu' 黃海舟中日人索句並見日俄戰爭地圖, in *Qiu Jin shiwen xuan* 秋瑾詩文選, ed. Guo Yanli 郭延禮 (Beijing: Renmin wenxue chubanshe, 1982), 83–5.

49. In terms of line length, the traditional tune pattern for 'Yu gezi' 漁歌子 is 7–7–3–3–7 (27 characters); here Su Shi's new pattern is 3–3–6–7–6 (25 characters).

50. Fang, in *Jin shu*, 5.1362, 'Biography of Ruan Ji' 阮籍傳.

51. See respectively 'Jianglou chuidi yinjiu dazui zhong zuo' 江樓吹笛飲酒大醉中作 and 'Dui jiu' 對酒; in *Lu You ji*, 1.245 and 3.1436.

52. Liu Yangzhong notes that Tang wine cups are smaller than those in previous times, and the term 'shao jiu' 燒酒 (distilled wine) appeared in the Tang; in *Shi yu jiu*, 29.

Chapter 5

1. Jiaoran 皎然, 'Jiuri yu Lu chushi Yu yincha' 九日與陸處士羽飲茶, *Quan Tang shi* 全唐詩 (Beijing: Zhonghua shuju, 1960), 817.9211.

2. Jiaoran, 'Qiao Cui Shi shi jun' 誚崔石使君, *Quan Tang shi*, 821.9260.

3. Fang Xuanling 房玄齡 et al., *Jin shu* 晉書 (Beijing: Zhonghua shuju, 1974), 49.1381.

4. Lu Yu's *Classic of Tea* identifies him as a Han dynasty immortal, see *Chajing* 茶經 in *Zhongguo lidai chashu huibian* 中國歷代茶書匯編, ed. Zheng Peikai 鄭培凱 and Zhu Zizhen 朱自振 (Hong Kong: Commercial Press, 2007), vol. 1.

5. Li Deyu 李德裕, 'Guren ji cha' 故人寄茶, *Quan Tang shi*, 475.5394. This poem has a second attribution, to the court official Cao Ye 曹鄴, see *Quan Tang shi*, 592.6872. For the discussion here, it matters little which attribution is correct, since it is clear that the author, whoever he was, was residing in the Tang capital.

6. Adopting the textual variant *chen* 沉 in place of *liu* 流 because it makes a better parallel with the matching line.

7. Liu Yuxi 劉禹錫, 'Xishan lanruo shicha ge' 西山蘭若試茶歌, *Quan Tang shi*, 356.4000.

8. Lu Tong 盧仝, 'Zoubi xie Meng jianyi ji xincha' 走筆謝孟諫議寄新茶, *Quan Tang shi*, 388.4379.

9. Paul J. Smith, *Taxing Heaven's Storehouse: Horses, Bureaucrats, and the Destruction of the Sichuan Tea Industry 1074–1224* (Cambridge, MA: Council on East Asian Studies, 1991).

10. Ibid., 195–6.

11. Mei Yaochen 梅堯臣, 'Wen jinshi fancha' 聞進士販茶, *Mei Yaochen ji biannian jiaozhu* 梅堯臣集編年校注, ed. Zhu Dongrun 朱東潤 (Shanghai: Shanghai guji chubanshe, 1980), 25.790; cf. Jonathan Chaves, *Mei Yao-ch'en and the Development of Early Sung Poetry* (New York: Columbia University Press, 1976), 172–4, where the poem is also translated and discussed.

12. Smith, *Taxing Heaven's Storehouse*, 53–6.

13. Huang Tingjian 黃庭堅, 'Shangjing cha song Zizhan' 雙井茶送自瞻, *Shan'gu shiji zhu* 山谷詩集注, in *Huang Tingjian shiji zhu* 黃庭堅詩集注, ed. Liu Shangrong 劉尚榮 (Beijing: Zhonghua shuju, 2003), 6.219.

14. Huang Tingjian, 'Yi Shuangjing cha song Kong Changfu' 以雙井茶送孔常父, *Shan'gu shiji zhu*, 6.223.

15. Su Shi 蘇軾, 'You zhu foshe yiri yin yanjiu qizhan xishu Qinshi bi' 遊諸佛舍一日飲釀酒七盞戲書勤師壁, in *Su Shi shiji* 蘇軾詩集, ed. Kong Fanli 孔凡禮 (Beijing: Zhonghua shuju, 1982), 10.508–9.

16. Cao Pi 曹丕, 'Zhe yangliu xing' 折楊柳行, *Weishi* 魏詩 4.393–94, in *Xian Qin Han Wei Jin Nanbei chao shi* 先秦漢魏晉南北朝詩, ed. Lu Qinli 逯欽立 (Beijing: Zhonghua shuju, 1983); cf. *Song shu* 宋書, 21.616.

17. The alternate title is found in the collation notes, *Su Shi shiji*, 10.519, n. 71. 'Sunzhi' is presumably another name for Master Qin in the other version of the title. The monk is unidentified.

18. Mei Yaochen, 'Ciyun he' 次韻和, *Mei Yaochen ji biannian jiaozhu*, 28.1008.

19. Counting the number of surviving texts reproduced in the very useful compilation, Zheng and Zhu, ed., *Zhongguo lidai chashu huibian*.

20. *Daguan chalun* 大觀茶論, in *Zhongguo lidai chashu huibian*, 1.103–10.

21. Cai Xiang 蔡襄, 'Diancha' 點茶, *Chalu* 茶錄, in *Zhongguo lidai chashu huibian*, 1.78; cf. p. xiv, where this passage is discussed.

22. Su Shi, 'He Qian Andao jihui Jian cha' 和錢安道寄惠建茶, *Su Shi shiji*, 11.529–31.

23. Ban Gu 班固, *Han shu* 漢書 (Beijing: Zhonghua shuju, 1962), 20.2317 and 47.3247.

24. Huang Ru 黃儒, *Pincha yaolu* 品茶要錄, in *Zhongguo lidai chashu huibian*, 1. 92–3, n. 20.

25. Ban Gu, *Han shu*, 81.3351 and 3366.

26. Ouyang Xiu 歐陽修, *Guitian lu* 歸田錄, in *Ouyang Xiu quanji* 歐陽修全集, ed. Li Yian 李逸安 (Beijing: Zhonghua shuju, 2001), 5.2.1931.

27. Ouyang Xiu, *Guitian lu*, 1.1915.

28. Peng Jiuwan 朋九萬, attrib., *Wutai shian* 烏臺詩案 (Hanhai 函海 ed.), 40a–41a.

29. For Mei Yaochen's two poems, written matching the rhymes of Ouyang's, see 'Ciyun he' and 'Ciyun hezaibai' 次韻和再拜, *Mei Yaochen ji biannian jiaozhu*, 4.1008–10. These poems exchanged by Ouyang and Mei are discussed and partially translated in Colin S. C. Hawes, *The Social Circulation of Poetry in the Mid-Northern Song* (Albany: State University of New York Press, 2005), 146–50.

30. Ouyang Xiu, 'Ciyun zaizuo' 次韵再作, *Jushi ji* 居士集, *Ouyang Xiu quanji*, 1.7.115.

31. Sima Qian 司馬遷, *Shiji* 史記 (Beijing: Zhonghua shuju, 1959) 92.2611. Ouyang may also be thinking of another *Shi ji* passage, in which Han Gaozu is holding seals of office in his hand, 'fingering them' (*nongzhi* 弄之) as he tried to decide who to appoint censor-in-chief, *Shi ji*, 96.2679.

32. Mei Yaochen, 'Ciyun hezaibai', *Mei Yaochen ji biannian jiaozhu*, 28.1010.

Chapter 6

1. An early version of this paper was presented at the New Zealand International Conference on Asian Studies (12th Conference) held at Massey University, Palmerston North, 26–29 November 1997 and was subsequently included in a series of working papers published by the Asian Studies Institute of Victoria University of Wellington. I am grateful to the Director of the Institute, Stephen Epstein, for his permission to publish this revised version of the paper. More recently, I am most grateful for the enlivening conversations I have had about this paper with the food historian Allen Grieco. Circumstances have prevented me from responding, immediately, to all the comparative questions he raised after favouring me with a close reading of the paper.

2. 'For kings, the people are Heaven, for the people, food is Heaven', opined Li Yiji 酈食其 (d. 203 BCE), the self-styled 'Tippler of Gaoyang' (*Gaoyang jiutu* 高陽酒徒), in the course of advising Liu Bang 劉邦 (247–195 BCE), the future founding emperor of the Han dynasty (206 BCE–220 CE), for which, see Ban Gu 班固, 'Li Lu Zhu Liu Shusun zhuan' 酈陸朱劉叔孫傳, *Han shu* 漢書 (Hong Kong: Zhonghua shuju, 1970), 5.2108. Li Yiji was later ordered boiled (*peng* 烹) to death by Tian Guang 田廣, the King of Qi, under suspicion of betraying him.

3. *Langhuan wenji* 琅嬛文集, ed. Yun Gao 雲告 (Changsha: Yuelu shushe, 1985), 201. Dongpo is the great Song dynasty scholar and poet Su Shi 蘇軾 (1036–1101), a man who, as we see below, Zhang Dai believed was one of the few to have preserved ancient knowledge about the art of eating; the father of the brothers Boyi 伯夷 and Shuqi 叔齊, those two ancient paragons of dynastic loyalty who, by legend, chose to starve themselves to death rather than eat the grain of the Zhou dynasty (c. 1027–256 BCE) once it had replaced their own Shang dynasty (c. 1600–1028 BCE), was Lord of Solitary Bamboo (*Guzhujun* 孤竹君).

4. Jack Goody, *Cooking, Cuisine and Class: A Study in Comparative Sociology* (Cambridge: Cambridge University Press, 1982), 108.

5. For short biographies of Zhang Dai in English, see A. W. Hummel, ed., *Eminent Chinese of the Ch'ing Period 1644–1912* (Washington: Government Printing Office, 1943), 53–4; and W. H. Nienhauser, ed., *The Indiana Companion to Traditional Chinese Literature* (Bloomington: Indiana University Press, 1986–98), 1.220–1. In Chinese, see Xia Xianchun 夏咸淳, *Mingmo qicai—Zhang Dai lun* 明末奇才——張岱論 (Shanghai:

Shehui kexueyuan, 1989); Hu Yimin 胡益民, *Zhang Dai pingzhuan* 張岱評傳 (Nanjing: Nanjing University Press, 2002); and Hu Yimin, *Zhang Dai yanjiu* 張岱研究 (Hefei: Anhui jiaoyu chubanshe, 2002). Philip A. Kafalas, 'Weighty Matters, Weightless Form: Politics and the Late Ming Xiaopin Writer', *Ming Studies*, 39 (1998), 50–85, provides a suggestive discussion of Zhang Dai's *Taoan mengyi* 陶庵夢憶. In his 'Presidential Address: Cliffhanger Days: A Chinese Family in the Seventeenth Century', *The American Historical Review*, 110 (2005), 1–10, Jonathan Spence presents a characteristically insightful reading of Zhang Dai's family biographies. Both Kafalas and Spence have subsequently published full-length treatments of Zhang Dai: Philip A. Kafalas, *In Limpid Dreams: Nostalgia and Zhang Dai's Reminiscences of the Ming* (Norwalk: EastBridge, 2007), and Jonathan D. Spence, *Return to Dragon Mountain: Memories of a Late Ming Man* (New York: Viking, 2007).

6. The particular vicissitudes of Zhang Dai's age—the cataclysmic collapse of the Ming dynasty (1368–1644) and its replacement by the Qing (1644–1911)—meant that only one of his books was published in his lifetime, this being his *Gujin yilie zhuan* 古今義烈傳, published (according to its various prefaces) sometime between 1628–32; for a note on this book and its publication history, see Hu Yimin, *Zhang Dai yanjiu*, 206–7.

7. In particular, *Sishu yu* 四書遇 (Hangzhou: Zhejiang guji chubanshe, 1985); *Kuaiyuan daogu* 快園道古 (Hangzhou: Zhejiang guji chubanshe, 1986); *Ye hang chuan* 夜航船 (Hangzhou: Zhejiang guji chubanshe, 1987); and most importantly, Zhang Dai's magisterial history of the Ming dynasty, *Shigui shu* 石匱書, in *Xuxiu siku quanshu* 續修四庫全書 (Shanghai: Shanghai guji chubanshe, 1997), vols. 318, 319, and 320.

8. The preface is undated; judging from its tone, however, I believe that the work to which it is attached was compiled before the fall of the dynasty in 1644, and the consequent and drastic change in Zhang Dai's circumstances. The prefaces to two other books by Zhang Dai particularly germane to the concerns of this paper, his *Cha shi* 茶史 and his *Taoan zhouhoufang* 陶庵肘後方, have also been preserved in this collection, the manuscripts of the books themselves, it seems, having been lost to us forever.

9. *Cooking, Cuisine and Class: A Study in Comparative Sociology*, 105.

10. Ibid., 191–2. For an excellent recent treatment of the last of these characteristics in the case of China, see Vivienne Lo, 'Pleasure, Prohibition, and Pain: Food and Medicine in Traditional China', in *Of Tripod and Palate: Food, Politics, and Religion in Traditional China*, ed. Roel Sterckx (New York: Palgrave Macmillan, 2005), 163–85.

11. *Food in Chinese Culture: Anthropological and Historical Perspectives* (New Haven & London: Yale University Press, 1977), 11.

12. Xia Xianchun, ed., *Zhang Dai shiwen ji* 張岱詩文集 (Shanghai: Shanghai guji chubanshe, 1991), 73.

13. 'Zhang Donggu haojiu' 張東谷好酒, in Xia Xianchun and Cheng Weirong 程維榮, eds., *Taoan mengyi: Xihu mengxun* 陶庵夢憶：西湖夢尋 (Shanghai: Shanghai guji chubanshe, 2001), 128–9. Zhang Dai's family were of course also Shaoxingers.

14. Zhang Dai's 'Author's Preface' (Zixu 自序) is dated 1646. To a considerable extent, his memories of the culinary indulgences of his youth must have been coloured by his experience of the extreme famine that struck his home district in 1641 and his involvement in local efforts of food relief. For a recent discussion focused particularly

on the local charitable activities of Zhang Dai's 'Friend in Landscape' (*shanshui zhiji* 山水知己*), Qi Biaojia 祁彪佳 (1602–45), see Joanna Handlin Smith, *The Art of Doing Good: Charity in Late Ming China* (Berkeley, Los Angeles & London: University of California Press, 2009).

15. According to the earliest sources, the 'Five Flavours' (*wuwei* 五味) were: the sour (*suan* 酸), the bitter (*ku* 苦), the pungent (*xin* 辛), the salty (*xian* 鹹), and the sweet (*gan* 甘).

16. The specific definition of what constituted this particular category of luxury food (*bazhen* 八珍) seems to have differed over time. One early Ming source, Tao Zongyi's 陶宗儀 (1316–1403) *Chuogeng lu* 輟耕錄, published around 1366, gives: (1) *tihu* 醍醐 (a type of liquor skimmed off boiled butter); (2) *zhukeng* 麞吭 (said to be either a wine made of horse milk of perhaps of a roebuck); (3) *yetuoti* 野駝蹄 (hoof of a wild camel); (4) *luchun* 鹿唇 (lips of a deer); (5) *tuorumi* 駝乳麋 (camel curds); (6) *tianezhi* 天鵝炙 (roasted crane); (7) *ziyujiang* 紫玉漿 (pulp of purple jade—said to be grape wine from the western regions); and (8) *xuanyujiang* 玄玉漿 (pulp of wondrous jade—said to be horse curds). Allen Grieco makes the suggestion that *zhukeng* here (number two above) is likely to be a reference to *koumiss*.

17. In another item in *Dream Memories of Taoan*, entitled 'The Sweet Tangerines of the Chen Clan of Fanjiang' (Fanjiang Chenshi ju 樊江陳氏橘), Zhang Dai writes: 'The Chen clan of Fanjiang had established an orchard (*guoyuan* 果園) on a patch of land they had cleared, enclosing it with a fence of hardy orange tree. The staple grown here is the betel vine, the leaves of which are made into paste; the glutinous rice is used to ferment wine. This wine, fragrant in the extreme and a dull amber colour, has won the praises of all serious drinkers. The fruit and the melons produced by the orchard are steeped in honey to make comfit. More than a hundred Xie's tangerine trees have been planted here, the fruit of which is not picked when still green or when still sour. Only once the fruit has turned orange on the trees after the first falls of frost are they picked, and even then this is done so by cutting them off the trees with their stems still attached. When such a procedure is followed, the skins of the tangerines prove thick and easy to peel, their colour is deep orange, their flesh firm, their segments easily divided, their taste sweet and fresh. The tangerines produced at Fourth Gate, Tao's Embankment, Daoxu, even Tangxi, cannot stand comparison with them. Each year I would insist on visiting this orchard, even if it was late in the season and the tangerines were expensive and few to be had. Once I had made my purchase, I would store the tangerines in earthenware vats upon a mat of rice straw from Zhancheng or dried pine needles. Every ten days or so, whenever the straw had begun to moulder, I would have it replaced, and in this way the tangerines could be made to last until towards the end of the third month, as sweet and crisp as when first picked. The Master of Hardy Orange Township earns himself a hundred bolts of silk a year from his hundred or so tangerine trees, these trees truly living up to their sobriquet 'Wooden Slaves' (*munu* 木奴)' (*Taoan mengxun: Xihu mengxun*, 82–3). In his annotations to this item, Xia Xianchun notes that Xie's tangerines were produced by the descendants of Xie Xuan 謝玄 in their family orchard.

18. On Zhang Dai's involvement in the development of this type of tea, see 'Orchid Snow Tea' (Lanxue cha 蘭雪茶), *Taoan mengyi: Xihu mengxun*, 44–5.

19. 'Xiehui' 蟹會, *Taoan mengyi: Xihu mengxun*, 132–3. For an alternative translation of this item (under the title 'Crab Parties'), see Yang Ye, trans., *Vignettes from the Late Ming: A Hsiao-p'in Anthology* (Seattle & London: University of Washington Press, 1999), 96–7. In her *How to Cook and Eat in Chinese* (Penguin, 1965), Buwei Yang Chao, the wife of the celebrated linguist Yuen Ren Chao (1892–1982), includes the following note in the 'Special Eating Parties' section of her book: 'Crab Parties are for many the favourite form of eating parties. Though often called Plain Boiled Crabs, they are really steamed rather than boiled. Each guest is served a dish of Chinkiang vinegar with minced ginger, with optional soy sauce. The steamed crabs are served whole and each guest eats them in great detail one by one, accompanied by wine or spirit. Six large crabs eaten in about sixty minutes form an average serving. Some restaurants give special tools, nutcrackers and hammers, etc., for eating crabs, but your teeth and fingers are the chief means of eating. The satisfaction you can get out of a meal of crabs depends on how messy you are willing to get. You really must make a mess of it to make a meal of it. According to old traditional Chinese medicine, the crab is one of those things which are supposed to have a "cold nature" and has to be supplemented by a cup of hot drink of brown sugar and ginger. Whatever the truth is, it certainly gives a nice contrasting taste after the crabs. Another popular theory is that crabs will crawl in your stomach, so that the more crabs you eat the hungrier you get. It is therefore customary to serve some light lunch or refreshments or even a full meal immediately after a crab party. Because no fat or starchy food is eaten with the crabs, the stomach with crabs in it does usually feel like having something more meaty to stay it. So a crab party usually turns out to be a sort of overgrown hors-d'œuvre (260–1).' This neglected treasure of a book, first published by Faber and Faber in 1956 and which carries a foreword by Hu Shi and a preface by Pearl Buck, must have been one of the earliest attempts to introduce to American and British homes both the practicalities and the splendours of Chinese cuisine. Buwei Yang Chao's husband's contribution to the book is a hilarious recipe for 'Stirred Eggs': 'To test whether the cooking has been done properly observe the person served. If he utters a voiced bilabial nasal consonant with a slow falling intonation, it is good (168).'

20. For a highly readable treatment of these issues, see Timothy Brook, *The Confusions of Pleasure: Commerce and Culture in Ming China* (Berkeley, Los Angeles & London: University of California Press, 1999).

21. For this, see Frederick Mote, 'Yüan and Ming', in Kwang-chih Chang, ed., *Food in Chinese Culture: Anthropological and Historical Perspectives*, 247. Mote argues that this period saw the 'second phase of an agricultural revolution' (198) that had started during the Song dynasty and which was brought about, in part, by the introduction of a range of new crops, including maize, sweet potatoes, peanuts and tobacco. With the introduction of tobacco came also the habit of opium smoking, and not surprisingly Zhang Dai's family seem quick to have picked up the habit, Zhang Dai's grandfather Zhang Rulin 張汝霖 (d. 1625) being apparently the first Chinese person to comment in writing that opium could be smoked, for which see Jonathan Spence, *Chinese*

Roundabout: Essays in History and Culture (New York: W. W. Norton, 1992), 231. On sumptuary laws, see Craig Clunas, 'Regulation of Consumption and the Institution of Correct Morality by the Ming State', in *Norms and the State in China*, ed. E. Zürcher (Leiden: E. J. Brill, 1993), 39–49. Other areas of life during the late-Ming period seem equally prone to such lavish and ostentatious display, and the inevitable countervailing discourse. Sarah Dauncey, in her 'Sartorial Modesty and Genteel Ideals in the Late Ming' (in Daria Berg and Chloë Starr, eds., *The Quest for Gentility in China: Negotiations Beyond Gender and Class* [London & New York: Routledge, 2007], 134–54), examines the extent to which contemporary men-of-letters became concerned at what they saw as the increasingly opulent clothing being worn by women. Xia Xianchun, in his *Wan Ming shifeng yu wenxue* 晚明士風與文學 (Beijing: Zhongguo shehuikexue chubanshe, 1994), 62, cites the Shaoxinger Tao Shiling 陶奭齡 (1571–1640) to the effect that: 'When I was a young man there were certainly no gardens to be found in Shaoxing, such things having only become numerous in recent years' and Qi Biaojia as declaring that the construction of gardens in the district began with Zhang Dai's great-great-grandfather Zheng Tianfu. For an important analysis of this garden 'mania', see Joanna F. Handlin Smith, 'Gardens in Ch'i Piao-chia's Social World: Wealth and Values in Late-Ming Kiangnan', *The Journal of Asian Studies*, 51 (1992), 55–81.

22. Interestingly enough, such anxieties about artificiality were in evidence during the Song dynasty as well, as shown by Stephen West, 'Playing with Food: Performance, Food, and the Aesthetics of Artificiality in the Sung and Yuan', *Harvard Journal of Asiatic Studies*, 57 (1997), 67–106.

23. Craig Clunas, *Superfluous Things: Material Culture and Social Status in Early Modern China* (Cambridge: Polity Press, 1991), 9.

24. Ibid., 8.

25. As both Clunas and Timothy Brook have pointed out, such handbooks also served the social and cultural purposes of precisely those they were intended to stigmatize. As Brook puts it: 'The texts of connoisseurship available on the book market in the late Ming, ironically perhaps, served both sides of the cultural barrier between gentry and merchants. They set what highly educated gentlemen of the age felt were the appropriate standards by which luxury goods should be consumed. But they also commoditized the knowledge that was needed to participate in this rarefied realm of cultural exchange', for which, see his 'Communications and Commerce', in Denis Twitchett and Frederick W. Mote, eds., *The Cambridge History of China: Volume 8: The Ming Dynasty, 1368–1644, Part 2* (Cambridge: Cambridge University Press, 1998), 706.

26. According to legend, Shennong was the second emperor of pre-dynastic China and was attributed with the invention of the first plough, the practice of animal husbandry and the discovery of the various usages of medicinal herbs.

27. Simon Leys, trans., *The Analects of Confucius* (New York: W. W. Norton, 1997), 46.

28. He Zeng (199–278), an extravagant man whose kitchens, according to his biography in the *Jin shu* 晉書, produced cuisine of a quality that exceeded even that of the palace.

29. A man of the Tang dynasty who served as an official during the reign of the Empress Wu Zetian 武則天 (r. 649–83).

30. A member of the Hanlin Academy, also during the Tang, and a skilled cook.

31. An official in the Kingdom of Qi during the Southern Dynasties whose family was renowned for their recipes. It is said that on one occasion the emperor asked him for some recipes but Yu Cong refused the request.

32. For a translation of this prose-poem, see Cyril Drummond le Gros Clark, trans., *The Prose-Poetry of Su Tung-p'o* (New York: Paragon Book Reprint Corp., 1964), 205–11.

33. In his *Dream Memories of Taoan*, Zhang Dai provides the following portrait of this man: 'The storied houseboats that now ply West Lake were in fact the invention of the Surveillance Vice Commissioner of the Education Intendant Circuit Bao Yingdeng. They come in three sizes; in the largest, one can lay out a banquet, accompanied by singing boys; the middle sized ones are sufficiently large to transport one's books and paintings; in the smallest, there is just room enough to hide away a beautiful young maiden or two to keep one company. Bao Yingdeng's singing girls were beyond comparison with ordinary maids-in-waiting, and, in imitation of the practice of Shi Chong 石崇 and Song Qi 宋祁 of old, he frequently ordered them to appear before his guests. Painted of face, they would amble in like ponies with mincing step as sauntering slowly, lingering leisurely, they threaded their way through the willows, all to bring joy and laughter to their audience. Standing in front of the bright railings and windows decorated with silken filigree, they would stretch out their song, play their flutes and pluck their zithers, the music they made akin to the warbling of the golden oriole. As guests arrived, the singing boys would begin the opera, dancing in rows, singing as they kept time with their drums. Their skills quite excelled those of others. When the mood took him, Bao Yingdeng would take his performers touring, sometimes not returning home for ten days or more, and attracting huge crowds, all of whom would ask where the troupe was next to perform. Bao's South Garden was sited beneath Thunder Peak Pagoda, his North Garden below Flew-Here Peak. Rocks abounded in both gardens, heaped up here and piled up there all higgledy-piggledy, but always forming the most eccentrically shaped precipices. In some places, rocks were used to construct a bridge over a brook, but in such instances, unlike the artificial mountains found upon the hill, these bridges were ingeniously designed and crafted. The ridgepoles of the main halls were held in place by cantilevers, thus obviating the need for pillars at all four corners, making the halls spacious enough for lion dancers to perform within. In North Garden, a chamber was built in the form of the Eight Trigrams, with a round pavilion partitioned into eight sections and shaped like a fan. Eight beds were placed horizontally in the narrow corners of each partition, curtained off on both sides. When the innermost curtains were lowered, the beds faced outside, and when the outermost curtains were lowered, the beds would face each other. Old man Bao would sit in state in the middle of the chamber with clear windows in his doors, and as he lay there propped up against his pillow burning incense, he could see each and every one of the eight beds. In such an excess of extravagance and wantonness did he grow old beside West Lake for more than twenty years, the splendour of his gardens not a jot inferior to those of Golden Valley or Mei Village, nothing less than the apotheosis of luxury and magnificence, what the locals of Hangzhou however were wont to dismiss by saying: "Well, that's just how it is." The grand families of West Lake wanted for nothing, and at the time is

seemed as if the West Lake had been encased within a Golden Chamber. It was only the impoverished and pedantic scholars who would mutter amongst themselves: "Tut! tut! What a very strange business".' ('Bao Hansuo' 包涵所, *Taoan mengyi: Xihu mengxun*, 53–4).

34. In his 'Ji Zhou Jianbo wen' 祭周戩伯文, Zhang Dai describes Huang Ruheng as one of his 'Friends in the Examinations' (*juye zhiji* 舉業知己), for which see *Langhuan wenji*, 274.

35. Yi Ya 易牙, a master chef who served under Duke Huan of Qi during the Spring and Autumn period and who was said to have had a palate so fine as to be able to distinguish between the water of these two rivers, both of which are to be found in present-day Shandong Province. It is also said of him that on one occasion, in order to please his master, he used the head of his own son to add flavour to a soup he was preparing.

36. According to his biography in the *Jin shu*, Fu Lang 苻郎 so understood the taste of food that his palate was able to make these distinctions.

37. This relates to an anecdote found in the 'Technical Understanding' (*Shujie* 術解) chapter of the *Shishuo xinyu* 世說新語: 'Xun Xu was once sitting with Emperor Wu of Jin eating bamboo shoots along with cooked rice. He said to those seated with him, "This has been steamed over firewood which has seen heavy service." Someone in the company did not quite believe him, and secretly sending to inquire about it, found that they had indeed used old carriage axles', Richard B. Mather, trans., *Shih-shuo Hsin-yü: A New Account of Tales of the World* (Minneapolis: University of Minnesota Press, 1976), 359.

38. Leys, *The Analects of Confucius*, 46: 'If it is not properly cut, he does not eat it.'

39. Zhang Dai provides a description of this studio in his *Dream Memories of Taoan*, for which see *Taoan mengyi: Xihu mengxun*, 33–4. It ends: 'Here I loosened my clothes and gave myself over the place, never wishing to leave it whatever the season. Thinking about it now, it seems as if it was another world.'

40. Ni Yuanlu 倪元璐 (1594–1644), an important late Ming official. He committed suicide on the day that Peking fell to the troops of Li Zicheng 李自成 (1606–45). For a short biography of him, see Hummel, 587.

41. According to Zhuang Yifu 莊一拂, this no longer extant opera was written by Xu Sanjie 許三階 of the Wanli period, see his *Gudian xiqu cunmu huikao* 古典戲曲存目彙考 (Shanghai: Guji chubanshe, 1982), 2.952–3.

42. 'Shanju zhuolu' 山居拙錄, *Qi Biaojia wengao* 祁彪佳文稿 (Beijing: Shumu wenxian chubanshe), 2.1087.

43. 'Author's Preface' (Zixu 自序), *Taoan mengyi: Xihu mengxun*, 3.

44. Zhang Dai speaks of the fate of his family's book collection in an item entitled 'Three Generations of Book Collecting' (Sanshi cangshu 三世藏書) in his *Dream Memories of Taoan* (*Taoan mengyi: Xihu mengxun*, 37–8). A translation of this may be found in D. E. Pollard and Soh Yong Kian, trans., 'Zhang Dai: Six Essays', *Renditions*, 33 & 34 (1990), 165–6.

45. 'Inscription for My Own Tomb', *Langhuan wenji*, 199.

46. 'Author's Preface', *Taoan mengyi: Xihu mengxun*, 3. For an alternative translation of this preface, along with a characteristically insightful discussion of it, see Stephen Owen, *Remembrances: The Experience of the Past in Classical Chinese Literature* (Cambridge, MA: Harvard University Press, 1986), 131–41.

47. 'Inscription for My Own Tomb', *Langhuan wenji*, 200–1.

Chapter 7

1. Richard Leakey, *People of the Lake: Mankind and Its Beginnings* (New York: Avon, 1978), 204.

2. This novel is more commonly known to the Western audience as *The Golden Lotus* or *The Plum in the Golden Vase*, according to its two most famous English translations by, respectively, Clement Egerton and David Tod Roy. However, because part of the aim of this chapter is to refute the conventional interpretation of this title, a more literal translation of the three Chinese characters which made up its original title—gold, vase, and plum blossom—is thus preferred. All quotations from this text are taken from Mei Jie 梅節, ed., *Mengmeiguan jiaoben Jinpingmei cihua* 夢梅館校本金瓶梅詞話 (Taipei: Liren shuju, 2007), 3 vols. The translations of the passages from the novel are all mine unless specified.

3. Lawrence S. Cunningham and John J. Reich, *Culture and Values: A Survey of the Humanities* (Belmont, CA: Wadsworth, 2002), 526.

4. Dai Hongsen 戴鴻森, 'Cong Jinpingmei kan Mingren de yishi fengmao 從金瓶梅看明人的飲食風貌', in *Mingjia yanzhong de Jinpingmei* 名家眼中的金瓶梅 (Beijing: Wenhua yishu chubanshe, 2006), 214–25. This article is originally published in *Zhongguo pengren* 中國烹飪 (4–5), 1982.

5. Zheng Peikai 鄭培凱, 'Jinpingmei cihua yu Mingren yinjiu fengshang 金瓶梅詞話與明人飲酒風尚', *Zhongguo wenhua* 中國文化, 2 (2006), 55–66.

6. Huang Lin 黃霖, *Huang Lin shuo Jinpingmei* 黃霖說金瓶梅 (Taipei: Dadi chubanshe, 2007), 169–89.

7. Zhao Jianmin 趙建民 and Li Zhigang 李志剛, *Jinpingmei jiushi wenhua yanjiu* 金瓶梅酒食文化研究 (Jinan: Shandong wenhua yinxiang chubanshe, 1998).

8. Hu Yannan 胡衍南, *Yinshi qingse Jinpingmei* 飲食情色金瓶梅 (Taipei: Liren shuju, 2004), 177.

9. Sigmund Freud, 'Female Sexuality', in *The Standard Edition of the Complete Psychological Works of Sigmund Freud* (London: Hogarth, 1953–74), 7. 149–50.

10. Ding Naifei, *Obscene Things: Sexual Politics in Jin Ping Mei* (Durham: Duke University Press, 2002), 194.

11. Carol J. Adams, *The Sexual Politics of Meat* (Cambridge: Polity, 1990), 47.

12. Xu Shen 許慎, *Shuowen jiezi zhu* 說文解字注 (Shanghai: Shanghai guji chubanshe, 1981), 2.50–1.

13. For example, see Louis Lo and Jeremy Tambling, 'How Excess Structures: On Reading Jin Ping Mei', *Textual Practice* 23 (2009), 119–40.

14. André Lévy, 'Introduction to the French Translation of *Jin Ping Mei cihua*', trans. Marc Martinez, *Renditions* 24 (1985), 109–29, 111–2.

15. Ge Hong 葛洪, *Baopuzi* 抱朴子 (Shanghai: Shanghai guji chubanshe, 1990), 81–2.

16. Chen Jiamo 陳嘉謨, *Bencao mengquan* 本草蒙筌, in *Xuxiu siku quanshu* 續修四庫全書 (Shanghai: Shanghai guji chubanshe, 1995), 991.660.

17. In China, gold and poison further share a common connotation to death in the sense that the swallowing of gold (*tun jin* 吞金) represents a popular means of committing suicide. During the Ming dynasty, a well-known case of suicide by such means is that of the eunuch Zhang Min 張敏 who, having saved Emperor Xiaozong's life by lying to Noble Consort Wan (*Wan guifei* 萬貴妃), killed himself by swallowing gold following the death of the emperor.

18. See Victoria Baldwin Cass, 'Celebrations at the Gate of Death: Symbol and Structure in Chin P'ing Mei' (unpublished doctoral thesis, Berkeley, 1979), 130–74.

19. See Wei Ziyun, *Jinpingmei yuanmao tansuo* 金瓶梅原貌探索 (Taipei: Xuesheng shuju, 1981), 57–69. See also Robert Yi Yang's paper on the 'Study of Song Huilian and Her Symbolic Function in JPM', presented at the 'Quadrennial Conference on Oriental-Western Literary and Cultural Relations', 12–14 May 1983, in Bloomington. A Chinese translation of this paper by Shen Hengshou 沈亨壽 can be found in *Jinpingmei xifang lunwenji* 金瓶梅西方論文集 (Shanghai: Shanghai guji chubanshe, 1987), 189–220.

20. This is also how Zhang Zhupo 張竹坡 understands this name. See Zhang Zhupo, 'Piping diyi qishu Jinpingmei dufa' 批評第一奇書〈金瓶梅〉讀法, in *Qishu siping* 奇書四評, ed. Song Jian 宋儉, 391–408. In particular, see 'Entry 48', 401.

Chapter 8

1. Unless otherwise stated all English quotations from Cao Xueqin's novel are drawn from the David Hawkes' translation of the first eighty chapters of the novel (Cao Xueqin, *The Story of the Stone Vols 1–3*, trans. David Hawkes [Harmondsworth: Penguin, 1973, 1977, 1980]). This translation is used because it is the most eloquent currently available and the original Chinese is also included with each excerpt to enable readers ready access to the flavour of the original. The chapter and page numbers are given in parentheses after the quotations, for example, (1.6.54) refers to Volume 1, Chapter 6, Page 54. For the Chinese I have used Cao Xueqin, *Ba jia pingpi Honglou meng* 八家評批紅樓夢, ed. Feng Qiyong 馮其庸 (Beijing: Wenhua yishu chubanshe, 1991). The same book, chapter, page reference system after each Chinese language quotation.

2. See Pan Baoming 潘寶明, '*Honglou meng* zhong cha, jiu, dian, yao de meigan yuyi' 紅樓夢中茶酒點肴的美感寓意, *Yangzhou daxue pengren xuebao* 揚州大學烹飪學報, 3 (2002), 7–10, 7, and Wu Fuping 吳斧平, 'Jingmei, hexie, dianya—Lun Honglou meng de yinshi wenhua tezheng' 精美和諧典雅——論紅樓夢的飲食文化特徵, *Lanzhou daxue xuebao*, 33 (2005), 57.

3. Kam-ming Wong, 'Anatomy of *The Stone*: Dotting the "I" of the Lichee and the Monkey', *Tamkang Review*, 36 (2005), 149.

4. Zhan Haiyan argues that tea is used to form bridges that connect segregated groups of people in the novel—across classes and through marriage. Anthony Yu reminds us of the Buddhist frame of the novel and mentions that the enjoyment of good food and wine are fundamental human 'desires'. No doubt Cao Xueqin used the excessive and exquisite nature of the foods consumed in the mansion as part of his thick

description of the 'red dust' of the world. Similarly, Li Wai-yee reminds us of the dialectical nature of Cao's description of desire—the illusion of worldly living can only be revealed through the experience of desire. While her discussion relates specifically to love, the excessive desire for food and wine on the part of the Jia mansion residents forms a significant part of their material experience of worldly illusion as well. See Haiyan Zhan, 'Tea in *The Story of the Stone*: Meaning and Function', *ICU Comparative Culture*, 39 (2007), 83–118; Anthony C. Yu, *Rereading the Stone: Desire and the Making of Fiction in Dream of the Red Chamber* (Princeton: Princeton University Press, 2001); and Wai-yee Li, *Enchantment and Disenchantment: Love and Illusion in Chinese Literature* (Princeton: Princeton University Press, 1993).

5.   R. Keith McMahon, *Causality and Containment in Seventeenth-Century Chinese Fiction* (Leiden: E. J. Brill, 1988), 49.

6.   See Louise Edwards, *Men and Women in Qing China: Gender in 'The Red Chamber Dream'* (Leiden: E. J. Brill, 1994, and Honolulu: University of Hawaii Press, 2001). Forthcoming in Chinese translation with Peking University Press, 2013; and Louise Edwards, 'Painting boundaries of sex segregation in Qing China: representing the family in *The Red Chamber Dream*', in *The Family in Chinese Art and Culture*, ed. J. Silbergeld and D. Ching (Princeton: Princeton University Press and P. Y. and Kinmay W. Tang Centre for East Asian Art, 2013), 339–71.

7.   Cao Xueqin's attention to details of daily life and his use of this detail to mark crucial themes within his novel is well recognized. For a digestion-related example, Chi-hung Yim has explained how Cao Xueqin presented readers with forewarning of the results of the love triangle between Daiyu, Baoyu and Baochai through his masterful use of illness, medicine and prescriptions. See Chi-hung Yim, 'The "Deficiency of Yin in the Liver": Dai-yu's Malady and *Fubi* in "Dream of the Red Chamber"', *Chinese Literature: Essays, Articles and Reviews*, 22 (2000), 85–111.

8.   Maram Epstein, 'Reflections of Desire: The Poetics of Gender in Dream of the Red Chamber', *Nan Nü: Men, Women and Gender in Early Imperial China*, 1 (1999), 66.

9.   See my chapter in Jerome Silbergeld and Dora Ching for a discussion of the role Picture plays in symbolizing the impermanence of divisions between purity and pollution and image and reality.

10. Hierarchies within space through food had already been established in hierarchies within individuals in the family as well. Prior to his entrance to the garden, Baoyu's unique and superior status in the family order was confirmed by his superior food provision through Grandmother Jia's household. Daiyu joined this premier wing of the household upon her arrival to the mansions as well. Food stands as a marker of status even within the already privileged residents of the mansions.

11. Fears about Baoyu being scalded and actual incidents where Baoyu is burned thread through the novel. In the chapter following the tea pouring incident with Crimson, Baoyu is actually burned, but not by food. While he is drunkenly harassing Sunset, Jia Huan's favourite maid, Jia Huan purposefully knocks over a candle and spills wax on Baoyu's face. These repeated references to heat invoke the alchemic aspect of the fire element within the novel's mystical frame. Jing Wang has argued that in most legends of stone in Chinese literature the wood element stands as a complement

to stone. But, in *Honglou meng* 'its [wood] subtle interplay with stone seems over-shadowed by the intervention of the third element, that of fire' (Jing Wang, *The Story of Stone: Intertextuality, Ancient Chinese Stone Lore, and the Stone Symbolism in* Dream of the Red Chamber, Water Margin *and* The Journey to the West [Durham: Duke University Press, 1992], 48). While Jing Wang is specifically referring to the moulding of stones in the process of repairing heaven described at the very start of the novel, we can also extrapolate this alchemic influence to the realm of food and drink through the repeated fears of Baoyu, the precious left-over stone, being burned.

12. After the Chrysanthemum poetry party following the crab banquet readers also learn from Patience that Xifeng has been illegally lending household money to earn interest and delays payments to the household members when the principal fails to be paid back in time (2.39.263).

13. In Chapter 77 Cook Liu and Fivey help to smuggle Baoyu back into the garden after he has sneaked out to see the dying Skybright. This incident happens at the height of the surveillance of the garden and reveals the inevitable cracks in the protective walls even during this period of close attention to 'border security'.

14. Hawkes translates this as Lycoperdon Snow but Fuling is not Lycoperdon but rather another fungus called Poria Cocos sometimes known as Tuckahoe in English.

15. Limin Bai, 'Children and the Survival of China: Liang Qichao in Education Before the 1898 Reform', *Late Imperial China*, 22 (2001), 124–55, 129–30.

16. Charlotte Furth, 'Concepts of Pregnancy, Childbirth and Infancy in Ch'ing Dynasty China', *Journal of Asian Studies*, 46 (1987), 8–9, 21.

17. The Hawkes' translation 'my own heart's blood' skips over the literal meaning of the phrase Cao Xueqin used in describing the origin of the breast milk. Nannie Li literally says 'milk changed from my own blood' or 'milk derived from my own blood'. This phrase reflects the close link between these two bodily fluids.

18. Baoyu is not the only man faced with pollution from his wet nurse. In Chapter 16 Nannie Zhao visits Jia Lian to seek employment for her two sons and explains her request in terms of reciprocity: 'To think I reared you up on the milk of my own bosom, Master Lian! And a fine young man you've growed into, thanks be!' She continues saying that 'they'll starve to death' if the sons can't get work (1.16.311). She had fed Jia Lian as a baby; now she request to be fed by him.

19. On this same day, a young servant man, Zhou, was found drunk and abusive at work. Xifeng moved to have him fired but was persuaded to keep him employed by the senior women servants who begged for him to be punished and given a second chance.

20. David Hawkes has romanized 'Liu An' as 'Lu-an'.

21. Dai Qing'e 戴清娥 and Yang Chenghu 楊成虎, '*Honglou meng* Yingyi ben yinshi ming-cheng fanyi de duibi yanjiu' 紅樓夢英譯本飲食名稱翻譯的對比研究, *Yunnan shifan daxue xuebao (Duiwai Hanyu jiaoxue yu yanjiu ban)* 雲南師範大學學報（對外漢語教學與研究版）, 7 (2009), 81.

22. Deng Yunxiang 鄧雲鄉, *Hongloumeng fengsu mingwu tan* 紅樓夢風俗名物譚 (Beijing: Wenhua yishu chubanshe, 2006), 259.

23. Hawkes translates 'purity and simplicity' as 'buoyant lightness': 'When did stored rain water have such a buoyant lightness?' (2.41.315)

24. Hawkes translates 'Girls' tea' as 'strong Pu'er' but this elides the significance of the 'girls' world party' that is about to happen in Green Delights.

25. See Zishan Chen, *Food and Chinese Culture: Essays on Popular Cuisine* (San Francisco: Long River Press, 2005).

Index